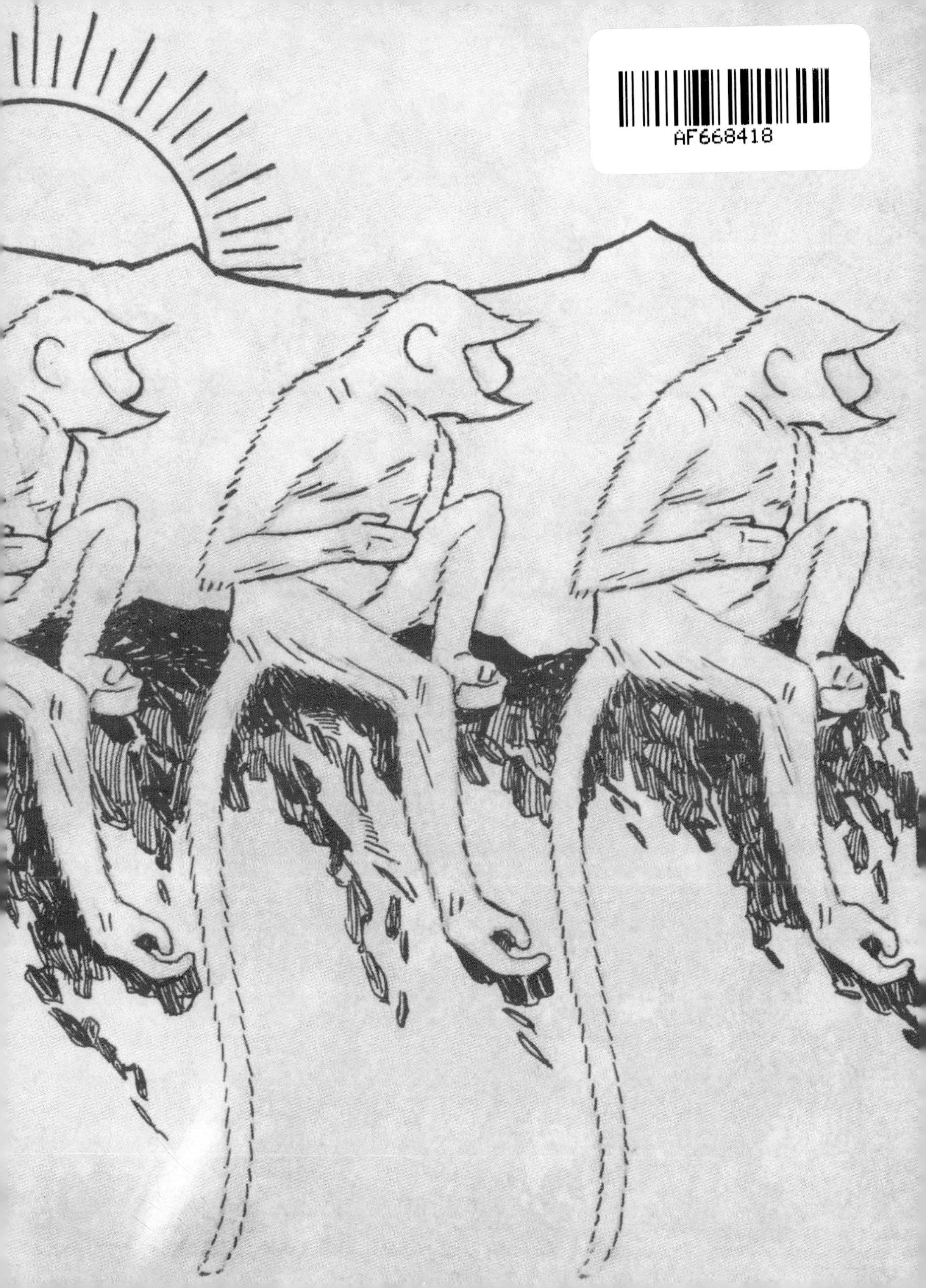

VISION AND VISUALS

Jatindrakumar Sen's Illustrations for Parashuram's Stories

NIYOGI
BOOKS

MUSUI
Art Foundation

Published by
NIYOGI BOOKS
Block D, Building No. 77,
Okhla Industrial Area, Phase-I,
New Delhi-110 020, INDIA
Tel: 011-26818960, +91 7428978881
Email: niyogibooks@gmail.com
Website: www.niyogibooksindia.com

Concept & Curation: KS Radhakrishnan

Text: Parimal Ray, Gautam Bhadra, KS Radhakrishnan

Editor: Juhi Saklani

Research Assistant: Nandini Ghosh

Coordinator: Ansuman Ray

Design: Musui Art Foundation team

Layout: Shaiju Augustine

ISBN: 978-93-89136-92-0
Publication: 2023

Printed at: Niyogi Offset Pvt. Ltd., New Delhi, India

VISION AND VISUALS

Jatindrakumar Sen's Illustrations for Parashuram's Stories

Curated by
KS RADHAKRISHNAN

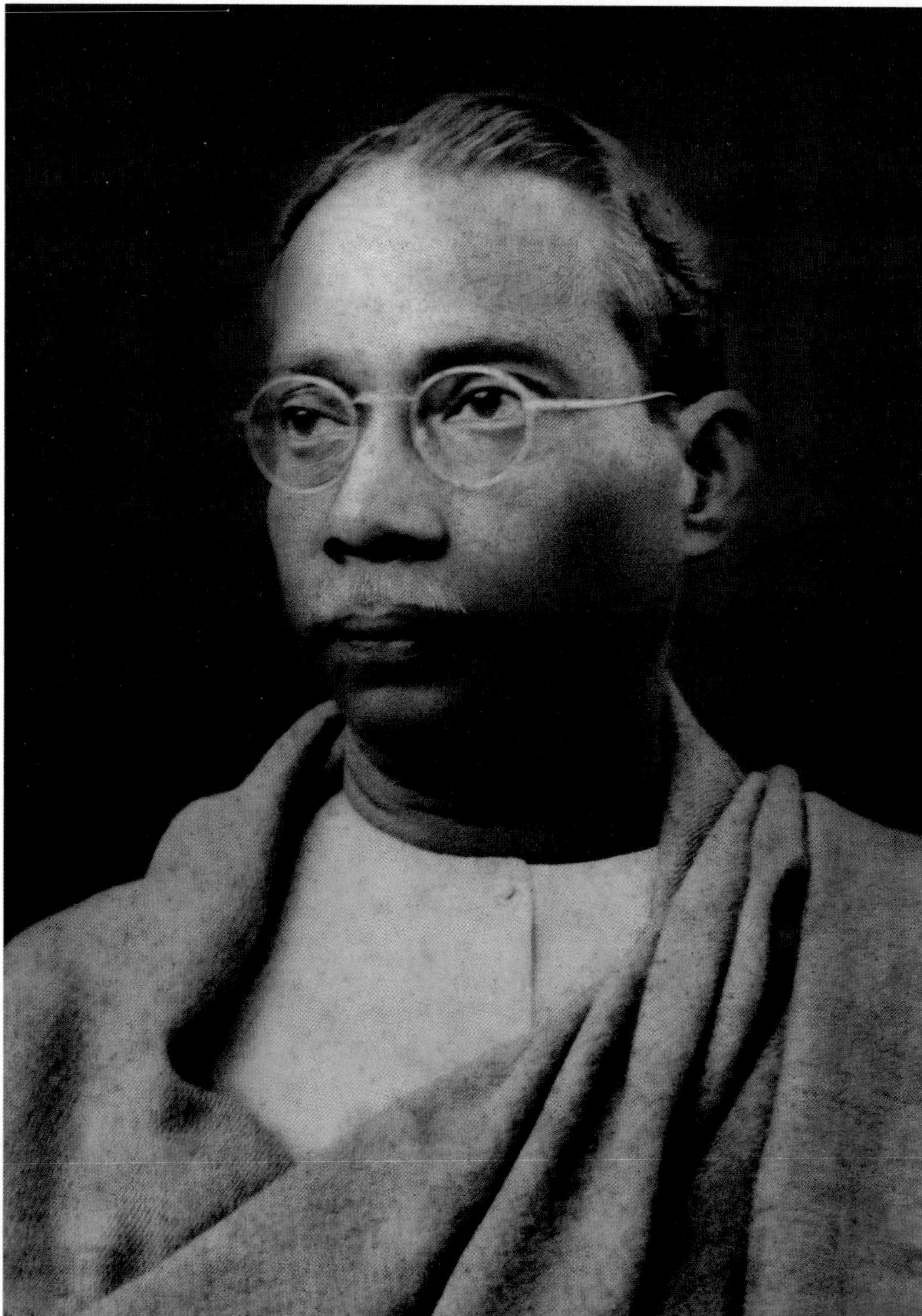

Jatindrakumar Sen

CONTENTS

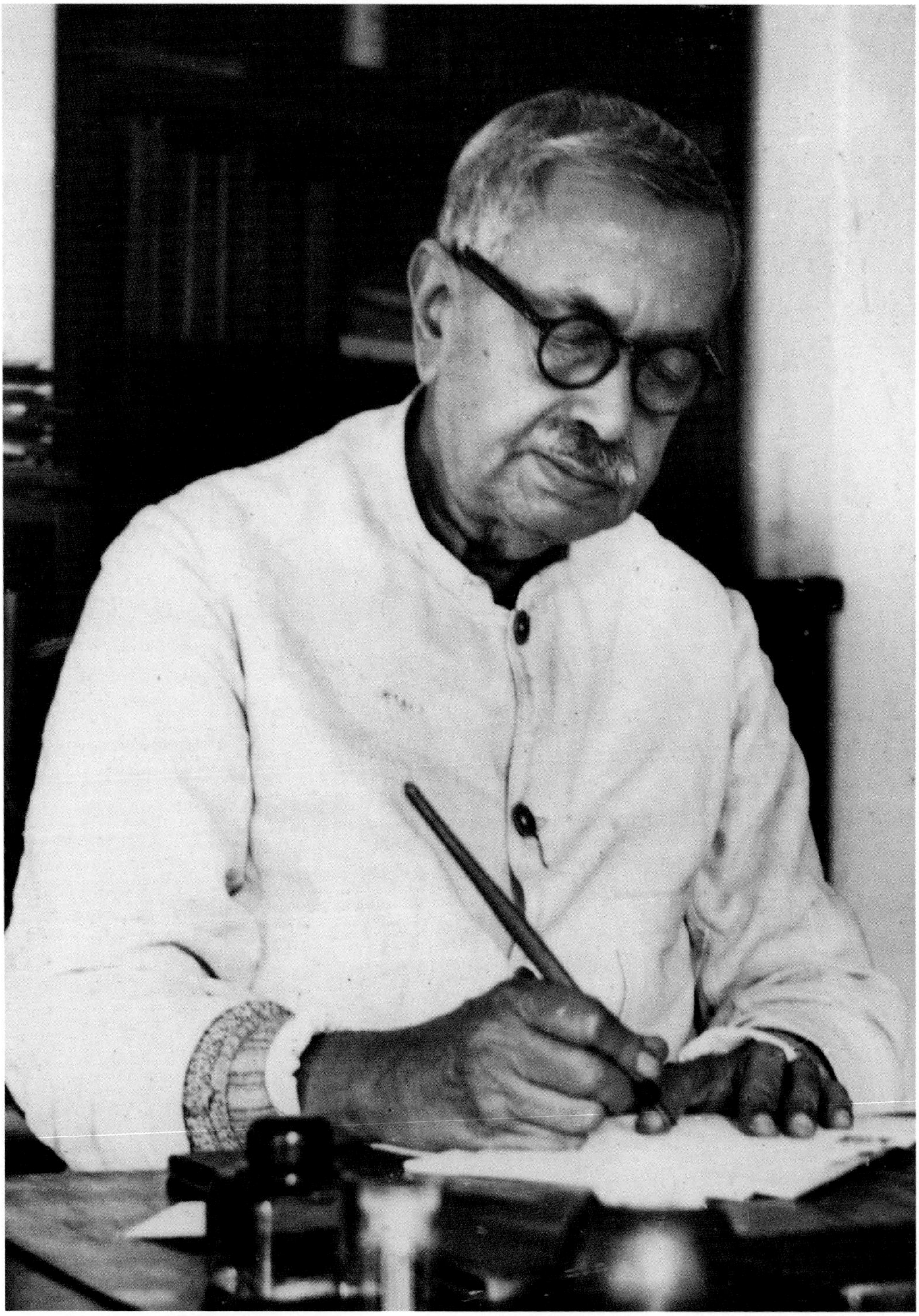

Rajshekhar Basu (Parashuram)

CURATOR'S INTRODUCTION

KS Radhakrishnan

Having studied and lived in Santiniketan, and being married to a Bengali writer, I have some small familiarity with the world of Bengali literature. My wife Mimi regularly talks to me of Bengali writers, for example Bibhutibhushan Bandopadhyay, Manik Bandopadhyay or Shakti Chattopadhyay, and often reads out what she wishes to share with me. I remember the time she read out the story *Bhushandir Mathe* by the great Parashuram (pseudonym of Rajshekhar Basu). It was so funny and had so many impish characters whom I really connected to!

Being an artist, I also felt an immediate connection to the superb illustrations by Jatindrakumar Sen that appeared in the story. As I saw more of Sen's work, I realised what a sensitive illustrator he was. He is given a prominent position in the studies of Bengali illustrations, even apart from Parashuram's stories. But his jugalbandi with Parashuram created a world of its own for generations of Bengali readers. Growing up in Kerala, I had been familiar with a similar collaboration between the writer VKN and the artist Namboothiri – teaming up to attain great popularity in Malayalam literature.

I doubly appreciated Jatindrakumar Sen's work because Parashuram being a humourist and a satirist, the scope of illustrations was more precise and refined. A sense of humour was needed, as was a celebration of the inherent absurdity of the world foregrounded in these narratives. How life brought me and these illustrations together is another story, and is the reason behind this book and exhibition.

The *adda* that nourished my roots

As a young student in Kala Bhavana, I was fortunate to be in contact with some of the best talents and cultural sensibilities thanks to my mentor and professor Sarbari Roy Choudhury. He introduced me to the regular sittings of his friends – the famous Calcutta *adda*! – that took place at The Image, Jyotish Chakraborty's photo studio in Calcutta. The *adda* regulars were much senior to me, and included Parimal Ray, one of Calcutta's best known collectors, who was often requested by Satyajit Ray to find some rare object he needed for his shooting; Basanta Chowdhury, the actor; Nemai Ghosh, the famous photographer known especially for Ray's photographs; Utpalendu Chakraborti, the director of *Chokh* and *Debshishu*; and Jyotish Chakraborty himself, the commanding centre of this hub, a printer and processor par excellence who came alive in his dark room. As the youngest member, I was the unofficial coffee maker, whipping up the coffee as I listened fascinated to their conversations. That's where I developed my historical understanding of Calcutta and Bengal – a vibrant oral history through the mouth of these intelligent and engaged people.

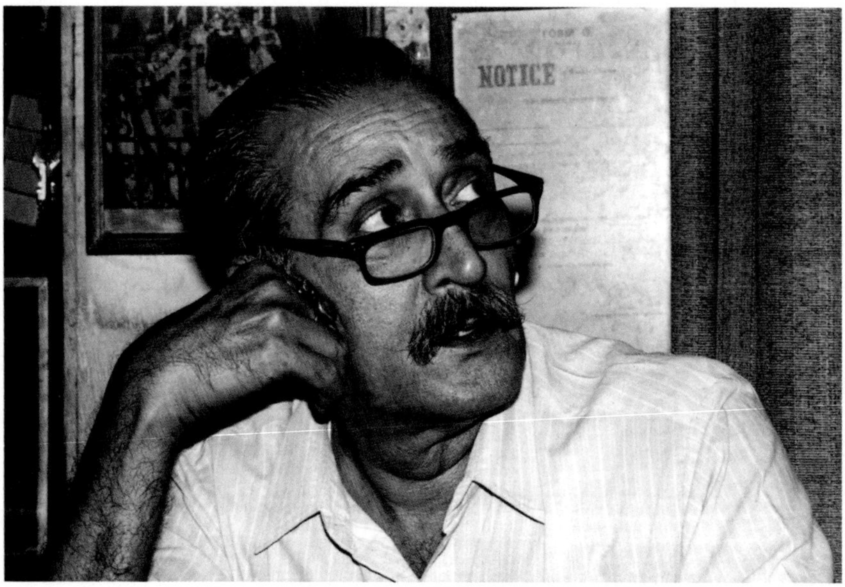

Jyotish Chakraborty

Today, most of these senior friends whom I looked up to are no more, but I am grateful that Parimal da – Parimal Ray – is still here with his bright and active mind. Often when I come to Kolkata, I go directly to him and his presence carries me to that beautiful space-time that we all shared in the 1970s and 80s. I watch with pleasure when he exhibits new ideas and energy. Indeed, Parimal da too had read out *Bhushandir Mathe* to me, with his characteristic dramatic flair and I was transported to that world of spirits.

Parimal Ray finds a treasure

Now, Parashuram's (Rajshekhar Basu's) family residence in Bhawanipore is in the lane next to Parimal da's house. Parashuram's great grandson Dipankar Basu is a very private person but Parimal da was a rare soul who had access to the house and to the treasure trove of Parashuram's belongings and mementos. Dipankar Basu agreed to let Parimal Da save these precious objects from eventually rotting away.

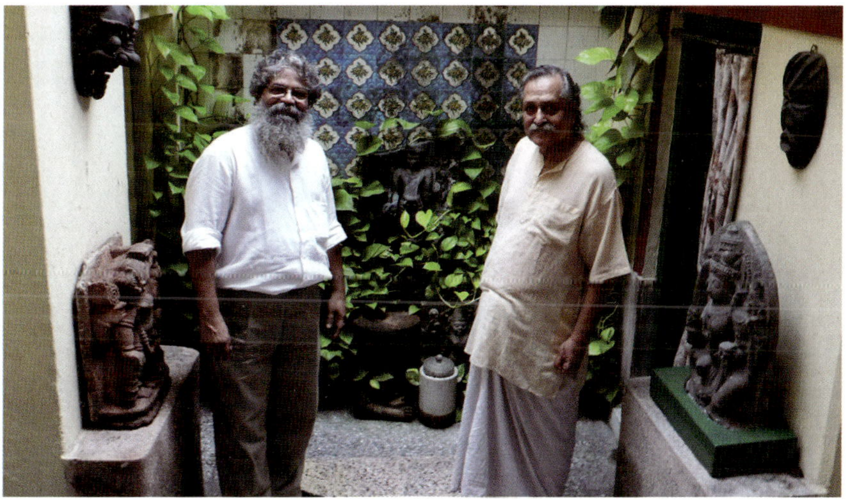

KS Radhakrishnan with Parimal Ray

Some of the first edition books had been eaten up by termites. There were books with the writer's handwriting gifting it to someone in the family. Among all of this lay the drafts and final illustrations of the drawings made by Jatindrakumar Sen, which

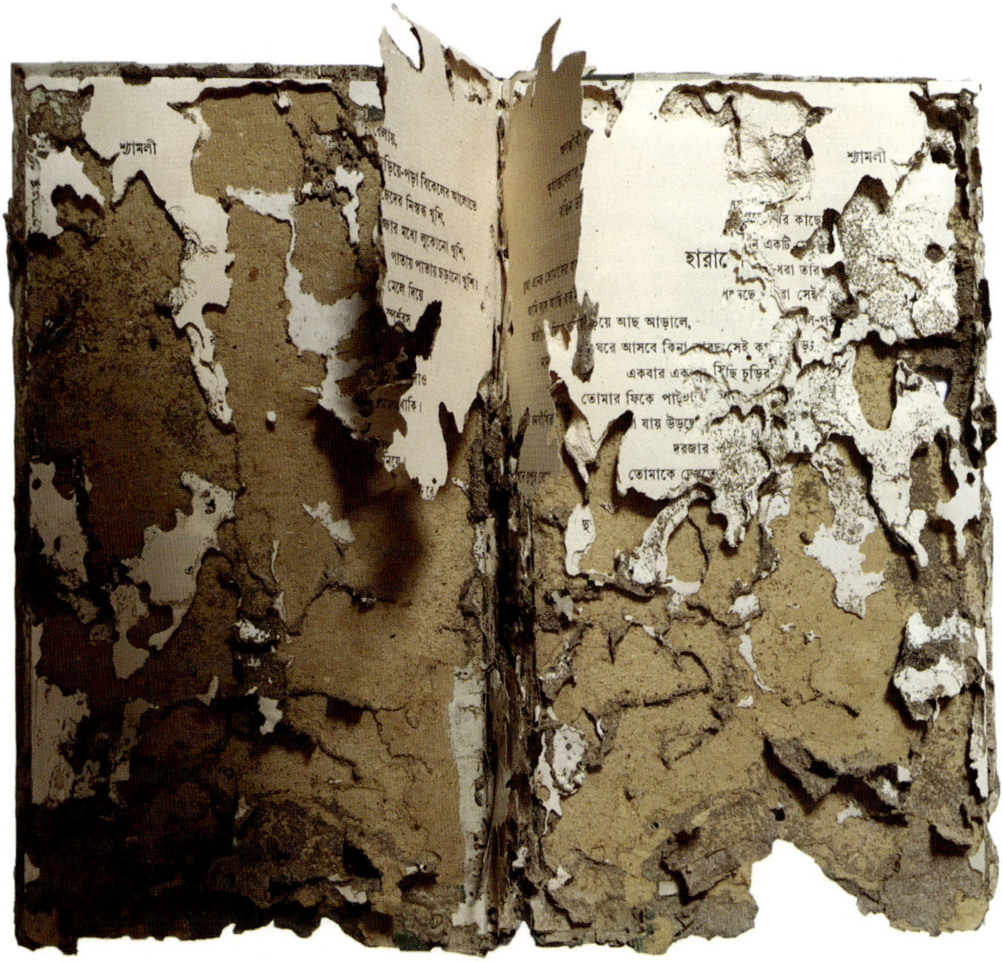

One of the first-edition books by Parashuram destroyed by termites

famously appeared in Parashuram's books and added so much vitality to them, as well as Parashuram's written and drawn instruction to his friend about the drawings. These were in good condition because Jatindrakumar Sen had kept them and later given them to Dipankar Basu, whom he thought of as a godson.

Over several years, Parimal da carefully cleaned and rescued these books and papers from years of dust and mould with such dedication that his health collapsed. He actually had to be hospitalised for severe pneumonia. But he felt that he was saving a national treasure and on recovering continued with the work.

Parashuram's Bhagwad Geeta

Of the treasures he found, Parimal da asked me if something could be done with a 'pothi', a handwritten manuscript, of the abridged version of the *Bhagwad Geeta* which Rajshekhar Basu had written. I decided that the book would be best 'recreated' in that other-worldly handwriting of Rajshekhar Basu, along with all the scars and holes on the paper, by scanning the pages and binding them. We brought out the book in 2017. Under the category of cost, it just said: "Invaluable". It was launched by Dipankar Basu in the Ramkrishna Mission, Golpark, and the original manuscript was gifted to the Mission for safekeeping.

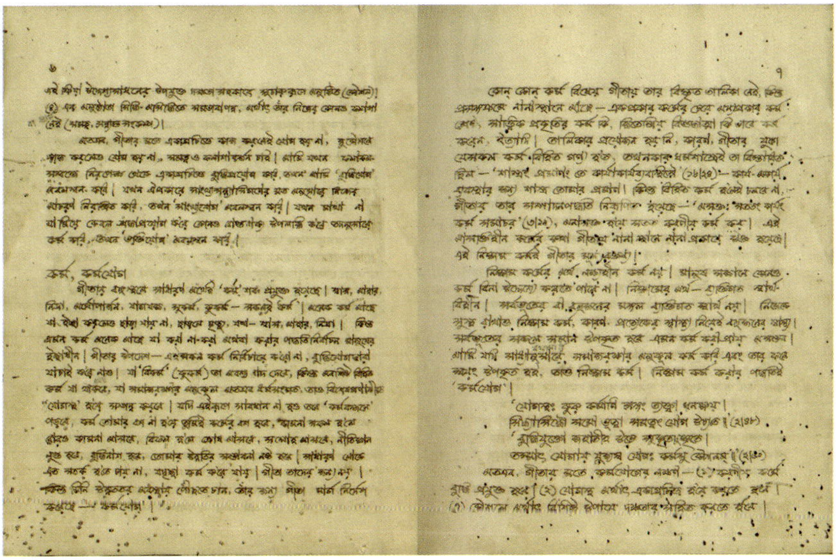

A page from the recreated *Srimad Bhagvad Geeta* by Rajshekhar Basu

Jatindrakumar Sen's originals

As Parimal da showed me the original drawings, I realised what a sensitive and creative artist Jatindrakumar Sen was. The ghosts and impish characters in Bhushandir Mathe, I feel, are some of the best illustrations in Indian literature. In fact, I felt inspired to see how these spirits would be reflected in my own sculptural characters: Musui and Maiya!

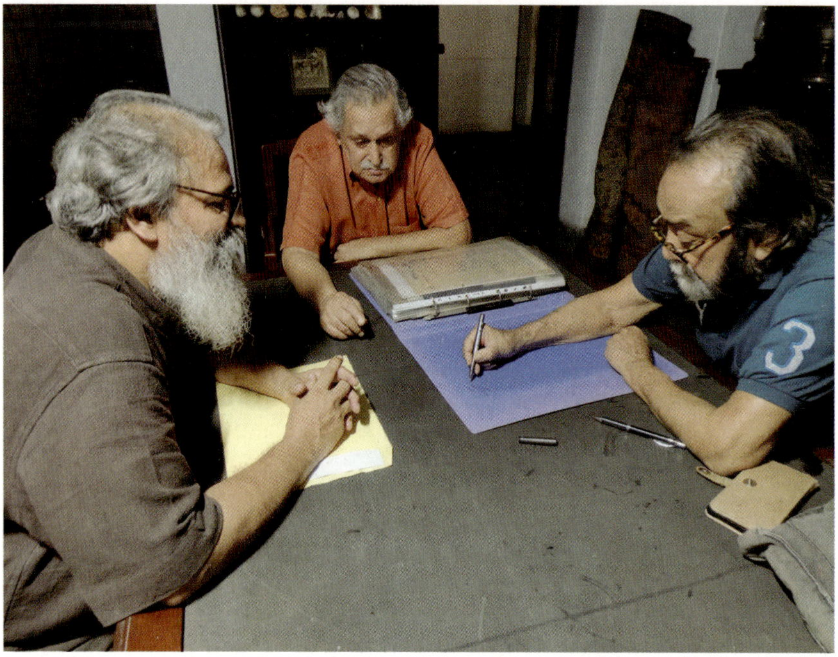

KS Radhakrishnan and Parimal Ray with Dipankar Basu while handing over the original works of Jatindrakumar Sen

Comparing the original drawings with the first edition books, I could make out that since the artwork had been reduced to a smaller size for publication, and because the printing quality was not of the highest order, it was almost as if the public had never seen the work done by Jatindrakumar Sen. I strongly felt that this needed to be remedied!

Dipankar Basu graciously and unconditionally gave me the original drawings so that they could enjoy not only a fresh lease of life in the public domain but also be seen in their original size. This was sure to make a substantial exhibition – a kind of retrospective of the collaboration between Parashuram and Jyotindrakumar Sen. I was sure it would be interesting for everyone to see how Parashuram had himself sketched out – very efficiently – his vision for the characters and given Sen specific instructions for them. And then to see how the writer's vision matured under a skilled and trained hand.

A tribute

This book and exhibition is my tribute to the hard work and energy of Parimal Ray, the man I have cared deeply for since I was 18 year old. I still remember how I had to submit my 5 copies of my final dissertation with a 100 photos of my sculptures – which meant 500 prints! I was quite lost. I went to Jyotish da who printed all 500 copies himself. I told him that I had no money to pay him. And he said: "Don't worry, your payment has already been made". It was Parimal da who had born the expenditure. He said to me, "I have seen a sketch you have made of Sarbari da, will you give it to me?" Accepting the sketch, he said I should consider that his debt has been repaid.

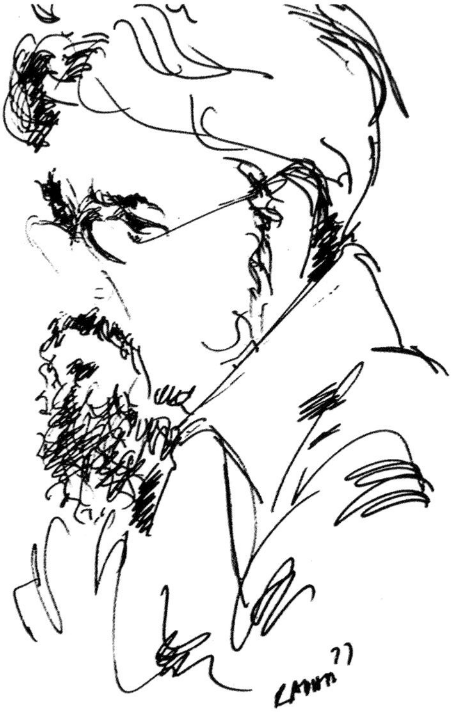

Sarbari Roy Choudhury by KS Radhakrishnan

How can one forget such memories and relationships? They still enrich my life. All my efforts at producing this book and putting up this exhibition are finally aimed at letting Parimal da's efforts come out in front of the public and give him the happiness and satisfaction he richly deserves.

Through this book, Musui Art Foundation hopes to open peoples' eyes to the talents of Parashuram and Jatindrakumar Sen with fresh appreciation, and to let a new generation explore the richness of Bengal's literary and artistic legacy with the same wonder that I felt when I first saw the drawings. I hope we all can collectively pay our respects to the doyen of Bengali literature and the man who worked with him like a shadow, bringing alive his stories in visuals.

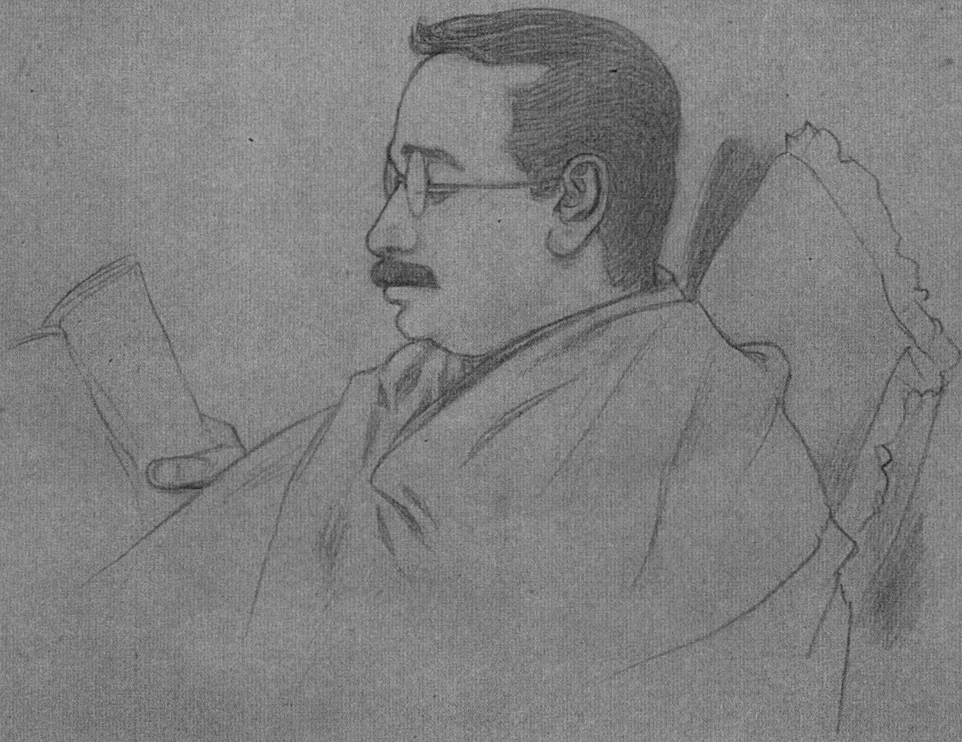

Rajshekhar Basu (Parashuram) | Sketch by Jatindrakumar Sen

I AM A MERE INSTRUMENT

Parimal Ray

Rajshekhar Basu's residence was a stone's throw away from my house. As a student, I often saw him going to the vegetable market every morning. Whenever my father and I came across him in Lansdowne Market, he would stop to exchange a few words with my father. Always dressed in a short *dhuti* and white shirt, Rajshekhar was a taciturn man. He was known for his discipline, punctuality and honesty, which were integral to his personality. There was a famous saying: "Rajshekhar does not follow the clock; it is the clock which follows him".

For Bengalis, 2013 was a memorable year. It marked the centenary of the famous children's magazine *Sandesh*, founded by Upendrakishore, and Sukumar Ray's 125th birth anniversary. The two great men, though known for their distinct work areas, were connected by *Sandesh*, which the father and son both edited. Indeed, I was no expert on them or their history; but I could not resist the temptation to take a small part in the celebration. I felt that it would be great if I could collect the covers of the magazine published in the last hundred years and show them in an exhibition.

With high hopes, I set out to collect the covers. Despite my sincere efforts, I could not make much progress even in four months. I searched for them in every library in Kolkata and its neighbourhood and even tried Visva-Bharati, but in vain. The bound volumes of *Sandesh* in the libraries were without covers. Of course, I got a few magazine issues from the old bookshops on College Street, but they were not enough to put up an exhibition. So, I gave up.

At the time, my late friend Chandu asked me to contact Dipankar Basu, Rajshekhar's great grandson, for this purpose. According to him, Dipankar was the first subscriber of *Sandesh* when it resumed operations for the third time. Although Dipankar lived nearby and I had known him since childhood, we were not friends. Growing up under his grandfather's guidance, care and affection, Dipankar had imbibed his ideals and personality. He, too, was a man of few words, and his character reflected his grandfather.

After several attempts, I finally got an appointment to meet him at his house. When I arrived, his servant opened the gate, and I met Dipankar Babu in the garden. The unmarried septuagenarian lived alone on the first floor, and the house's ground floor was occupied by his servant Siddheswar (Sidhu) and his family.

After exchanging a few words, I explained my purpose of visiting him. I said I would only photograph the covers of the *Sandesh* magazines in his collection. Having heard this, he replied that he was extremely sorry he could not help me. According to the family custom, all unwanted textbooks, periodicals and magazines were discarded, not outside the house, but in a storeroom. Rajshekhar's strict instruction was that nothing could be sold or thrown outside the home. I saw a faint light of hope that, whatever their conditions might be in the storeroom, the magazines were inside the house. My hope, however, soon vanished when Dipankar said that handling this 'garbage' was strictly prohibited and he could not disobey his grandfather by allowing a gentleman like me to touch it. It would harm the family's reputation.

Three days passed. On the fourth day, Dipankar called me over the telephone and asked me to visit him. Excited, I quickly went to his house. In the small drawing room of Rajshekhar, I saw him standing in front of a heap of old monthly magazines, in which a few issues of my prized *Sandesh* issues, now transformed into trash, could be seen. Without losing time, I asked Dipankar to permit me to start my work. He smiled and agreed and went upstairs, leaving Sidhu to help me.

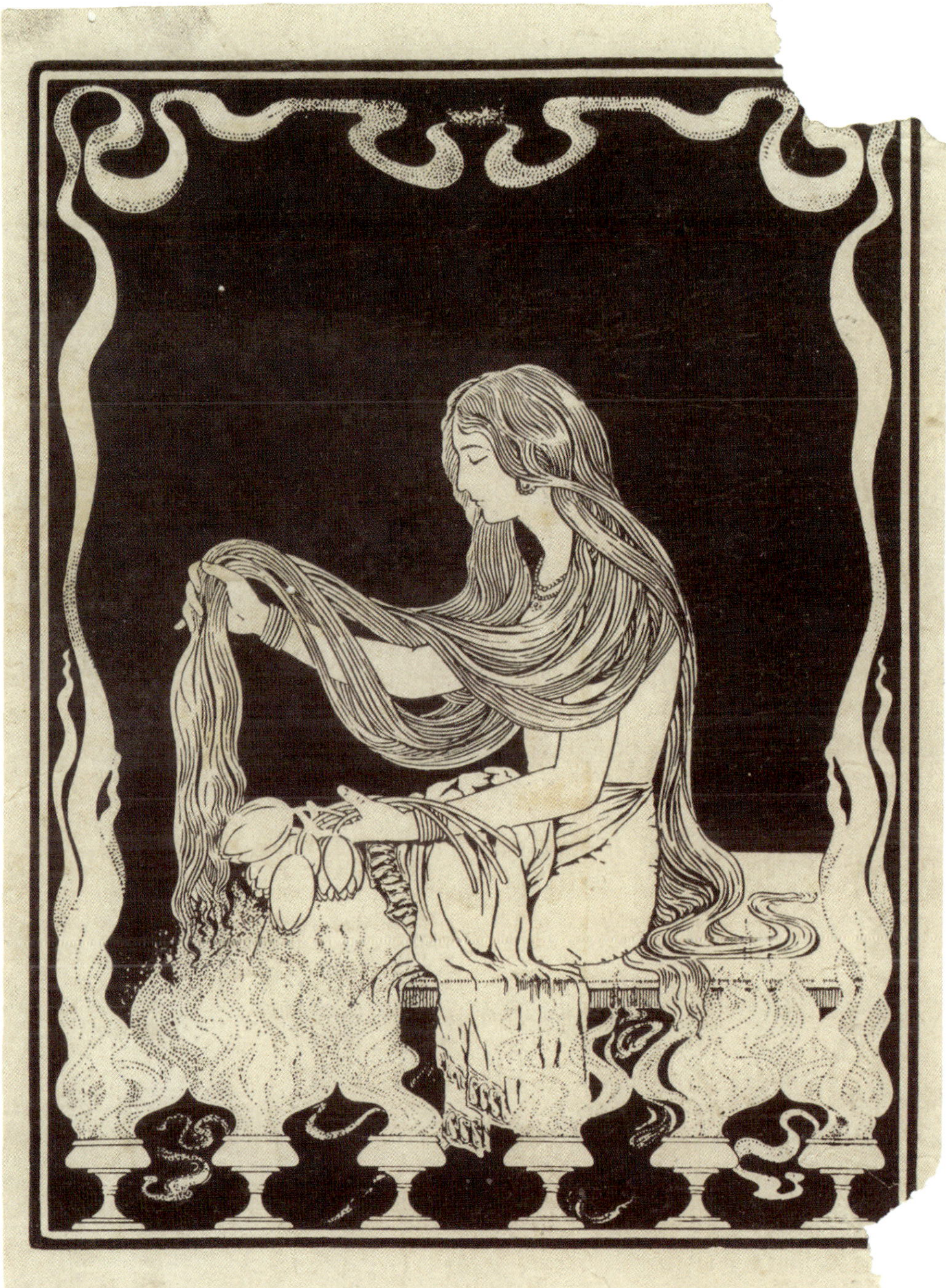

A commercial illustration by Jatindrakumar Sen

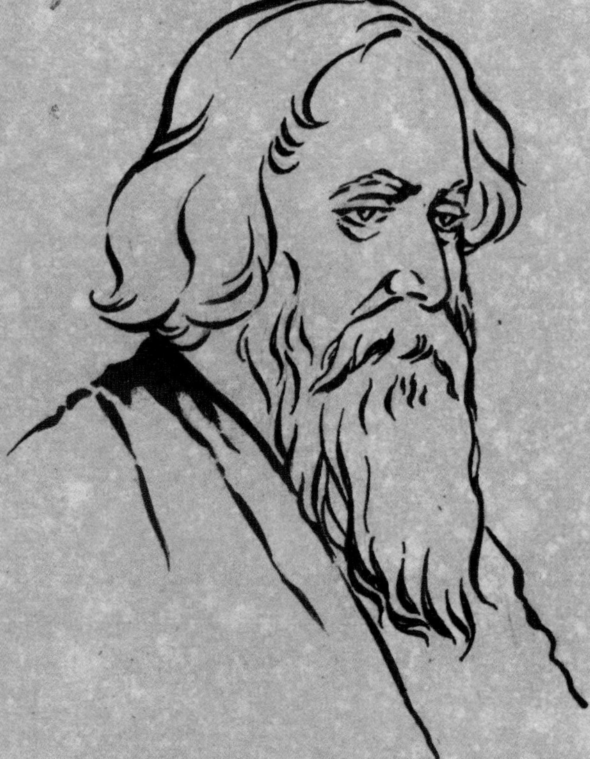

Rabindranath Tagore | Sketch by Jatindrakumar Sen

I worked four hours, five days a week. Every day, Sidhu brought new piles of old magazines from the storeroom, and I worked with my brush and camera, cleaning and photographing the magazine covers. Indeed, most of the materials were found damaged, but I was not entirely disappointed because I was looking only for *Sandesh*. I photographed almost all the *Sandesh* covers published during its third interval, between 1961 and 2012. Besides this, I was also able to collect the earlier covers published in the magazine's first and second incarnations from elsewhere. I displayed them in the exhibition titled *Nana Chhander Sandeshi Mela* at Nandan 4 Gallery, Kolkata. Dipankar came to see the show one day, and I warmly welcomed him. His face beamed with happiness when he saw the reproductions of the discarded magazines in his house.

A creative jugalbandi

Rajshekhar's collected works include nine books of fiction, in which he appeared under his pseudonym, Parashuram. Of these nine books, three books – *Gaddalika*, *Kajjali* and *Hanumaner Swapno* – were illustrated by noted artist Jatin (Jatindra) Kumar Sen. It needs to be mentioned here that, like Rajshekhar, Jatin Sen also initially appeared under a pseudonym, Narada. But he later discontinued using it and signed his works with his real name. Rajshekhar's first fiction, 'Sri Sri Siddheswari Limited' was published in 1923 in the famous monthly magazine *Bharatbarsha*. Here, it was mentioned that the story was "written by Parashuram and illustrated by Narada". However, when it appeared in *Gaddalika* in 1924, it was printed on the book's cover: "written by Parashuram and Illustrated by Jatindrakumar Sen".

Gaddalika – a collection of five stories – appeared in 1924 and immediately became popular. Seeing its popularity, some Bengali writers and artists joined hands and jumped into similar ventures to capture the market. There was a well-known publisher who, inspired by *Gaddalika*'s success, thought of publishing a story by Rabindranath with Jatin Sen's illustrations. Jatin Sen accepted the offer and said he would only follow the poet's instructions to illustrate his story, and the poet would finally judge the suitability of the pictures. When Rabindranath heard about this, he was delighted but refrained from advising the artist, allowing him to work with complete freedom. However, unfortunately, the project did not materialize.

Treasures from a storeroom

During my project on *Sandesh*, I came closer to Dipankar, and we forged a close friendship. He once told me that Rajshekhar did not throw anything, even the most insignificant objects, from his ancestral house in Parsi Bagan Lane when he shifted to this new house in Bakul Bagan in 1935. I, too, saw some old diaries, medical prescriptions, letter drafts, and grocery lists infested with insects in the piles of old books and magazines that Sidhu brought to me from the family's storeroom. Among them was a large brown envelope with an inscription: "All pictures will return to Jatin". The curiosity to know what was inside the envelope and see if anything valuable had survived the torture of the insects and time made me want to explore the storeroom. When I expressed my desire to Dipankar, he was shocked and discouraged me by saying that the store was not only foul in condition but also unsafe. He did not even dare to open its doors. However, seeing my enthusiasm, he finally agreed. Sidhu and his family were more than happy. They saw it as an opportunity to clean the storeroom and save the household from snake bites and insects.

It took me over a year to complete my second project at Rajshekhar's residence. Since the storeroom had remained closed and unused for over eighty years, insects had eaten away ninety per cent of the materials. The little that we rescued and conserved has been published in this book. We found some of Rajshekhar's manuscripts and Jatin Sen's hand-drawn illustrations made for the three books, except for Bipulananda's picture, the last drawing in *Chikitsa Sankat*.

The most valuable finding was undoubtedly the pictures inside the brown envelope. When I opened it, I was surprised to see the images of six ghosts depicted in Parashuram's well-known story,

Bhushandir Mathe. The pictures were in good condition as the envelope had three layers, and the insects had not invaded the last one. The images of the ghosts – Brahmadaitya Shibu Bhattacharya of Peneti village, Petni of the Pituli pool, Shankchunni, Dakini, Kariya Piret, and Yaksha Naderchand –were drawn not by Jatin Sen but by his mentor, Rajshekhar.

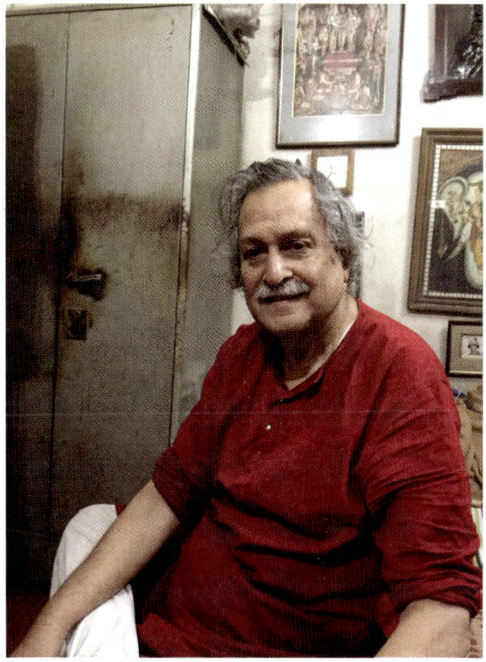

Parimal Ray

Bhushandir Mathe (In Bhushandi's Plain) is the most famous of the five stories published in *Gaddalika*. Rajshekhar drew not only the sketches of the main characters but also the headpiece, title and letterings. He did it because he probably felt it was difficult for anyone other than the author to imagine the fantastic creatures visually. He also gave a short descriptive note below each picture. Comparing these sketches with Jatin Sen's final illustrations published in the book, I think much nuance of Rajshekhar's drawings has been lost in Jatin's adaptations. The unworldly characters of *Bhushandir Math*, who look bucolic in Rajshekhar's drawings, appear sophisticated and urban in Jatin's illustrations. Had the author's drawings been published in the book, the readers would have been able to relate them more accurately to the story based on a village environment.

In this context, I want to draw the reader's attention to the illustrations of *Prem Chakra* in the book *Hanumaner Swapno*. Parashuram created all nine pictures of the story, reflecting the power of his visual imagination. His illustration of *Rahu* perfectly captures the humour of the memorable lines in the text. Parashuram is an accomplished artist, and one should judge his drawings as the best illustrations of his writings.

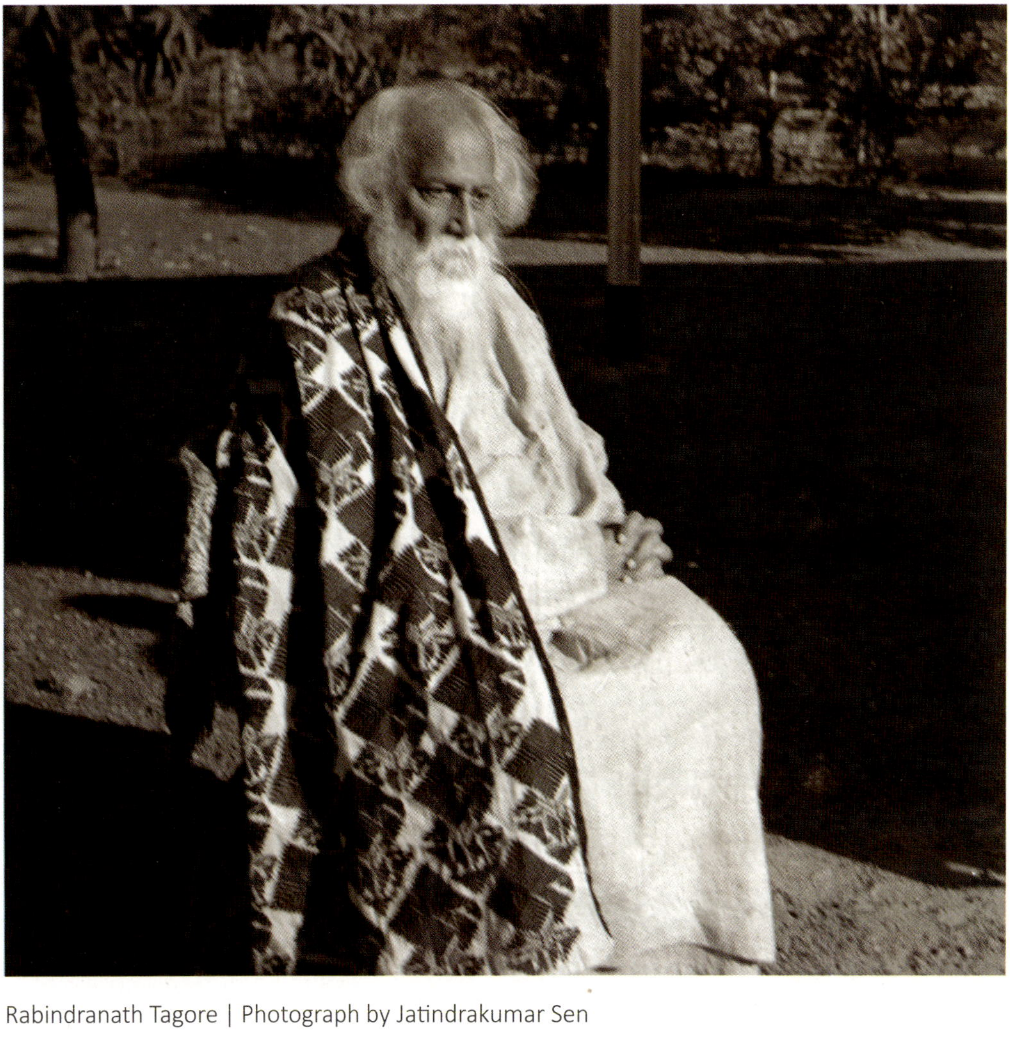

Rabindranath Tagore | Photograph by Jatindrakumar Sen

However, I do not intend to belittle Jatin Sen. Except for those in *Prem Chakra*, Jatin Sen created all the other remarkable illustrations published in the three books mentioned earlier, following Parashuram's instructions closely. Rabindranath Tagore highlighted his pictures in his review of *Gaddalika*, saying, 'There is an excellent harmony between the pen and the brush in the book. The words and lines flow with the same rhythm; no one is less important than the other." Half the share of the immense popularity that the three illustrated books have enjoyed for years belongs to Jatin Sen.

In conclusion

On April 27, 1960, Rajshekhar passed away. On August 31, 1960, Jatin Sen transferred all his property to Dipankar through a will. Except for a few essential things, such as his still camera, he put everything in the storeroom of Rajshekhar's residence. The illustrations we recovered from the 'Tower of Silence' have been published here.

The central pillar of this project is Dipankar Basu. He allowed me to work in his residence for more than a year and engaged his servant Siddheswar, who died recently, to assist me. *Vision and Visuals* is the result of his generosity, patience and kindness. I want to thank him, Sidhu, and his family; without their keen interest and dedication to the project, the book would not have come out.

The second pillar is my close friend KS Radhakrishnan. This book is his tribute to the great writer Rajshekhar Basu and his illustrator, Jatin Sen. I do not need to say anything about Radhakrishnan, widely known for his sculpture and organisational activities. But I must thank his wife, Mimi Radhakrishnan, who always remained behind the scenes and was closely associated with the project.

In this project, I just played the role of a gatherer. I am no more than a mere instrument.

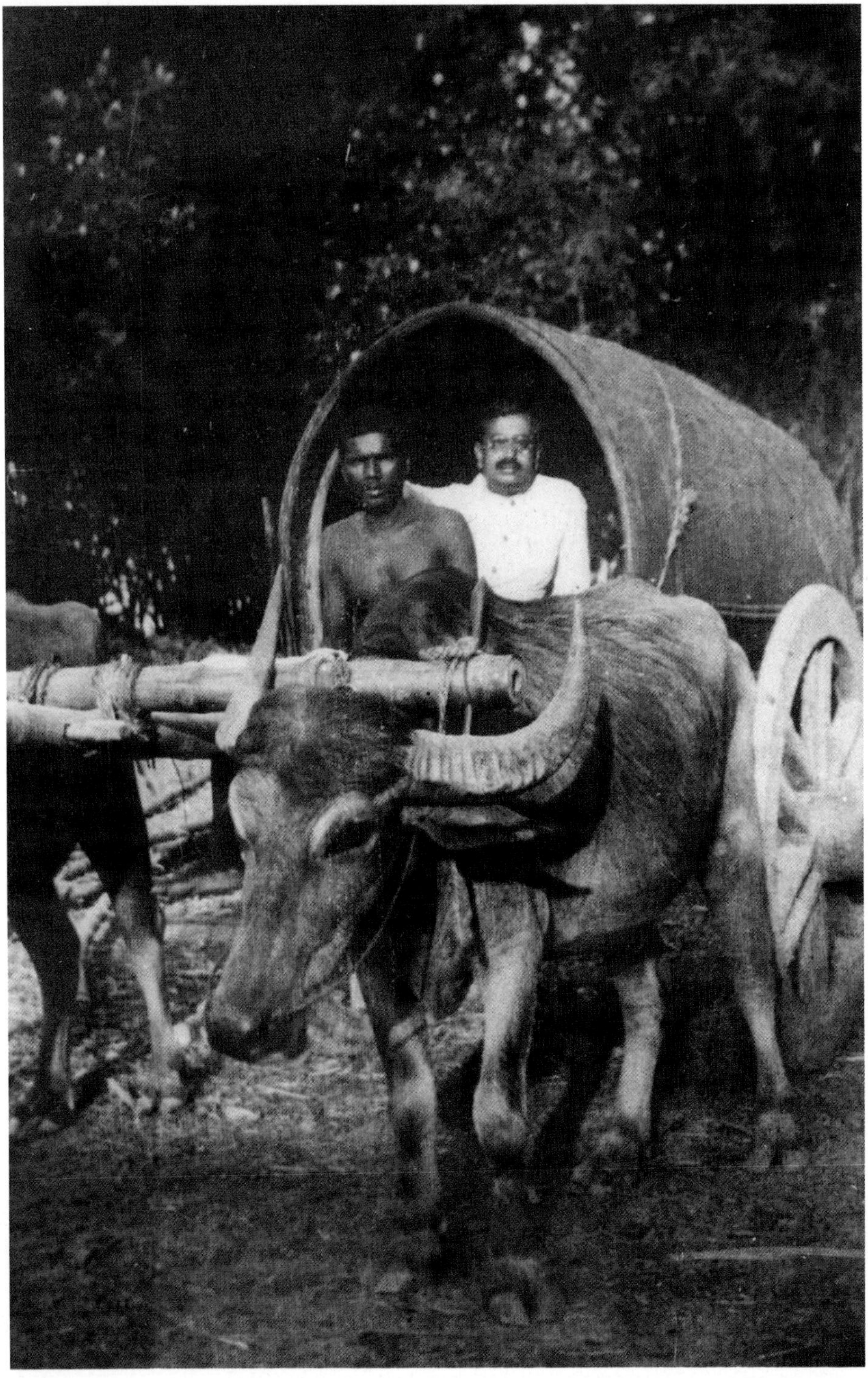

Rajshekhar Basu travelling in a cart

A CREATIVE COLLABORATION

Gautam Bhadra

The long personal and professional relationship between Rajshekhar Basu or Parashuram (1880-1960), a great satirist, lexicographer, translator, essayist and a capable director of a pharmaceutical firm, and his favourite illustrator and designer Jatindrakumar Sen was not, at all, dramatic and tense. Nothing in their collaboration is comparable to the tensions between Lewis Carroll (1882-1966) and John Tenniel (1820-1914) in making the visual representations and printed versions of *Alice's Adventures in Wonderland*. There is not even a murmur of dissatisfaction similar to the reaction expressed by Jibanananda Das to the cover drawn by a young artist, Satyajit Ray, for *Banalata Sen*, Das's well-known collection of poems published by the Signet Press, a famous publisher in the 1940s and 50s in Bengal. The relationship between Rajshekhar Basu, alias Parashuram, and Jatin Sen was personal and humane; it had nothing to do with market calculations, differences in aesthetic judgement or squabbling over the print quality of the production.

A friend and protégé

Jatin Sen was born in a relatively poor family. Due to the family's financial difficulties, he was unable to complete his course in the art college. Rajshekhar had taken on the promising artist as his protégé and appointed him as a designer for the product covers and advertisements of his company, Bengal Chemical. His artworks, such as those for the tonic Ashwar, became quite popular.[1] Their relationship was very close and beyond a mere business relationship. As a memoir has suggested, Jatin Sen was a regular member of the "Utkendra Sabha" (Arbitrary Club), a weekly informal *adda* or 'Majlish' held at Rajshekhar's ancestral house at Parsi Bagan, mid-Calcutta, around the 1920s and 30s. Jatin Sen had a reputation for making good tea; therefore, his presence was regarded as a 'must' for the visitors of the 'Majlish'.[2] Incidentally, a few initial sketches for Jatin Sen's illustrations had oblique references to the physical attributes of some of the Sabha's members.

Parashuram: Visualiser par excellence

Rajshekhar, or Parashuram, was a consummate visualizer. He conceived the artworks for his narrative and drew the initial sketches, which he gave Jatin Sen, who chose the pseudonym Narada, with specific instructions for the final illustrations. Narada was a faithful executor of the draft sketches, following the directives closely. It was the norm for cooperation between them, the writer and illustrator.[3] Parimal Ray's discovery of the treasure trove of Parashuram's sketches and draft drawings, published in this book, clearly shows the stages in this process of collaboration. The initial sketches by Parashuram and Jatin Sen's rough drawings based on them, as well as the final illustrations for the print-works, have been arranged to produce an excellent archive, which is a visual pleasure. These initial sketches indicate the acuteness of observation and sense of precision on the part of Parashuram.

Ganderiram Batparia, for example, one of the famous characters of the con company named 'Shri Shri Siddheshwari Limited' (1922), the first story written by Parashuram, is given this description in Parashuram's sketch: "Ganderi, well-built, upper-jaw protruding, racial type. Smiling would be better"[*see pg 42*]. The 'Smiling Face' would appear as quite a ruse for this type of persona with the appropriate surname 'Batparia,' a thorough cheat.

Parashuram, at the same time, had no fondness for excess; a note, thereby, instructed Jatin Sen firmly, "Jatin, don't draw too many illustrations." [*see pg 42*]. He maintained his reins of control over the sketches drawn by Jatin Sen till the third story collection,

Hanumaner Swapno (1937), the last published work by Parashuram illustrated by Jatin Sen. In the book, *Khalwidong Swami*, a fashionable Guruji or religious preceptor, actually a charlatan, was described thus: "curly, long clusters of hair, plum and fleshy built, neatly dressed in dhoti, loose sleeved Kurta but with a stole, without beard and moustache, young in age" [*see pg 163*]. The writer has left out no detail in his visualization of the Swami; the artist simply has to follow the instructions with a pen and brush.

Even the situation under which the large goat, with its furious posture, butted the Swami has been described in precise language. A delightful sketch was drawn but not published in the book for

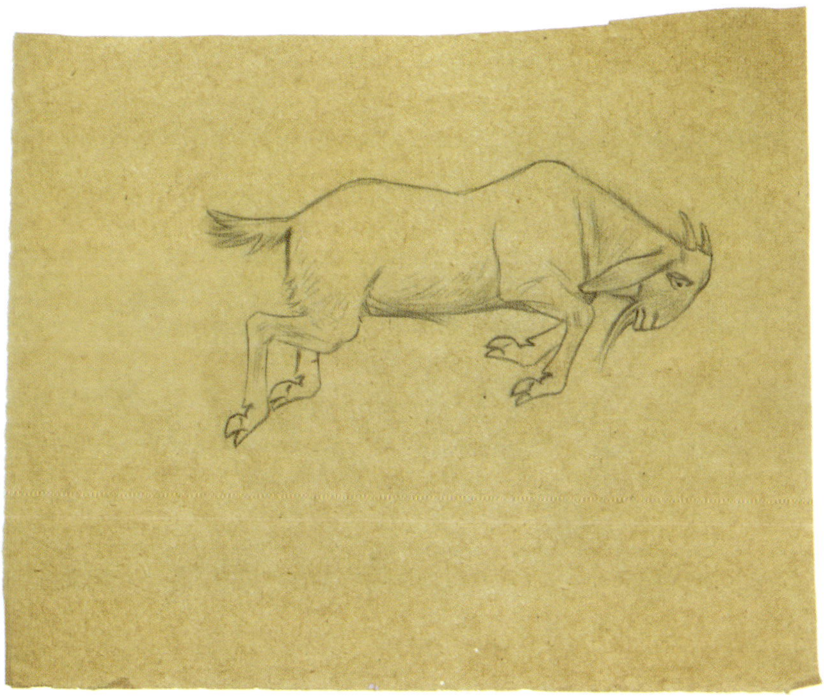

unknown reasons. The illustration, however, used in the printed version depicting the situation is different, clearly less funny and more tepid. The initial neatness and compactness of the book illustrations, which grew from a mutual understanding between a perfect visualizer and a talented and efficient artist, gradually faded and took a downward slide.

Jatin Sen ceased to create illustrations for Parashuram's subsequent story books published after *Hanumaner Swapno* (1937). Even his sketches for the *Ramayana*, translated by Rajshekhar Basu and preserved by Dipankar Basu, and for the first time published in this catalogue, have not been used for the printed version.

About the collaboration

Pramathanath Bishi, a perceptive literary critic and an admirer of Rajshekhar's writings, has written an informative introduction to the collected writings of Parashuram. He has opined that Jatin Sen's illustrations lost their lustre in the later works, and the lack of proper illustrations certainly makes the later stories less appealing.[4] The facts, however, are slightly different. Parashuram produced a collection of nine story books, of which Jatin Sen illustrated the first three. These have also been printed in single collections of stories and collected works. Many other stories have been published in different well-known journals, especially the autumn numbers or Puja Special. These are – *Krishnakali Ityadi Galpo, Niltara Ityadi Galpo* or *Anandibai Ityadi Galpo*, etc. These books have Parashuram's finest stories like *Anandibai, Parashpathar, Saralakha Home* or *Rajmahishi*. Stalwarts like Shaila Chakraborty, Satyajit Ray and Samir Roychoudhury illustrated a few of them with considerable verve and skill. Hardly any of them has been included in his published books, and none has been used in Parashuram's sanctioned volumes.

The reticent Parashuram made no comments on the illustrations by other artists, not even on the delightful picture of the 'Jujuburi' (cadaverous appearance) of the heroine in the story *Saralakha Home*. He had no control over these illustrators, appointed by different authorities. Parashuram had his own artist, Narad, and had no preference for any other.[5]

Parashuram was the original visualizer, and Jatin Sen the faithful and skilful executor, transcribing the vision into a few deft and subtle lines. This is precisely the point Rabindranath Tagore underlined in his review, praising the perfect balance between the textual description and visual representation of the characters in the book *Gaddalika*. There is no glitch, no dissonance between the two. The balance happens to be perfect. "The pen and brush perfectly match (*Jor*) each other; the writing flows as smoothly as the drawings. The two are on the same perfect level."[6]

The assessment of Pramatha Chaudhury, the editor of the avant-garde magazine *Sabuj Patra*, is most forthright. To him, *Gaddalika* is a picture book, a "cinema"; all the characters and accompanying drawings "are living pictures."[7]

The significance of the co-creation

Two contemporary citations from perceptive critics have underlined a few points. First, book illustrations and covers used to receive scant attention in the book reviews of that time. Jatin Sen's illustrations, however, elicited a rapturous response and have been accepted as integral to the narration of the stories. Thus, this critical appreciation was certainly a significant event in the history of Bengali graphic art.

Secondly, the specific assessment of Jatin Sen's works is also important. Parashuram's work has been regarded as a character sketchbook, all the humorous characters and situations being

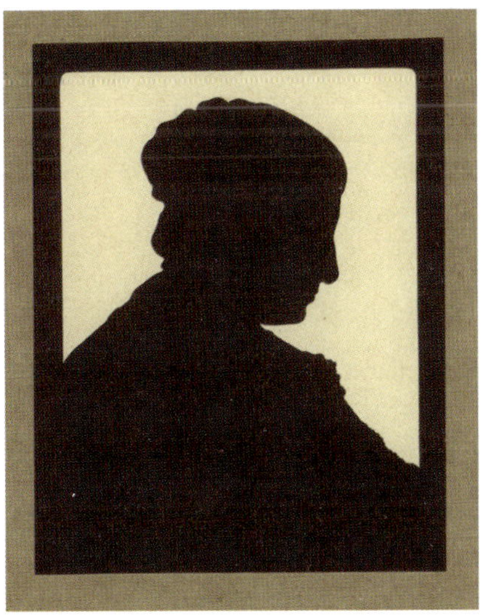

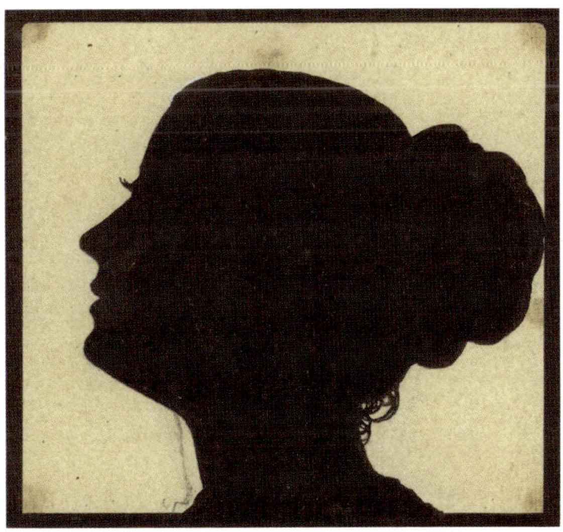

Silhouettes by Jatindrakumar Sen

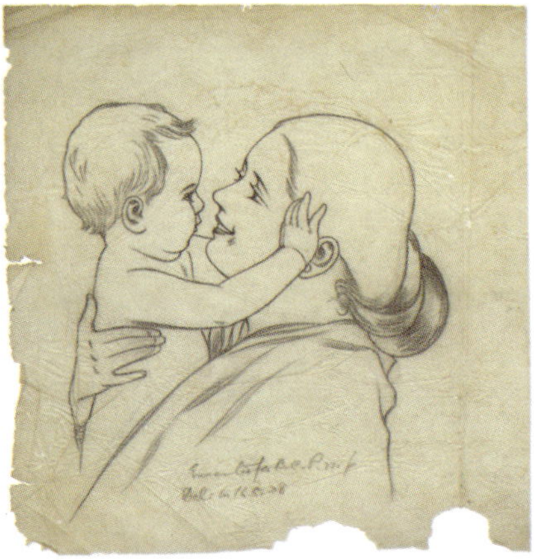

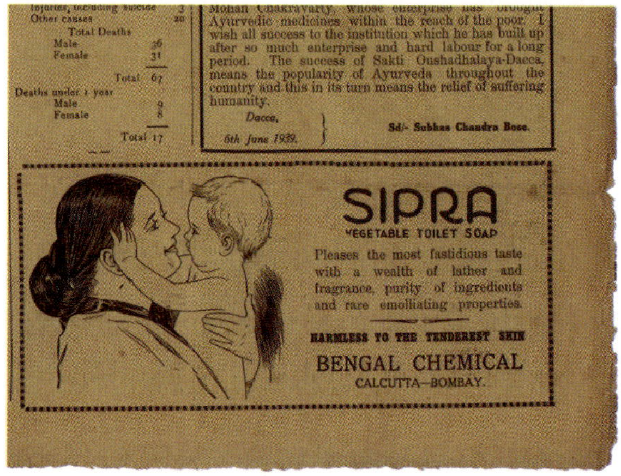

Other causes 20

Total Deaths

Male 36

Female 31

Total 67

Deaths under 1 year

Male 9

Female 8

Total 17

Ayurvedic medicines within the reach of the poor. I wish all success to the institution which he has built up after so much enterprise and hard labour for a long period. The success of Sakti Oushadhalaya-Dacca, means the popularity of Ayurveda throughout the country and this in its turn means the relief of suffering humanity.

Dacca, 6th June 1939. Sd/- Subhas Chandra Bose.

Sketch and published illustration for a Bengal Chemical advertisement by Jatindrakumar Sen

rooted in the familiar environment of the daily life of the Bengali middle class. Jatin Sen, following the narrative of Parashuram closely, has translated the characters into black and white drawings. Pramatha Chaudhury has dubbed it a perfect product of 'Sehai-Kalam' (ink-work), a fine piece of line drawing. The intellectual investment behind the vision has to be yet recognized. Third, there were traditions of printed book illustrations in Bengal around the mid-twentieth century. Book production and illustration by the Santiniketan artists and the works of Abanindranath and his associates for Bengali books created a distinct genre, the so-called Bengal School of Art.

On the other hand, Upendrakishore Ray Chowdhury and Sukumar Ray engaged with illustrating children's books, sometimes producing humorous pictures, accommodating the European techniques of book production and graphic art. Amidst these, *Gaddalika*, with its distinctive satire and emphatic visual representation of character types, happens to be a new intervention in the orientation and outlook. Despite the fulsome critical praise, no contemporary reviewer has recognized the newness: the plasticity of gestures and postures in the visualization and its consequent sketches, a laughable 'unreal' in the so-called 'natural' representation of the world around. This distinctiveness from the two hitherto well-known contemporary traditions of book illustrations needs to be emphasized here.

The creative process

It is necessary to underline a small intervening processual space of the printed illustrations. The stories with pictures have been first produced in magazines and then incorporated into the book. In that way of transference, there happened to be a slight shift and alteration to make the illustration more meaningful following the story. We can cite one example from *Shri Shri Siddheshwari Limited*. In this story, initially published in *Bharatbarsha*, a well-known magazine, the headpiece shows a picture of Calcutta, a collected mass of buildings, temples and chimneys of the factories. In the headpiece of the story published in the book, *Gaddalika and Other Stories*, the figure of Shyamlal Ganguly 'Brahmachari', a key character, appeared in front of the urban scene, underlining the spatial context of the stories. The change is subtle but telling.[8]

Parashuram is a great storyteller of the marital accords and discords, with all their follies, attractions, adjustments and humour, in the middle-class Bengali milieu. The ghost story *Bhushandir Mathe* is an acme of his creative imagination. All the male ghosts are haunted by the memories of their quarrelsome wives in their afterlife. The lightweight, ghost-like figures are not at all gruesome, but are similar to their human appearance, more free to talk and move. They are ghost-men, 'Bhuta' (Bhu + ta), coming from the past world, yet quite familiar in the present milieu.

This freedom of incongruities is represented in their flexible, funny postures and gestures, in the plasticity of their swift action. Kalia Ghost (Kele Bhut), for example, is described as "a jet-black, very slim figure with a turban in head slid down the toddy-palm tree" [*see pg 80-82*]. The Bengali word "Sarak' in the narrative happens to be onomatopoeic. In Parashuram's draft sketch and Jatin Sen's drawing, the Kele Bhut with elongated hands and unnatural postures of climbing down the tree marvellously captures the sense of the quick movement of the non-corporeal ghost, appropriate to the word 'Sarak.' Again, Parashuram is the guide and master visualizer, and Jatin Sen follows his draft sketch closely with deft skill and precision.

Jatin Sen often added situational perspective to the figures drawn by Parashuram. For example, in the writer's sketch, Dakini the ogress, is like a harmless older woman holding a date-palm branch as a broom, standing erect. The narrative says, "She is sweeping the floor of a porch." The very action of sweeping is expressed in a posture of a slightly bent body, underlined in Jatin Sen's draft sketch. In the final illustrations for the book, a blue-line indicator has supplied the background screen, roof and door to complete the narrative description. These deft touches have emerged from the academic and naturalistic style, standard drawing exercise – a faithful representation of a village cottage [*see pg 53-54*]. Imagination, as if, belongs to Parashuram while Jatin Sen has the skill to produce and refine it as per rule. This very structure and tenor of collaboration have been ever present in the illustrations of Parashuram's first three books – *Gaddalika* (1924), *Kajjali* (1928) and *Hanumaner Swapno* (1937).

The ideology behind the illustration

The nature of collaboration between the narrator and illustrator is symptomatic of the definitive ideology behind the illustration. The verb 'illustrate' carries a sense of: "to make lustrous or luminous". And illustration means "the action or fact of making clear and evident".[9] Jatin Sen has the sole objective of highlighting the character and situation of the textual narrative so that the logic of the narrative becomes evident to the readers as per the author's specific intention. Illustrator's autonomous role has been limited to the role of an obedient but extremely efficient artist to fill up the few gaps to make original designs suitable for the book.

There may be another notion of illustration. The artist may have the autonomy of a distinctive reader to bring out a more profound and innate meaning from the author's narratives. Satyajit Ray (1921-1992), Shaila Chakraborty (1909-1989), and Ahibhushan

Malik (1924-1986) cultivated the notion of the creative tradition of book illustration. Their world differs significantly from that of Parashuram and Jatin Sen. The latter are undoubtedly two great duos, one absolute leader and the other a skilful and disciplined follower in the narration and illustration of Bengali graphic art. This catalogue is an acceptable testimony to a unique creative collaboration and a particular vision of book illustration in the art world of Bengal.

NOTES

1 'Jatindra Kumar Sen', *Bharater Bhaskar* and *Chitrashilpi*, compiled and edited by Kamal Sarkar, Jogmaya Prakashani, Calcutta, 1984, p. 167

2 For this 'Majlish' or informal arrangement of meeting of friends and associates in Rajshekhar Basu's parental house, see Sailendra Krishna Saha, 'Utkendra Samiti', Katha Sahitya, Rajsekhar Basu Commemoration Volume, Sravan, 1360 BS, cited in *Parashuram Granthabali*, Calcutta, MC Sarkar and Sons, 1394 BS, pp-13-14

3 Parashuram is the non de plume of Rajshekhar Basu and Narad is that of Jatindrakumar Sen. 'Parashuram' was the name reserved for fiction and was persistently used to distinguish fictive stories from the non-fiction or translation works, which were written and published under the name of Rajshekhar Basu. Narad, name of the mythic sage, had been taken up by Jatin Sen soon to be discarded for his actual signature.

4 Pramathanath Bishi, *Introduction*, Parashuram Granthabali, Vol 1, op.cit. p. 21

5 For discussion on Parashuram's other illustrators, see Gautam Bhadra, 'Parashuramer Dohar-ra (illustrated)', *Ei Somoy*, Autumn No., 1420 BS, pp 256-267

6 Rabindranath Tagore, '*Gaddalika*', *Prabasi*, Agrahyan, 1332 BS; *Rabindra Rachanabali*, Vol 32, Visva-Bharati edition, 1419 BS, p 251-252

7 For Pramatha Chaudhury's assessment, see Parimal Ray ed., *Gaddalika Prabaha*, IMH, New Delhi, 2019, p269

8 The magazine publication date for the story is 1922. The story was republished in *Gaddalika* in 1924. All the relevant dates are discussed in my article 'Parashuramer Dohar-ra (illustrated),' op.cit. cf. illustration 1 and 6, see the article here.

9 Shorter Oxford English Dictionary

STORIES FROM *GADDALIKA*

COVER ILLUSTRATION FOR
GADDALIKA (SHEEP IN A FILE), 1924

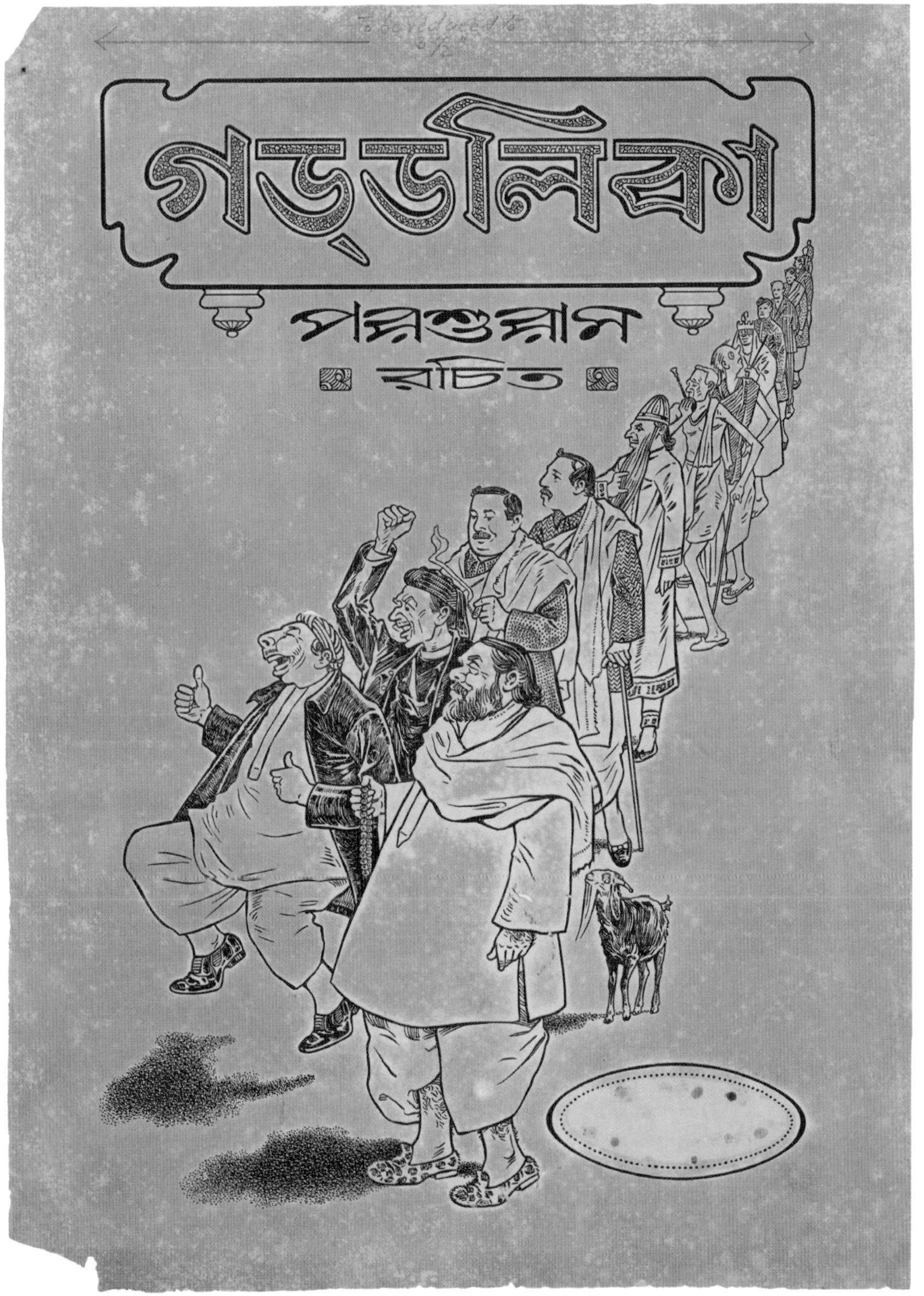
গড্ডলিকা
পরশুরাম
রচিত

SHRI SHRI SIDDHESHWARI LTD.

Shyambabu was a businessman who was overtly religious and secretly wished that people would think of him as the great Shyamananda Brahmachari. He ran a company with his brother-in-law Bipin (inventor of The Automatic Sridurgagraph, which could stamp the name of Goddess Durga 108 times in only nine impressions!) Keeping in mind the enormous revenues of the great temples of India, they start a new company – Shri Shri Siddheshwari Ltd – to establish a successful Devi temple and pilgrimage centre, earning from hotels, shops and sale of *prasad*. They persuade several hypocritical pillars of society to join their board – especially Tinkari babu who considers himself very clever with money. Many shareholders invest in the company. Eventually, having pocketed the money, Shyambabu claims that wealth is a hindrance to spiritual growth and walks away leaving Tinkari holding the mess.

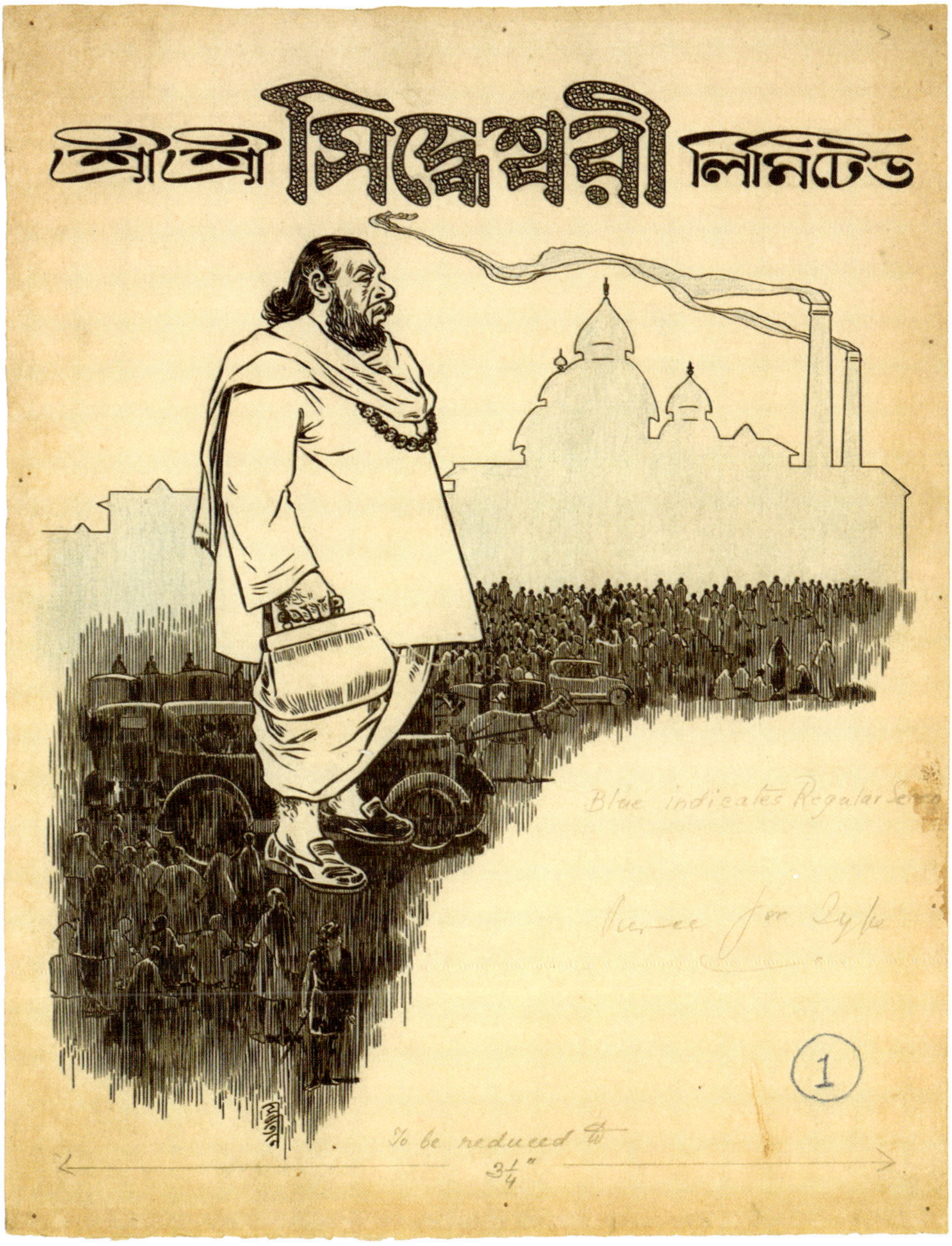

Illustration and title design for the opening page of *Shri Shri Siddheshwari Limited* (published in the collection *Gaddalika*, 1924)

Character: Shyamlal Ganguly (who preferred calling himself 'Brahmachari').

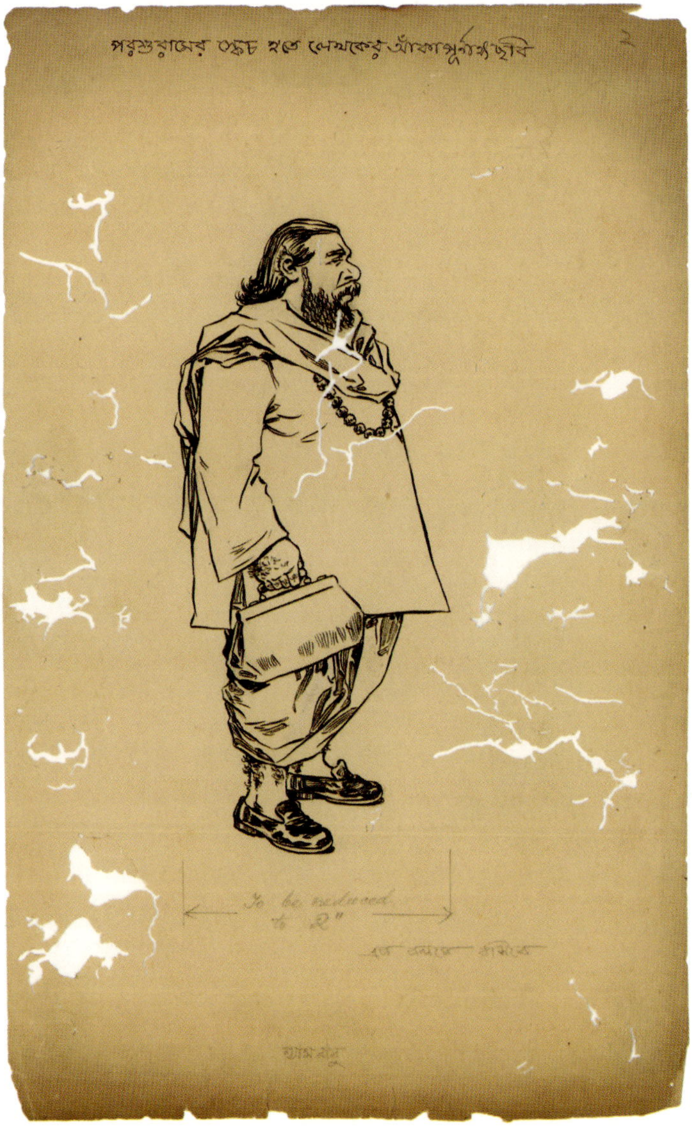

Draft illustration for *Shri Shri Siddheshwari Limited* (*Gaddalika*, 1924)

Character: Shyamlal Ganguly (who preferred calling himself 'Brahmachari').
Bangla text on top: "From Parashuram's sketch, the writer's full body image" (*indicating that Sen based the image on Parashuram's sketch*).
Bangla text below the figure: "Fit in 1 column".
Bangla text at bottom: "Shyam babu".

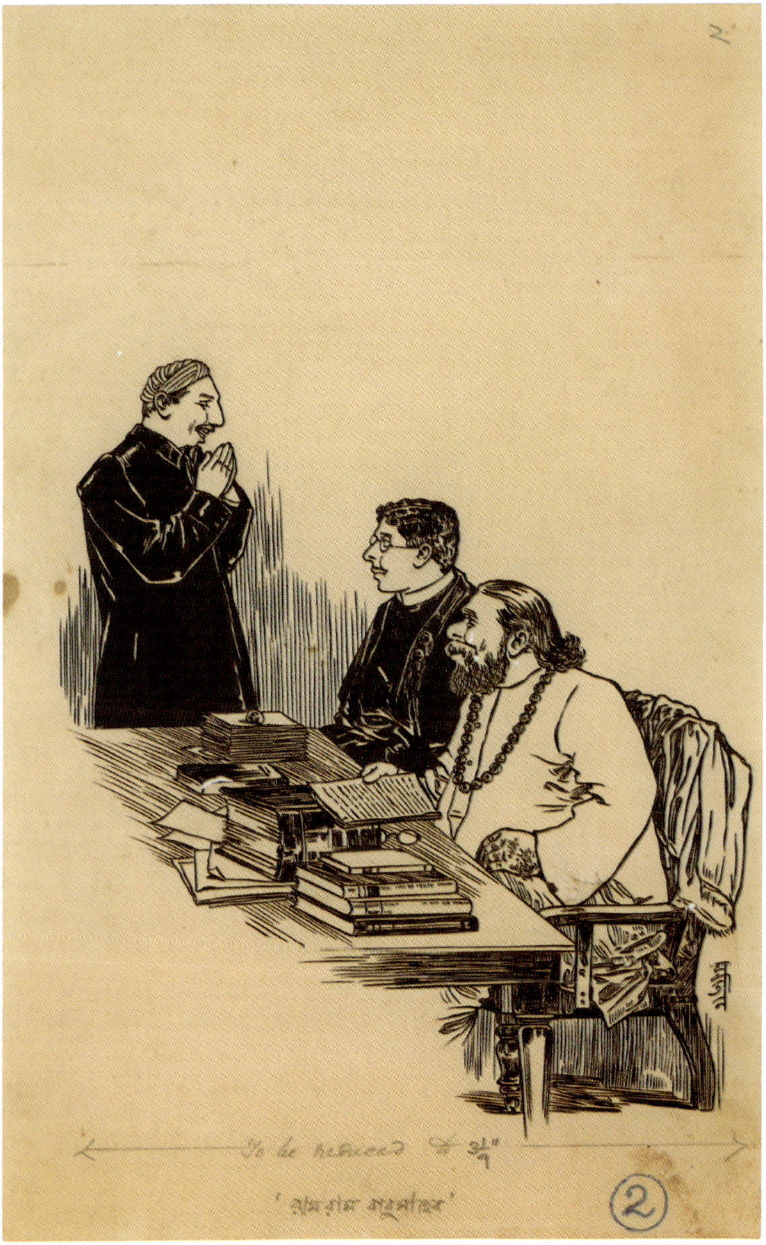

Illustration for *Shri Shri Siddheshwari Limited* (*Gaddalika*, 1924)

Bangla text: "Ram Ram babu saheb".
Characters: Ganderiram, Atal babu, and Shyam babu.

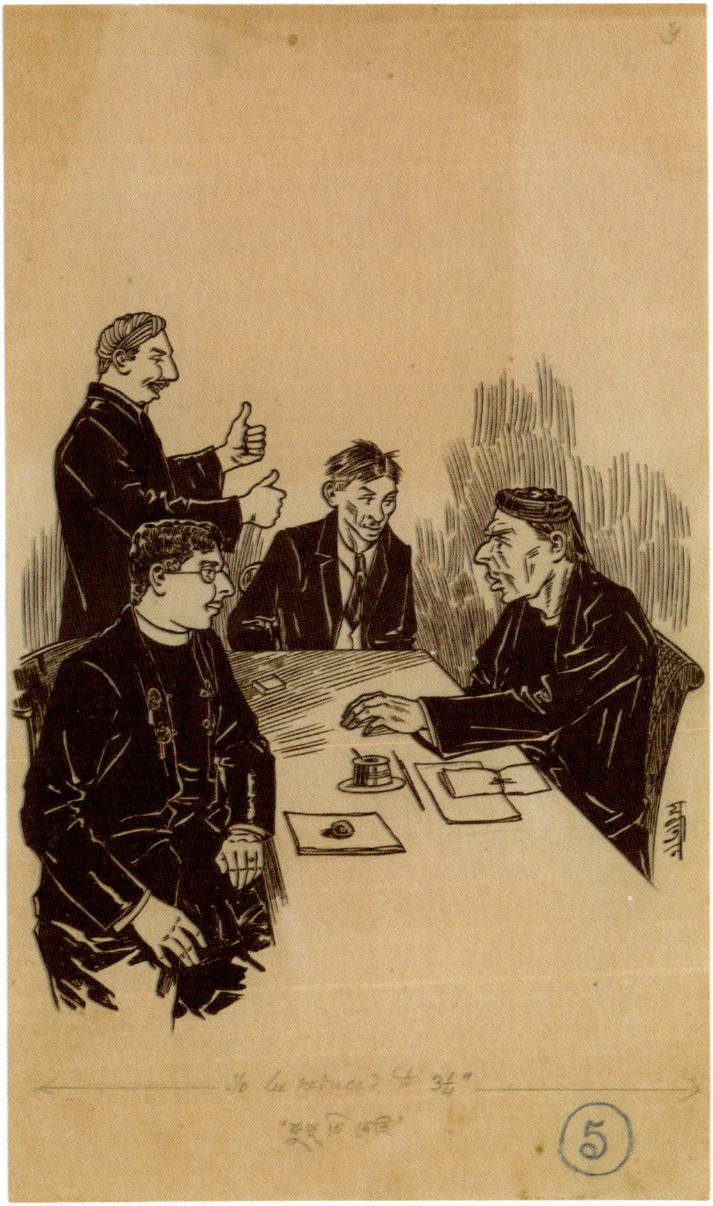

Illustration for *Shri Shri Siddheshwari Limited* (*Gaddalika*, 1924)

Bangla text: "Kucch bhi nahin" (Nothing).
Characters: Atal babu (in front), Ganderiram (with his thumbs up), Bipin babu and Tinkari babu.

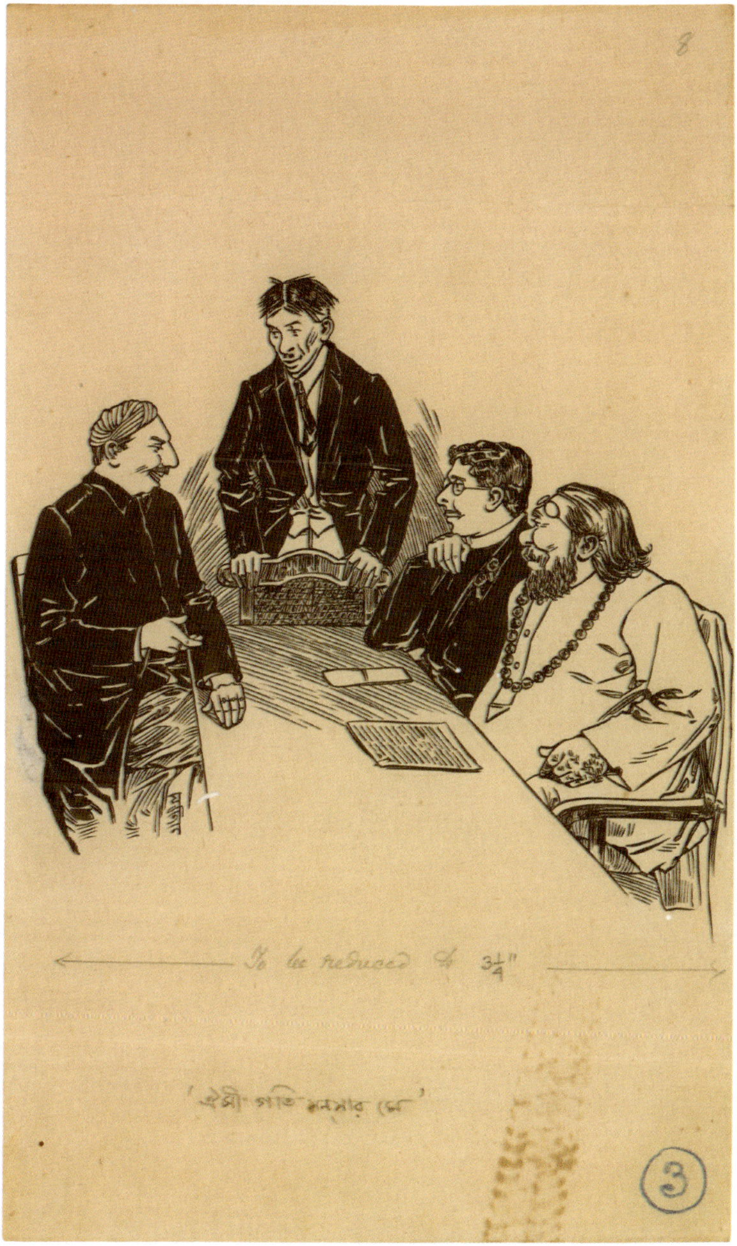

Illustration for *Shri Shri Siddheshwari Limited* (*Gaddalika*, 1924)
Bangla text: "Jaisi gati sansaar mein" (a verse from Tulsidas's *Ramcharitmanas* spoken by Ganderiram).
Characters: Ganderiram, Atal babu, and Shyam babu.

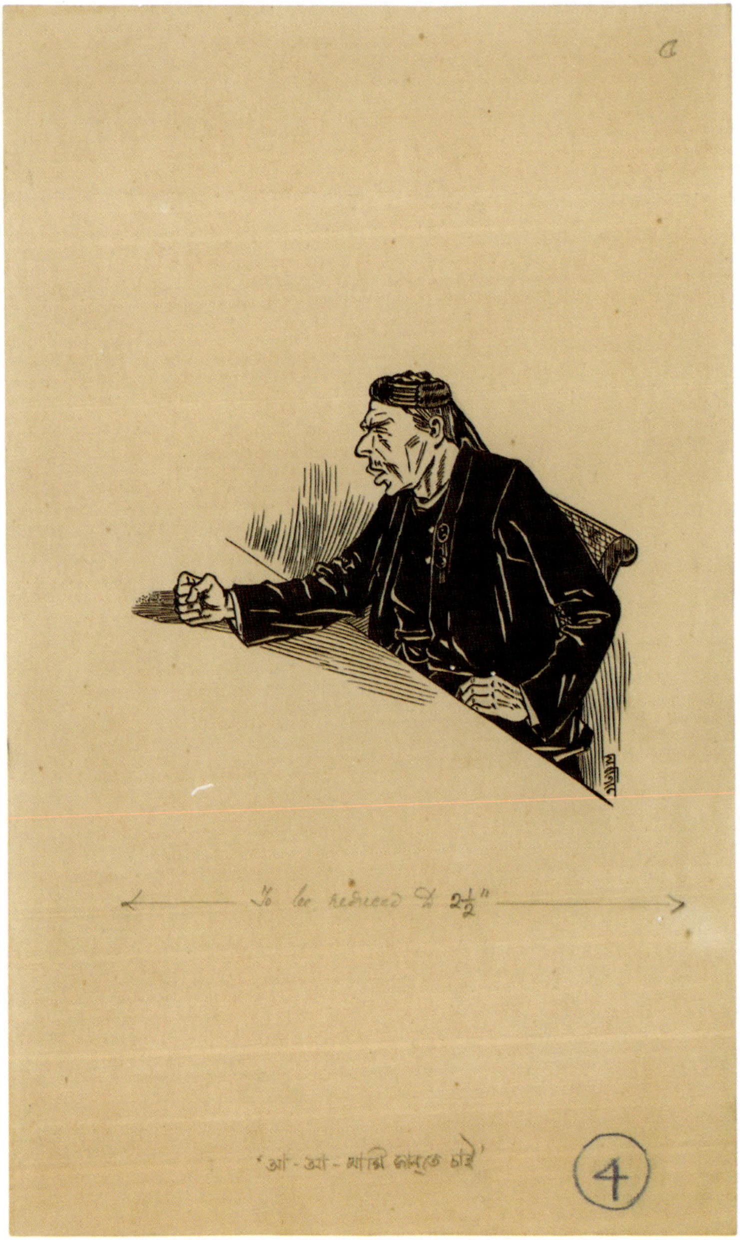

Illustration for *Shri Shri Siddheshwari Limited* (*Gaddalika*, 1924)

Bangla text: "I.. I... want to know".
Character: Tinkari Bandopadhyay.

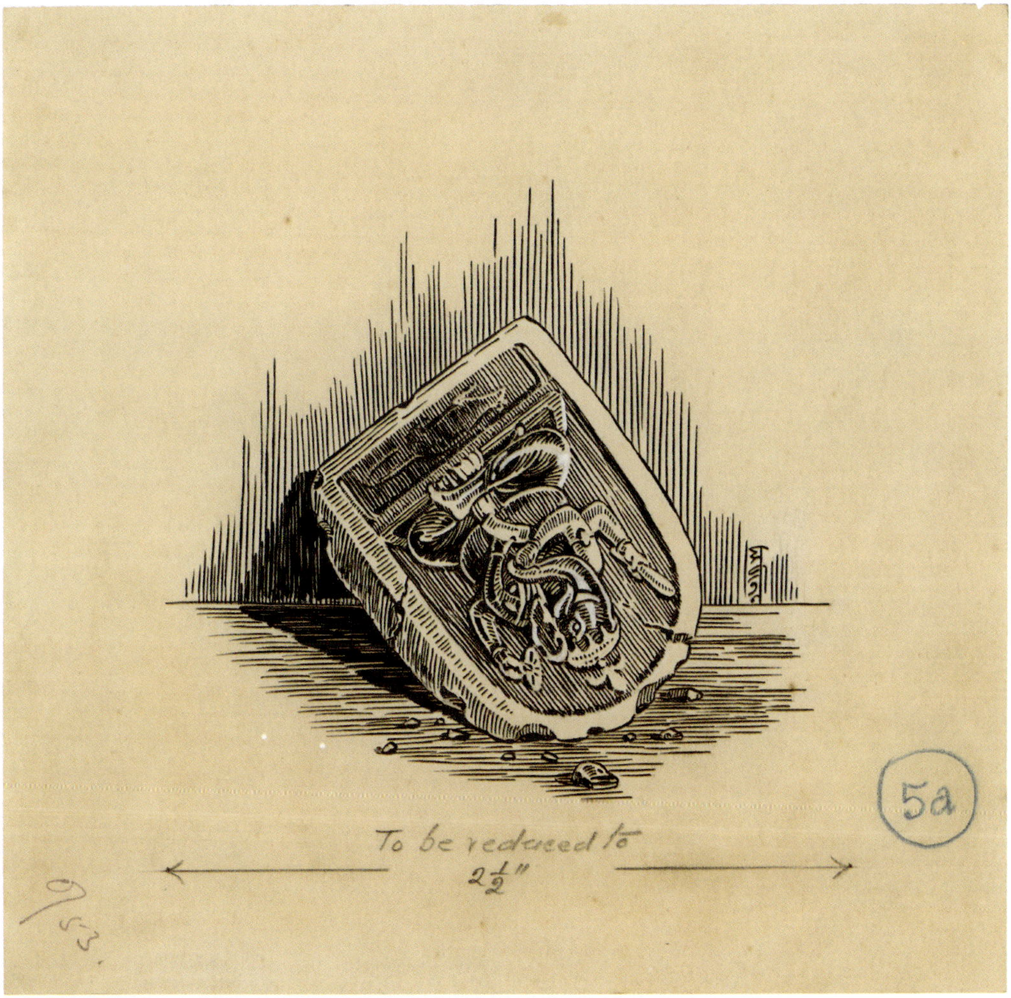

Illustration for the tailpiece of *Shri Shri Siddheshwari Limited* (*Gaddalika*, 1924)

[*A toppled Ganesh indicating that the company has sunk.*]

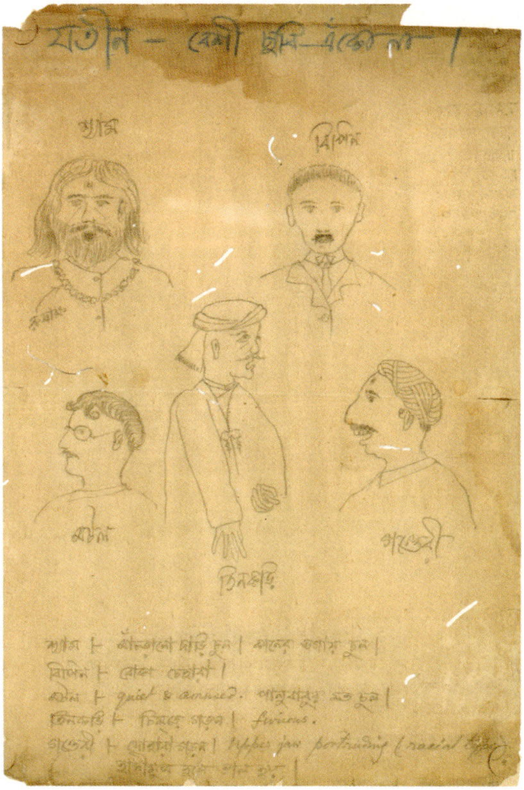

Parashuram's instructions and sketches for *Shri Shri Siddheshwari Limited* (*Gaddalika*, 1924)

Bangla text on top is a note from Parashuram saying: "Jatin, don't draw too many illustrations".
Characters in top row: Shyam (Shyamlal Ganguly); Bipin (Bipin Chaudhuri).
Characters in second row: Atal (Atalbehari Datta); Tinkari (Tinkari Bandopadhyay); Ganderi (Ganderiram Batparia).
Bangla text at the bottom:
Shyam: Well combed beard and hair. Hair growing on ears.
Bipin: Foolish appearance
Atal: Quiet and amused. Hair like Panubabu (*a name used by Bengalis to indicate someone fond of dressing up like a dandy*)
Tinkari: Lean. Furious.
Ganderi: Well built. Upper jaw portruding [*spelling as written by Parashuram*]. Racial type. Smiling face would be better.

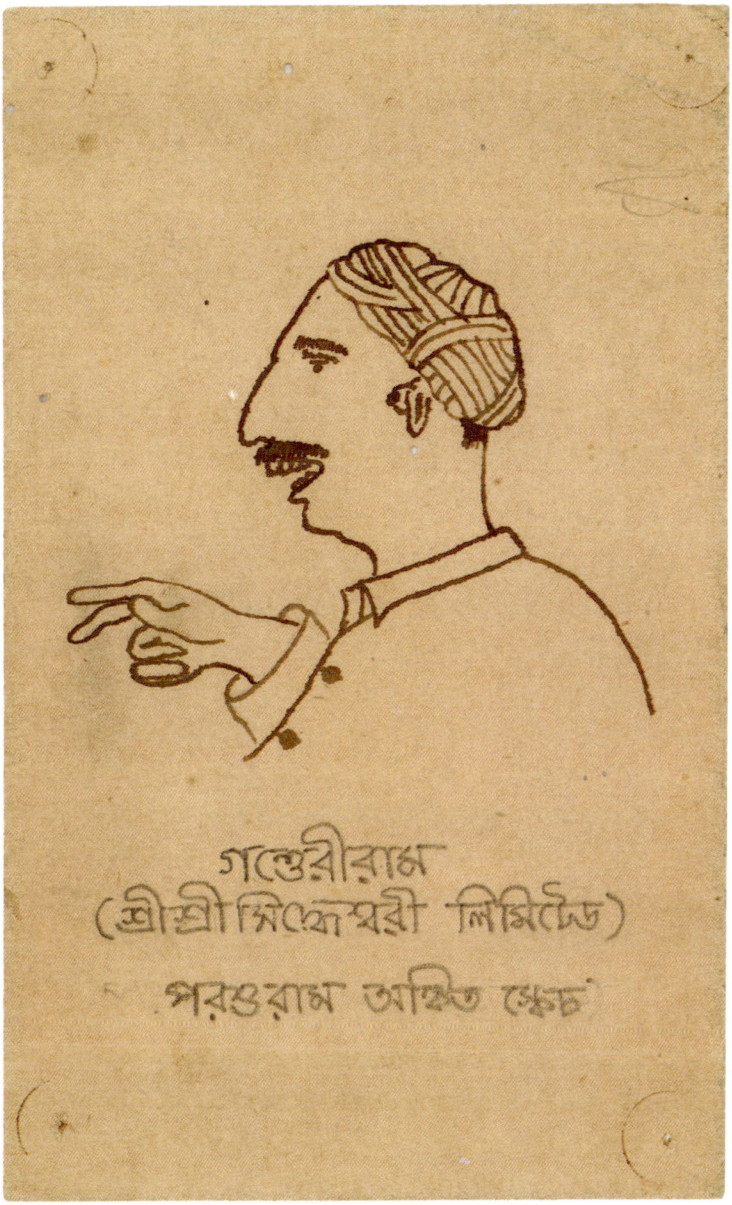

Parashuram's sketch for *Shri Shri Siddheshwari Limited* (*Gaddalika*, 1924)

Bangla text: "Ganderiram (*Shri Shri Siddheshwari Limited*) sketched by Parashuram".
Character: Ganderiram Batparia.

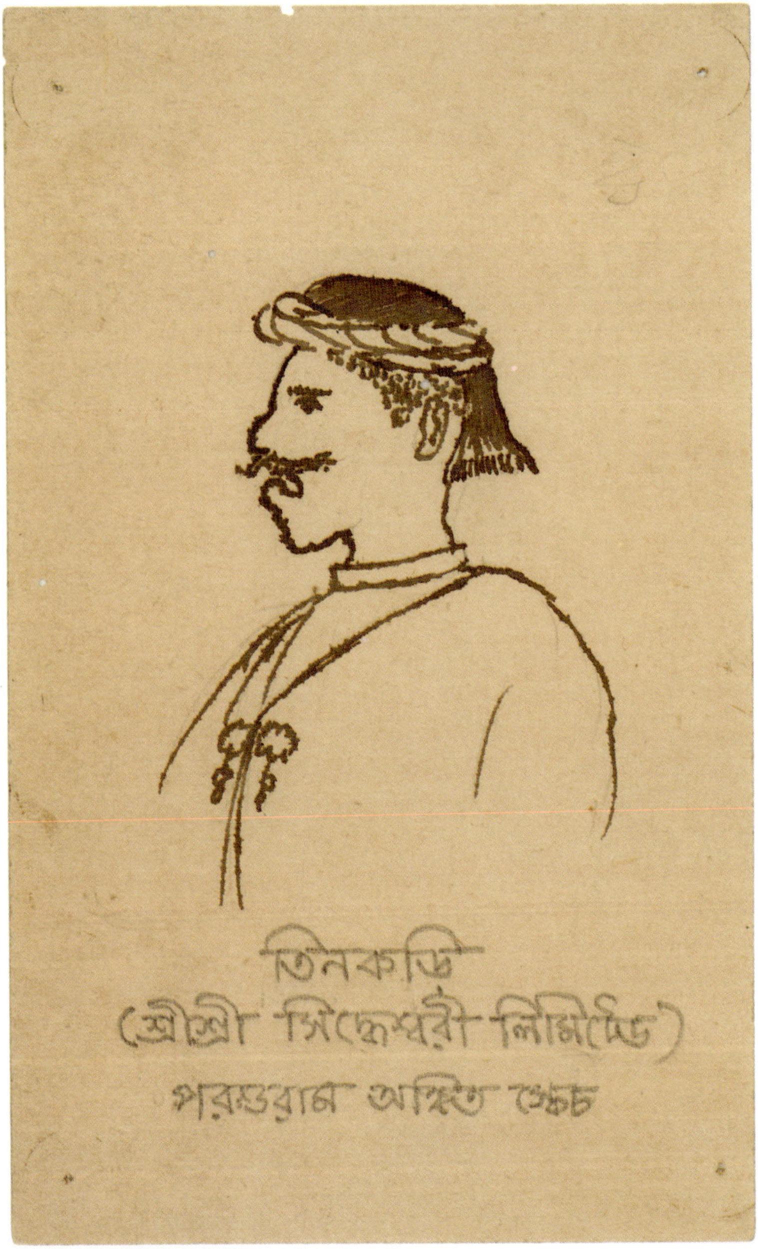

Parashuram's sketch for *Shri Shri Siddheshwari Limited* (*Gaddalika*, 1924)

Bangla text: "Tinkari (Shri Shri Siddheshwari Limited) sketched by Parashuram". Character: Tinkari Bandopadhyay.

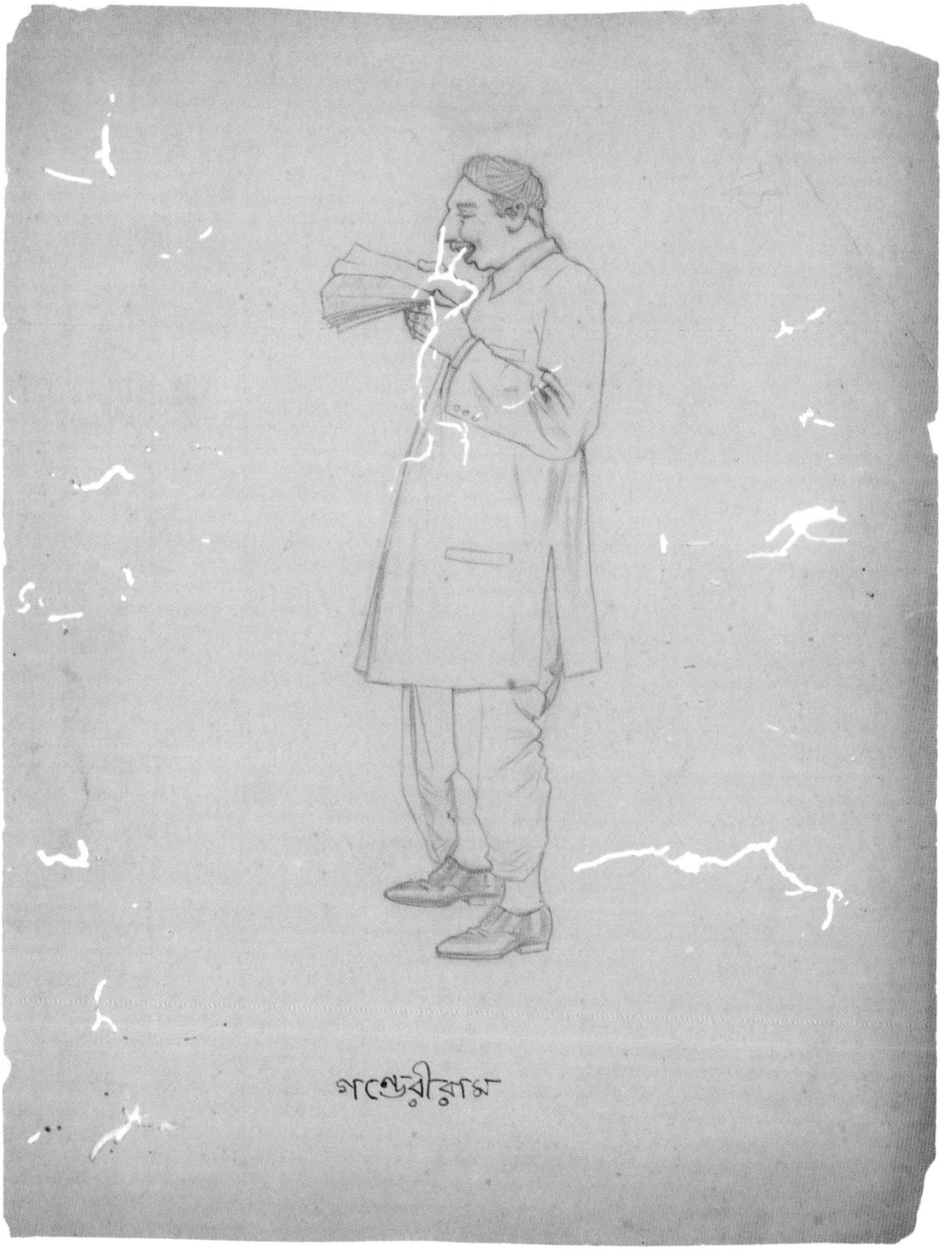

Unused draft sketch for *Shri Shri Siddheshwari Limited*

Bangla text says: “Ganderiram”.
Character: Ganderiram Batparia.

CHIKITSA SANKAT

After a fall, Nandadulal Mitra suffers from some minor injuries. He has a lot of money and consequently a lot of well wishers. They advise him in turns to visit an allopath, a homoeopath, a Hakim... the last impressively named Haziq-ul-mulq bin Lokman Nurullah Gazan Farullah al Hekim Yunani! Each medical man has a different and scary diagnosis – including the allopath's "cerebral tumour with strangulated gangolitandolia" – but no treatment helps Nanda babu. Eventually, he visits Doctor Miss Bipula Mallik who smilingly points out that there is nothing wrong with him and he just needs someone to look after him. The medical comedy turns into a love story...

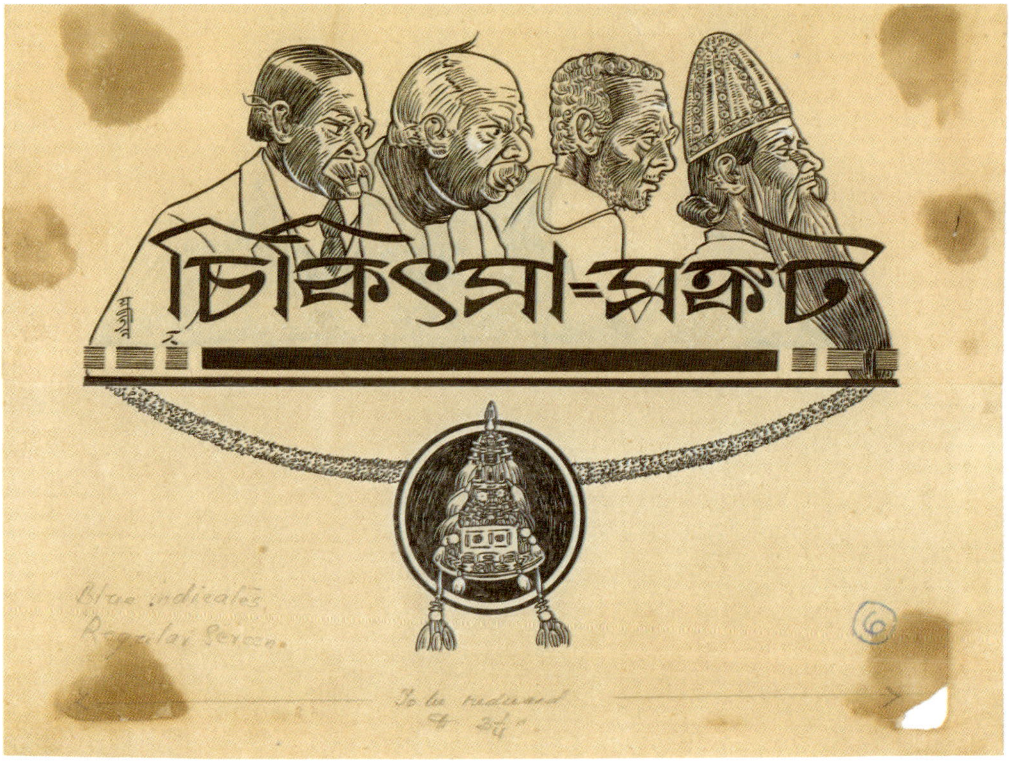

Illustration and title design for the opening page of *Chikitsa Sankat* (published in the collection *Gaddalika*, 1924)

Characters (from left): Dr Tafadar (MD, MRAS), Dr Nepal Chandra Roy ("famous homeopath"), Tarini Kaviraj, and Haziq-ul-mulq bin Lokman Nurullah Gazan Farullah al Hekim Yunani!

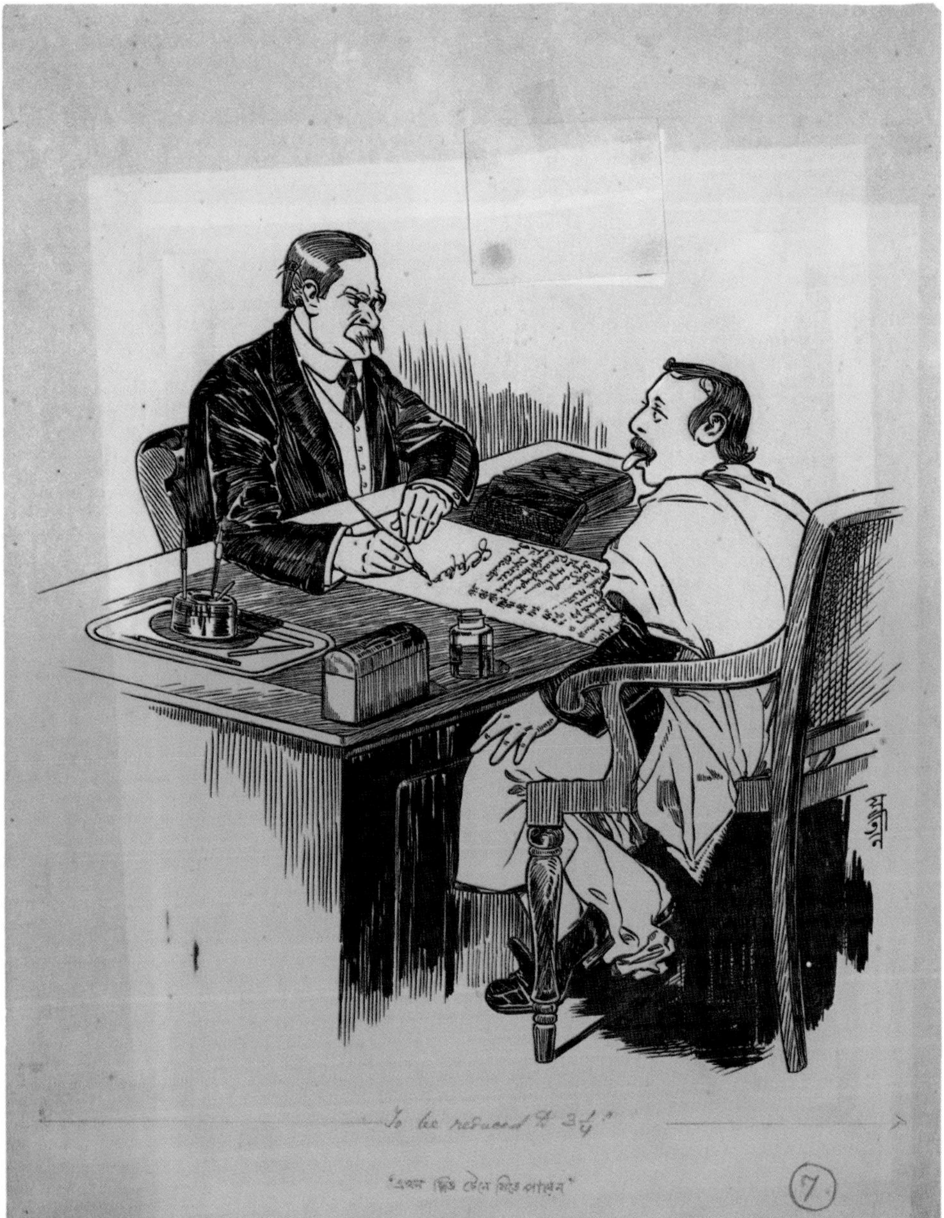

Illustration for *Chikitsa Sankat* (*Gaddalika*, 1924)

Bangla text: "You can draw in your tongue now".
Characters: Dr Tafadar with Nanda babu (Nandadulal Mitra).

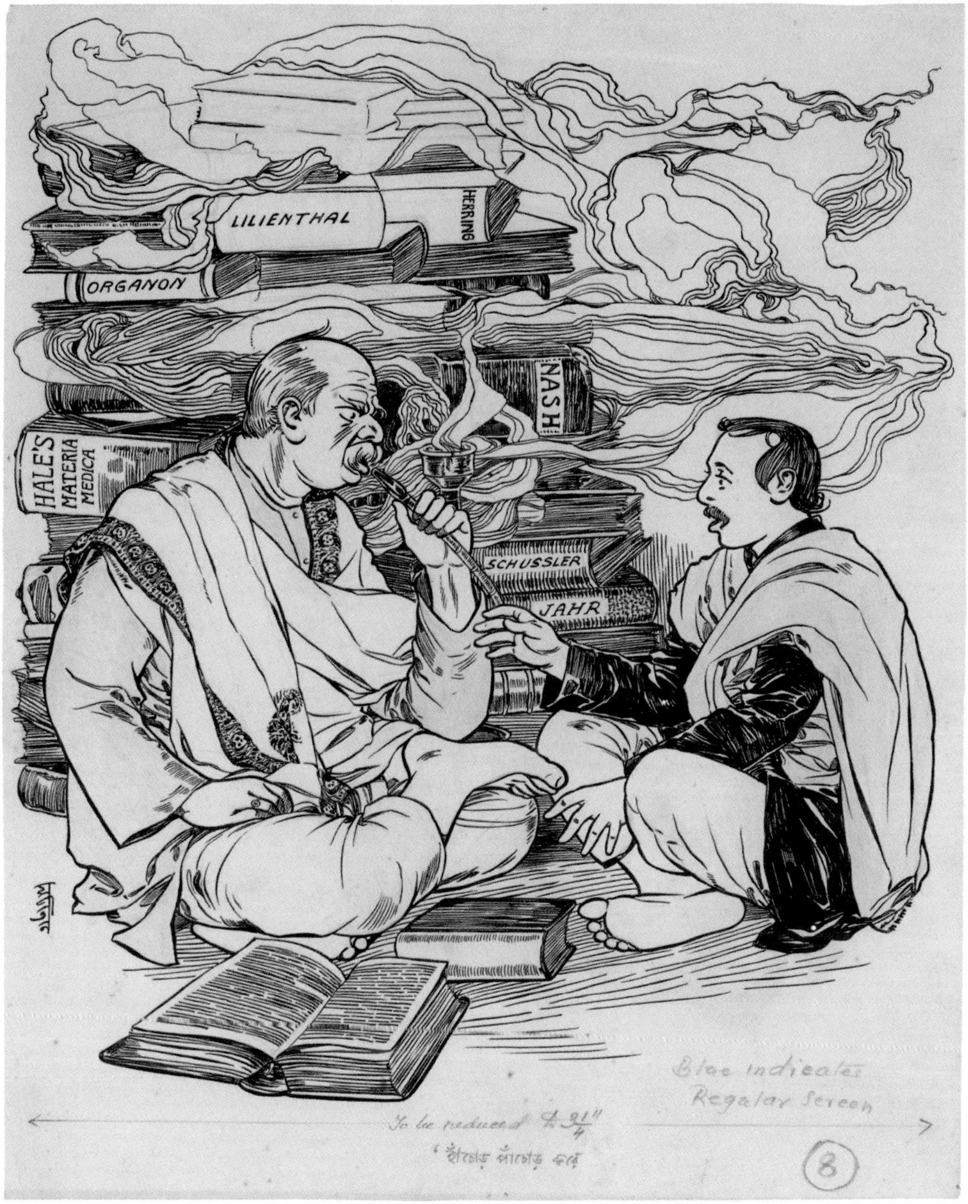

Illustration for *Chikitsa Sankat* (*Gaddalika*, 1924)

Bangla text: "My stomach churns".
Characters: Dr Nepal Chandra Roy (homeopath) with Nanda babu (Nandadulal Mitra).

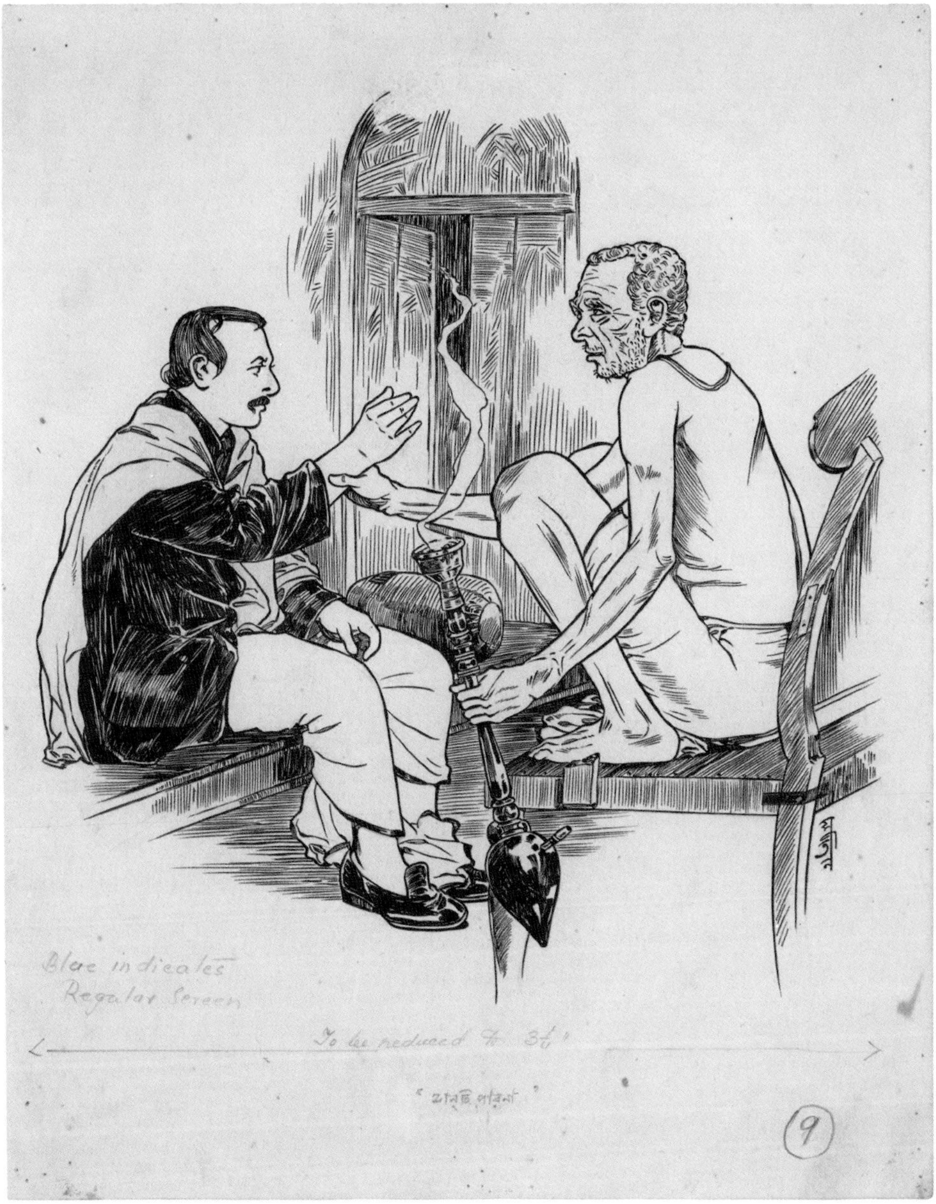

Illustration for *Chikitsa Sankat* (*Gaddalika*, 1924)

Bangla text: "You zust don't know it" (*'z' in the original writing to indicate the East Bengal accent*).
Characters: Tarini Kaviraj with Nanda babu (Nandadulal Mitra).

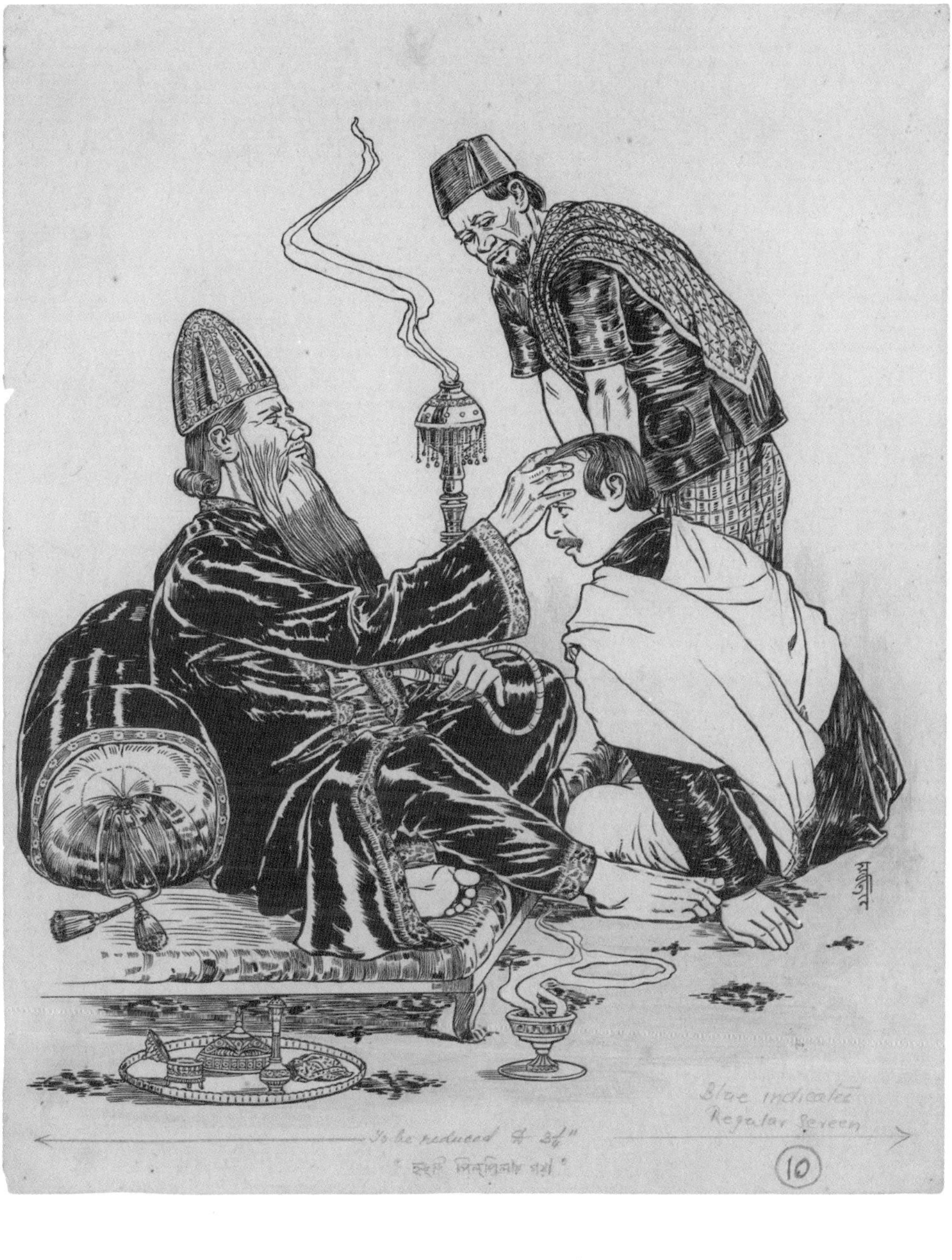

Illustration for *Chikitsa Sankat* (*Gaddalika*, 1924)

Bangla text: “The bones have gone completely soft”.
Characters: Haziq-ul-mulq bin Lokman Nurullah Gazan Farullah al Hekim Yunani with Nanda babu.

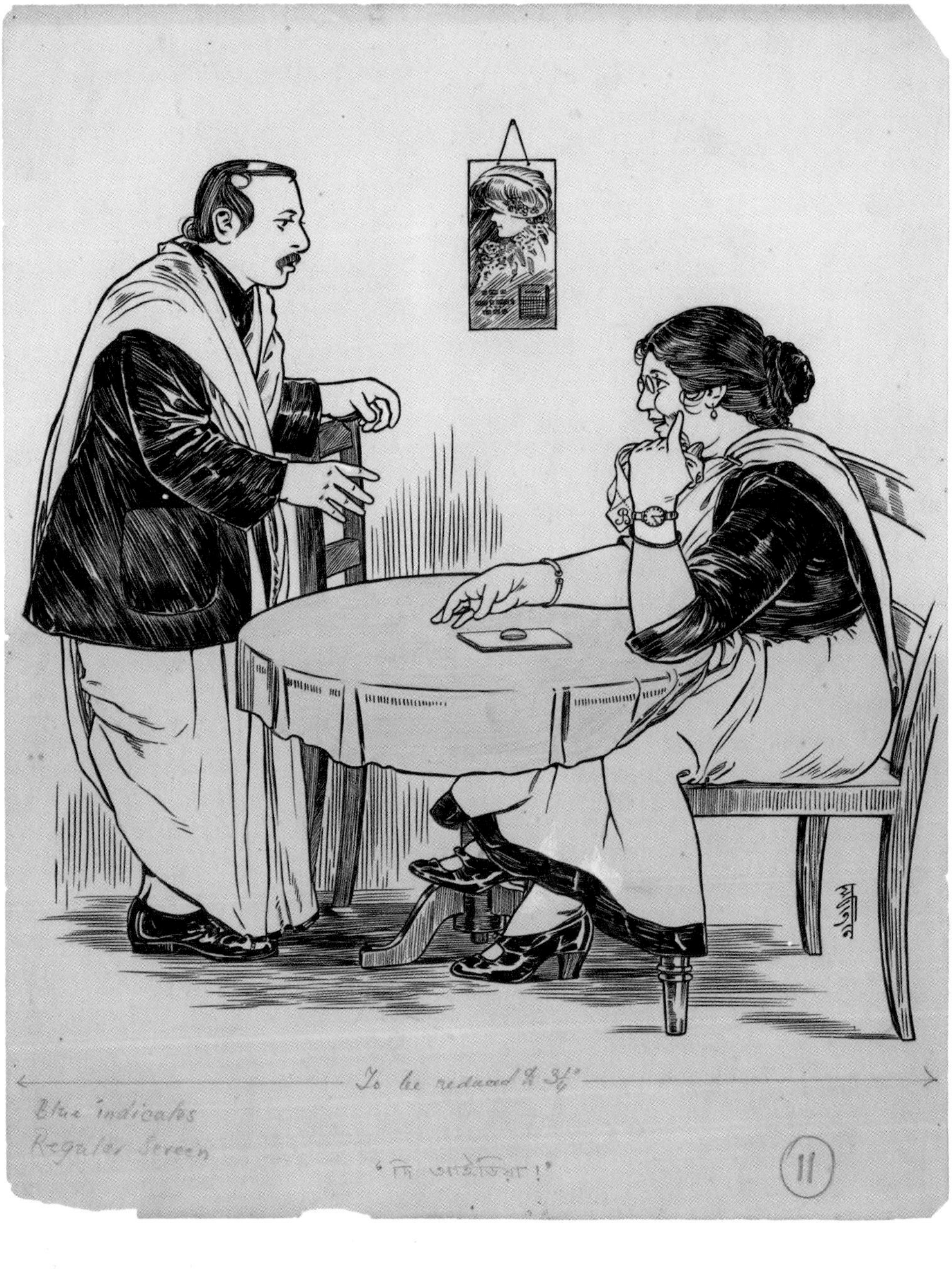

Illustration for *Chikitsa Sankat* (*Gaddalika*, 1924)

Bangla text: "The idea!".
Characters: Nandu babu with Dr. Miss Bipula Mallik.

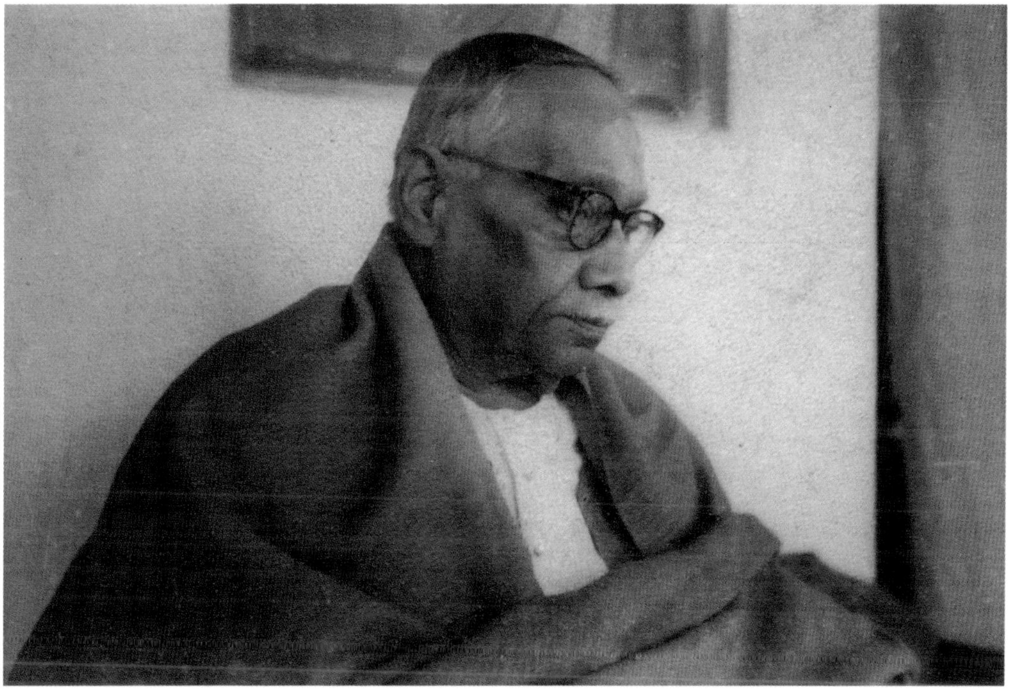

Jatindrakumar Sen

MAHAVIDYA

Mahabidya is yet another Parashuram story which satirizes the hypocrisy of the respectable. Jagadguru educates his students on Mahabidya or the supreme knowledge. He explains that while this knowledge is inherently present in every human being, it has to be tailored to suit the demands of civilized society. The story ends by pointing to this piece of wisdom from a common Bengali proverb: “There is nothing like stealing if you don’t get caught”.

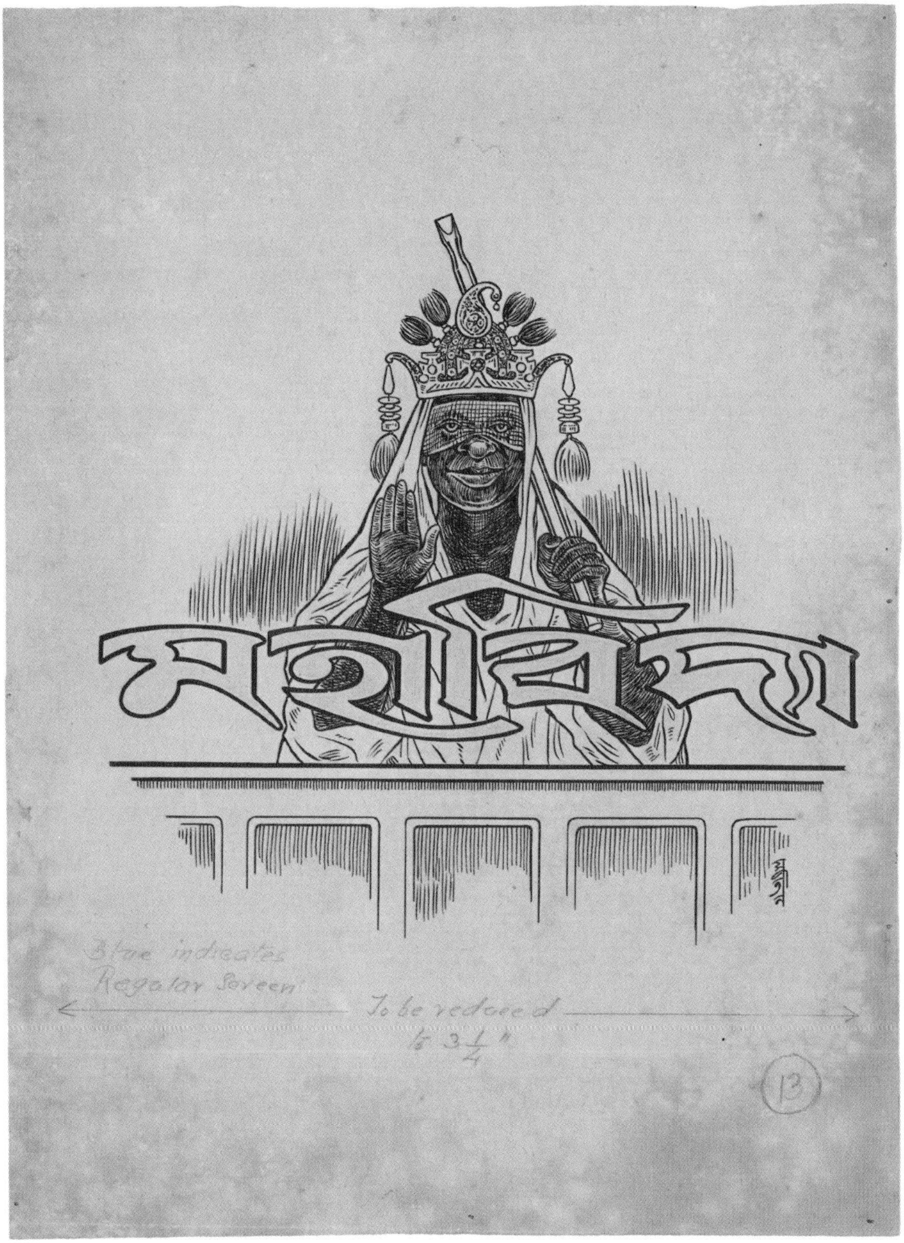

Illustration and title design for the opening page of *Mahavidya* (published in the collection *Gaddalika*, 1924)

Character: Jagadguru.

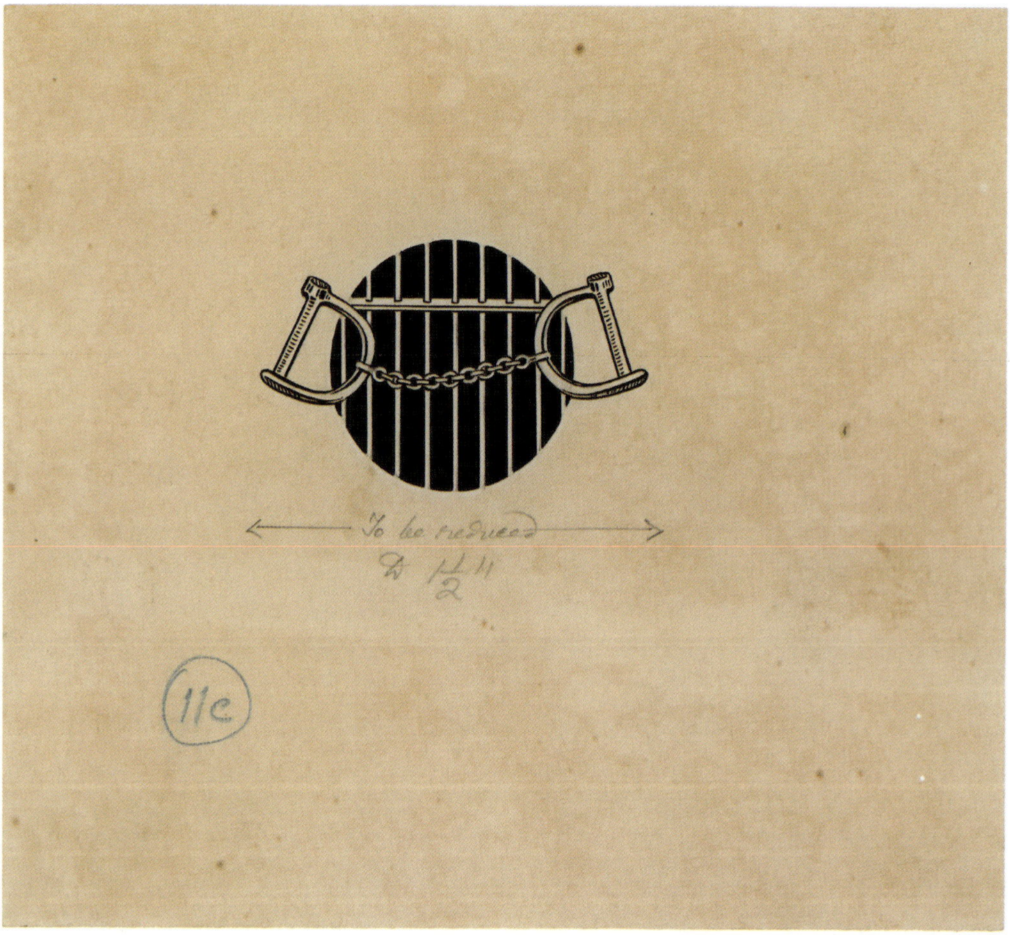

Illustration of a symbol for the tailpiece in *Mahavidya* (*Gaddalika*, 1924)

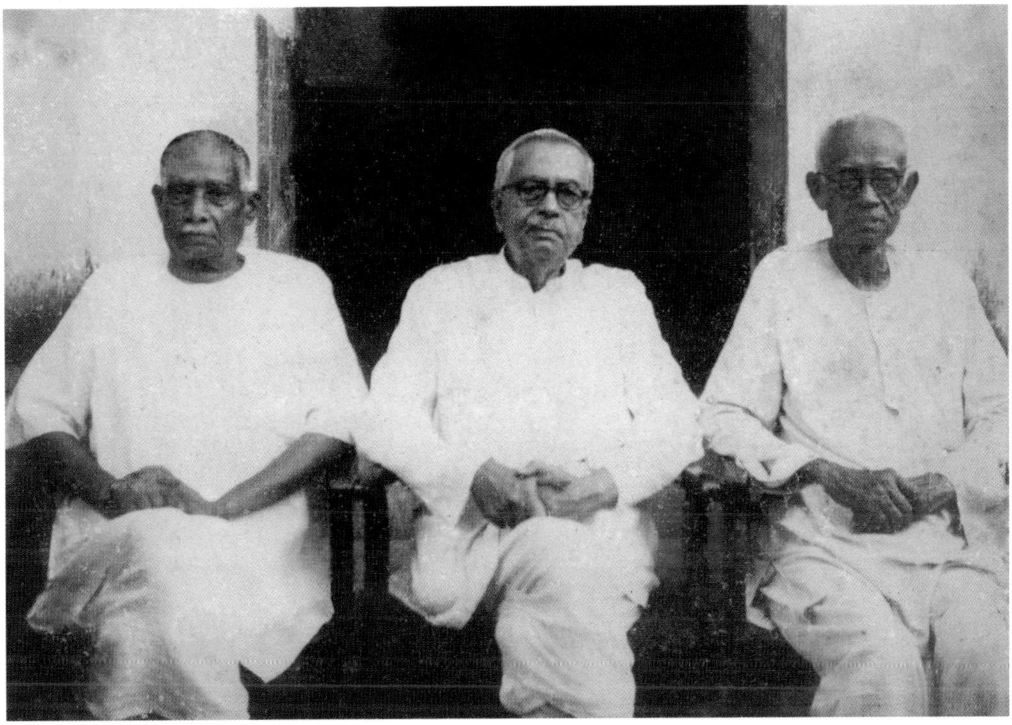

Jatindrakumar Sen, Rajshekhar Basu and Charuchandra Bhattacharya

LAMBAKARNA

The hero of the story, Lambakarna (long ears), is a goat. Rai Banshalochan Bannerjee Bahadur is a magistrate who hosts gossipy addas at his house. One day, when he goes for his evening walk, the goat follows him to his house. Although he wants to keep it as a pet, his wife Manini objects. Lambakarna creates a lot of mischief in the house and marital discord between husband and wife keeps increasing. Eventually, by saving Banshalochan babu's life, Lambakarna becomes dear to his wife and is accepted as a member of the household.

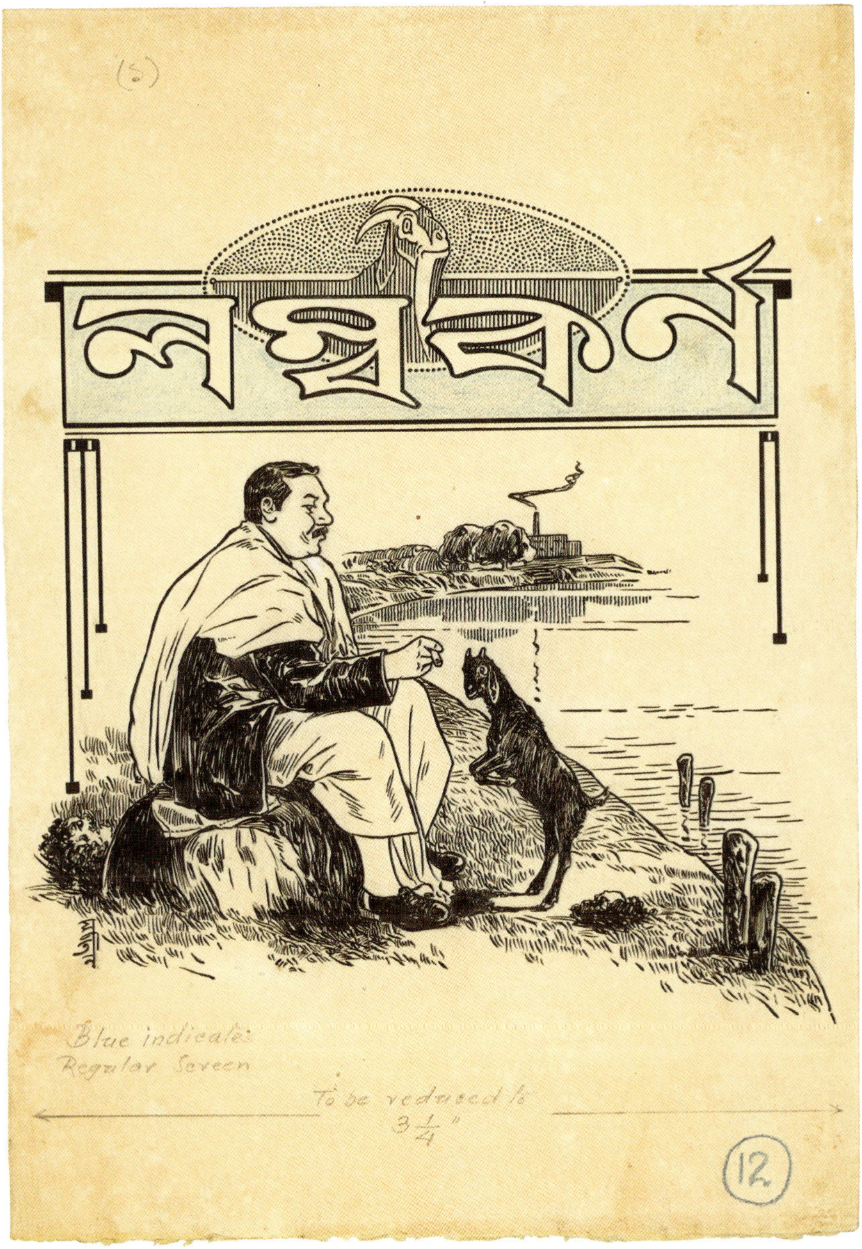

Illustration and title design for the opening page of *Lambakarna* (published in the collection *Gaddalika*, 1924)

Characters: Rai Banshalochan Bannerjee Bahadur and Lambakarna, the goat.

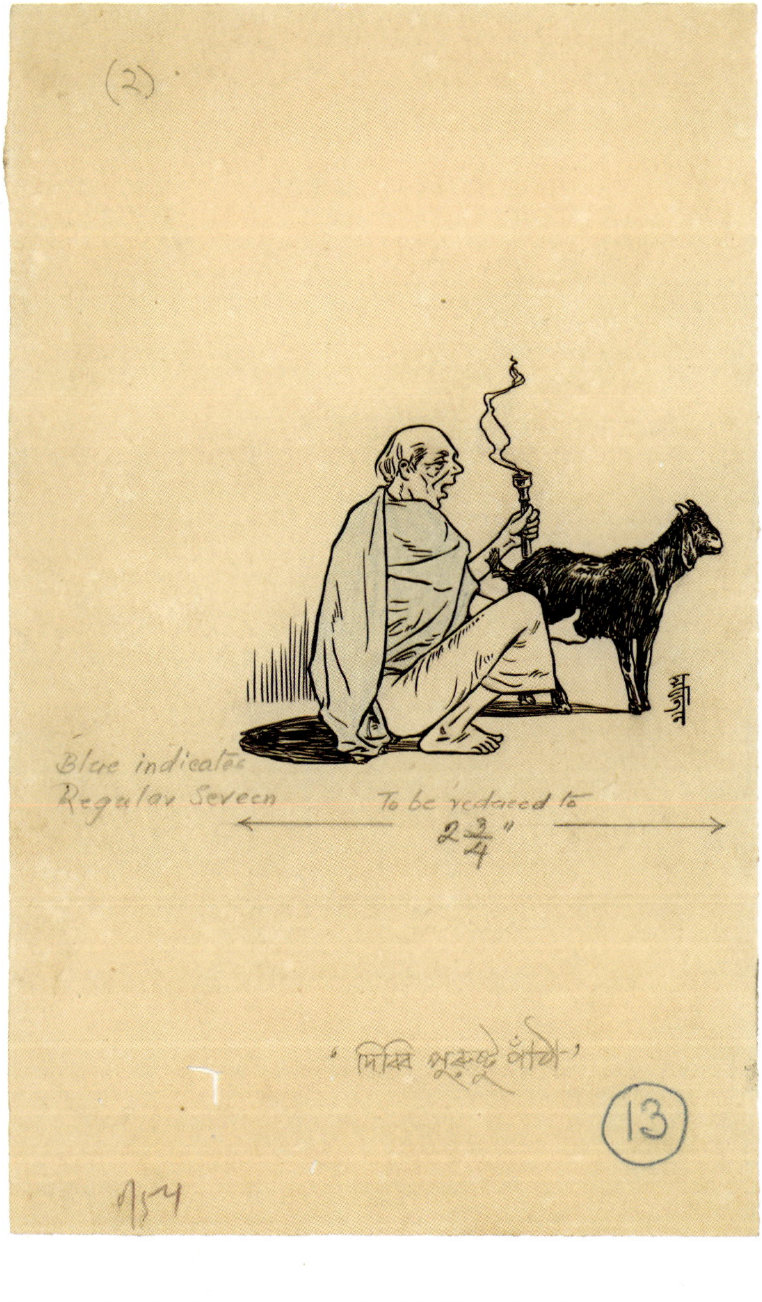

Illustration for *Lambakarna* (*Gaddalika*, 1924)

Bangla text: “What a healthy goat”.
Characters: Chatterjee moshai (Kedar Chatterjee) and Lambakarna, the goat.

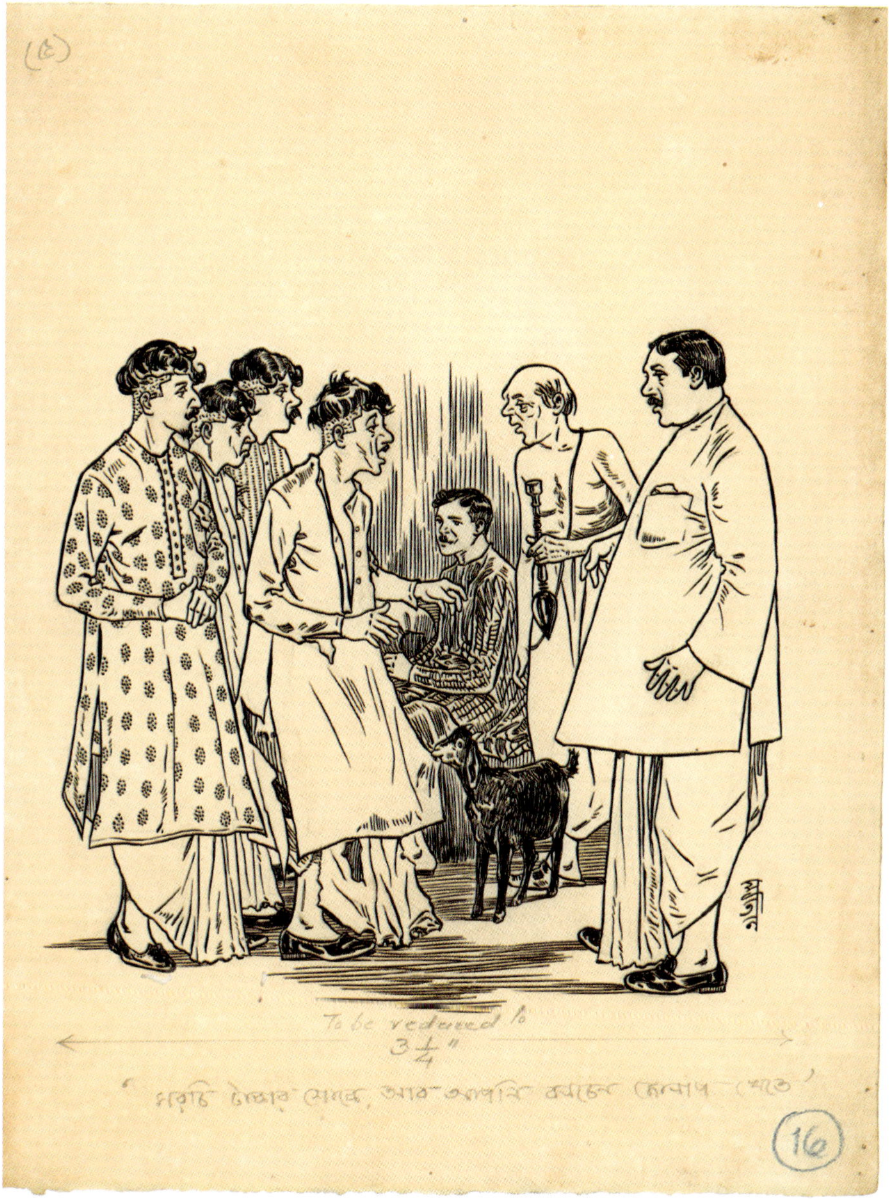

Illustration for *Lambakarna* (*Gaddalika*, 1924)

Bangla text: "We are dying for money and you are offering us Jolaab (a laxative)". Characters: Laatu (leader of the music band) speaking to Rai Banshalochan Bannerjee Bahadur, as Chatterjee moshai and Narahari look on.

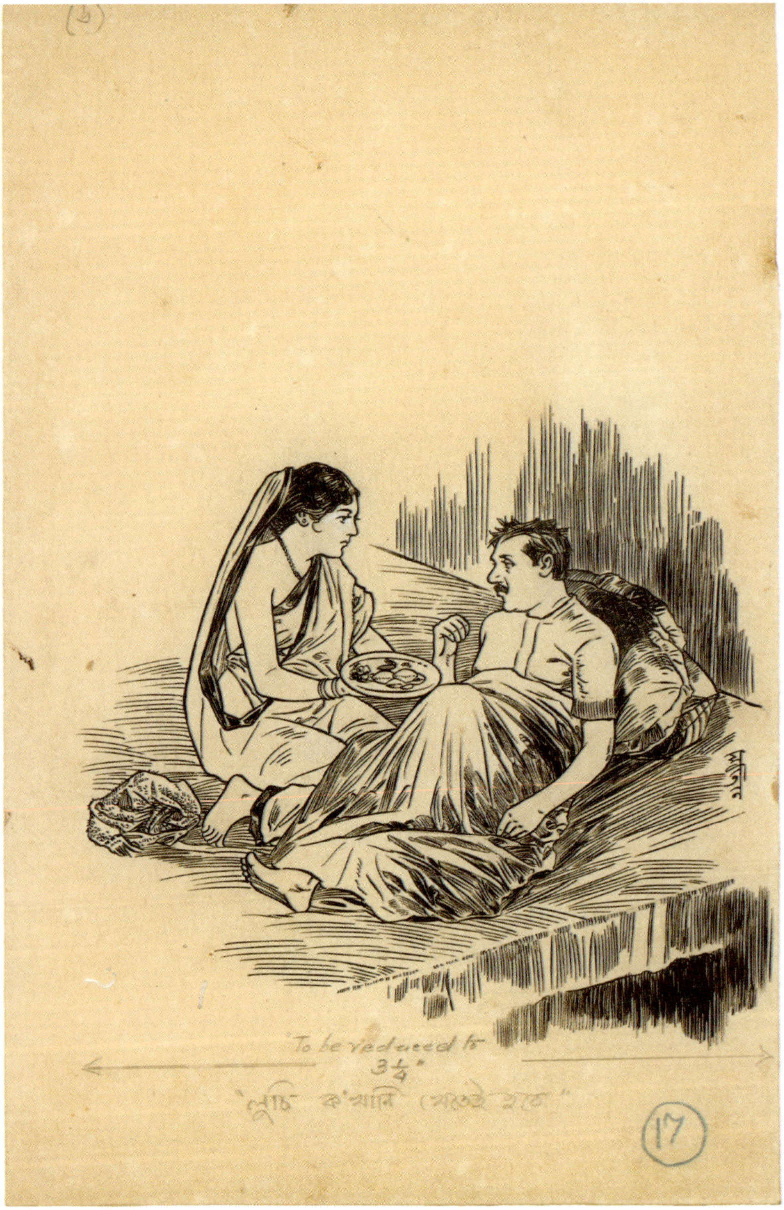

Illustration for *Lambakarna* (*Gaddalika*, 1924)

Bangla text: “You must have these luchis” (*luchi is a deep fried bread, like the north Indian poori*).
Characters: Manini Devi with her husband Rai Banshalochan Bannerjee Bahadur.

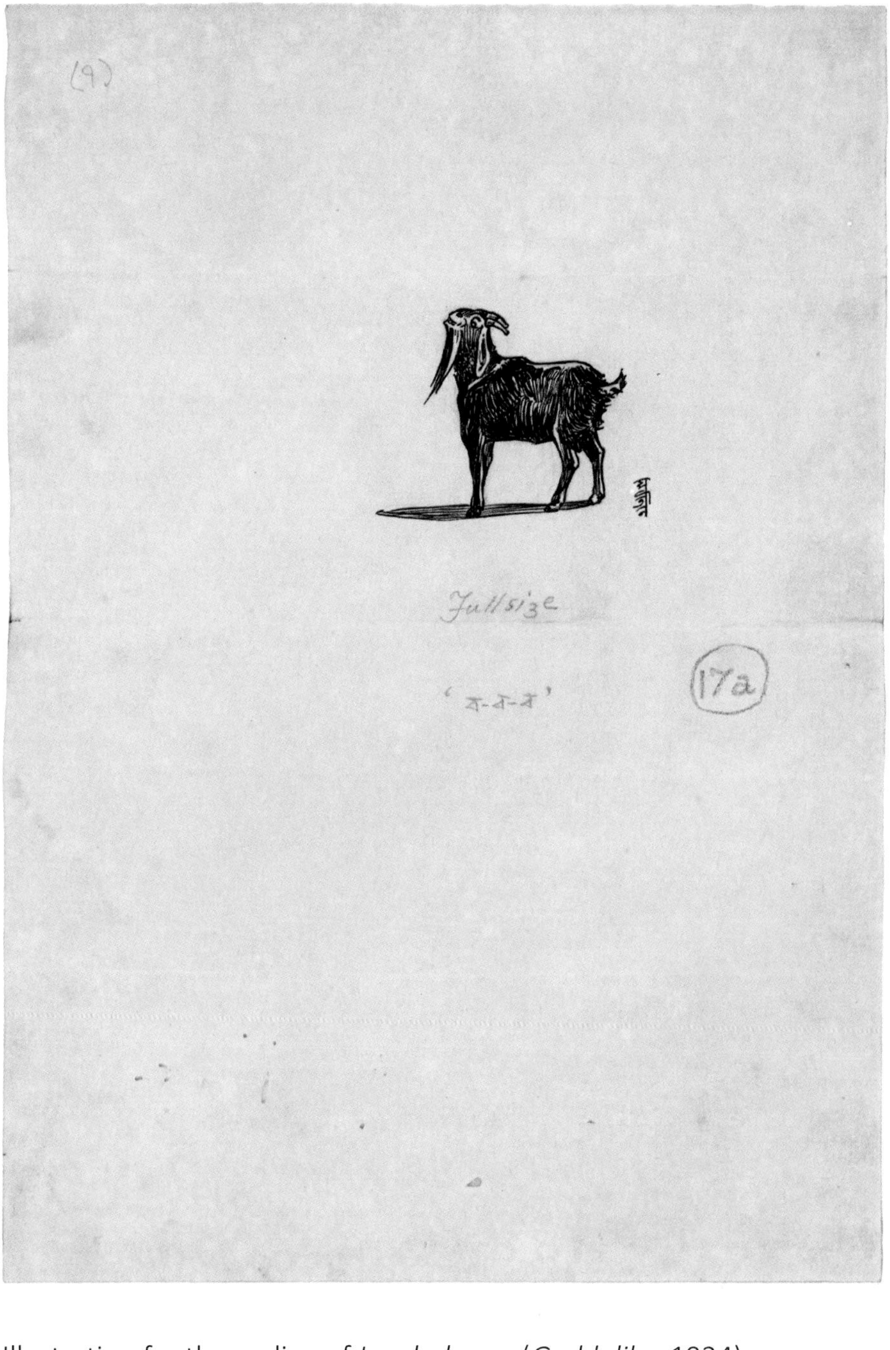

Illustration for the ending of *Lambakarna* (*Gaddalika*, 1924)

Character: Lambakarna, the goat.

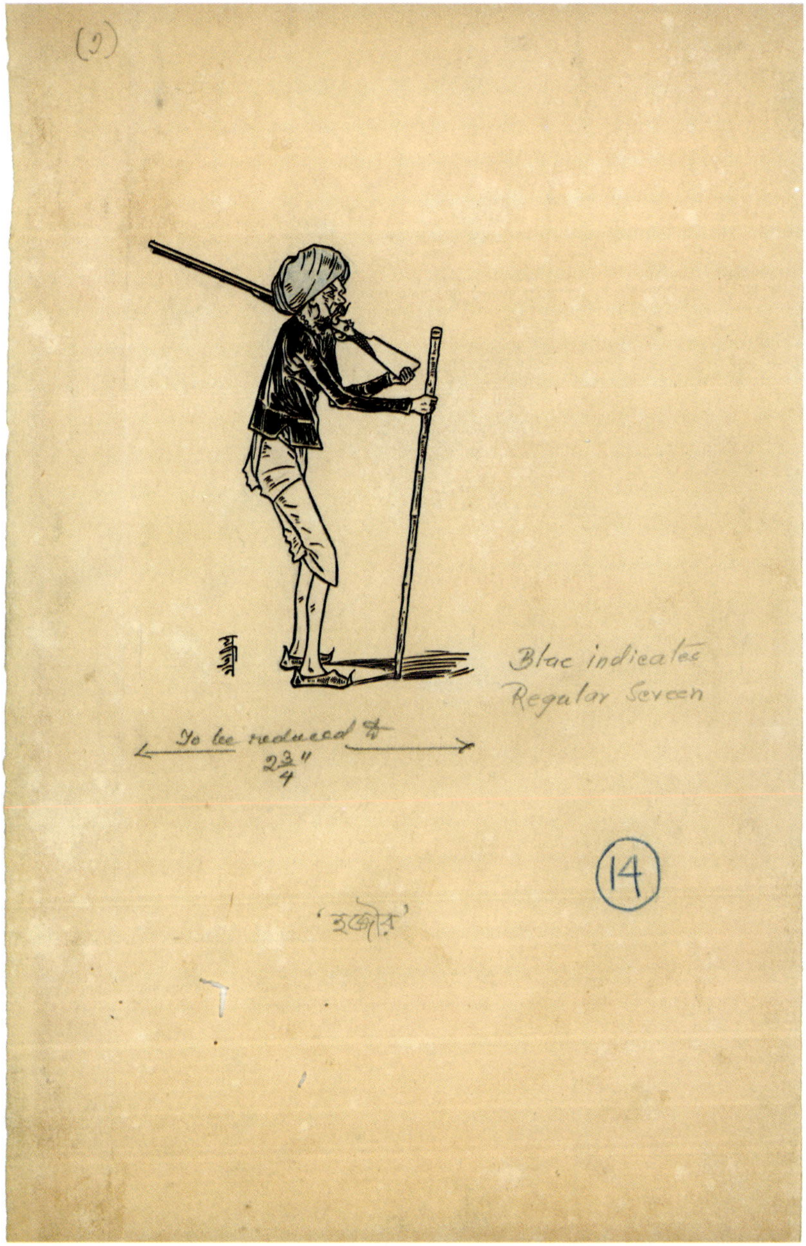

Illustration for *Lambakarna* (*Gaddalika*, 1924)

Bangla text: “Hujoor (Sir)”.
Character: Chukandar Singh.

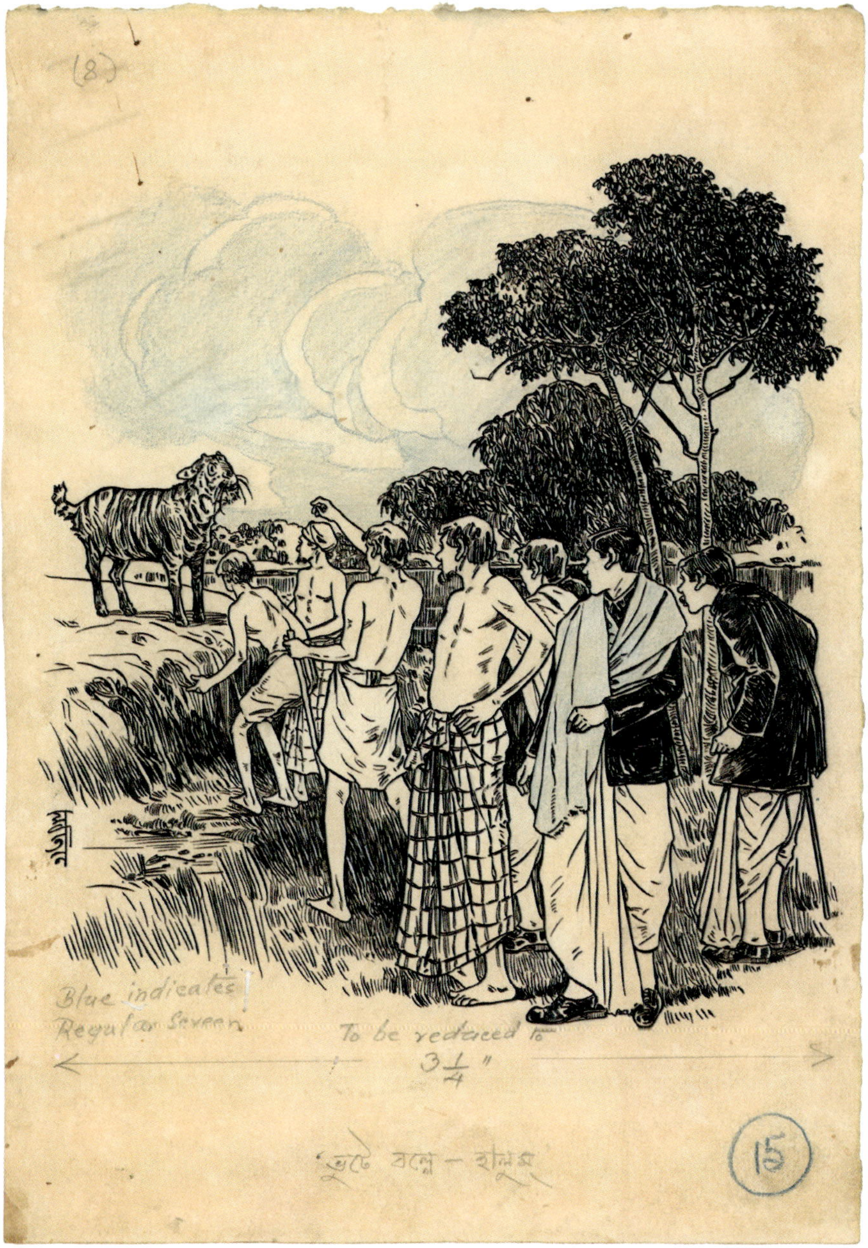

Illustration for *Lambakarna* (*Gaddalika*, 1924)

Bangla text: “Bhute (a goat) roared like a tiger”.
Characters: Villagers.

BHUSHANDIR MATHE

In this madcap comedy, Bhushandi's field is an uninhabited area which is home to many ghosts. In the afterlife, the ghosts do have a life. Shibu Bhattacharya, who lives on a bael tree and is now a Brahmadaitya, wishes to settle down with one of the three female ghosts Petni, Shankchunni and Dakini. After much deliberation when he finally chooses Dakini, he finds to his shock that his new wife is a ghost of the same woman who was his wife, Nrityakali, in his earthly life. Meanwhile, Shankchunni and Petni burst in on the scene – they are his wives from earlier lives. But that is not all. The ghosts Kariya Piret, resident of a palm tree, and Naderchanda Mullick, the Yaksha from the brick kiln, turn out to be Nrityakali's husbands from *her* previous lives....

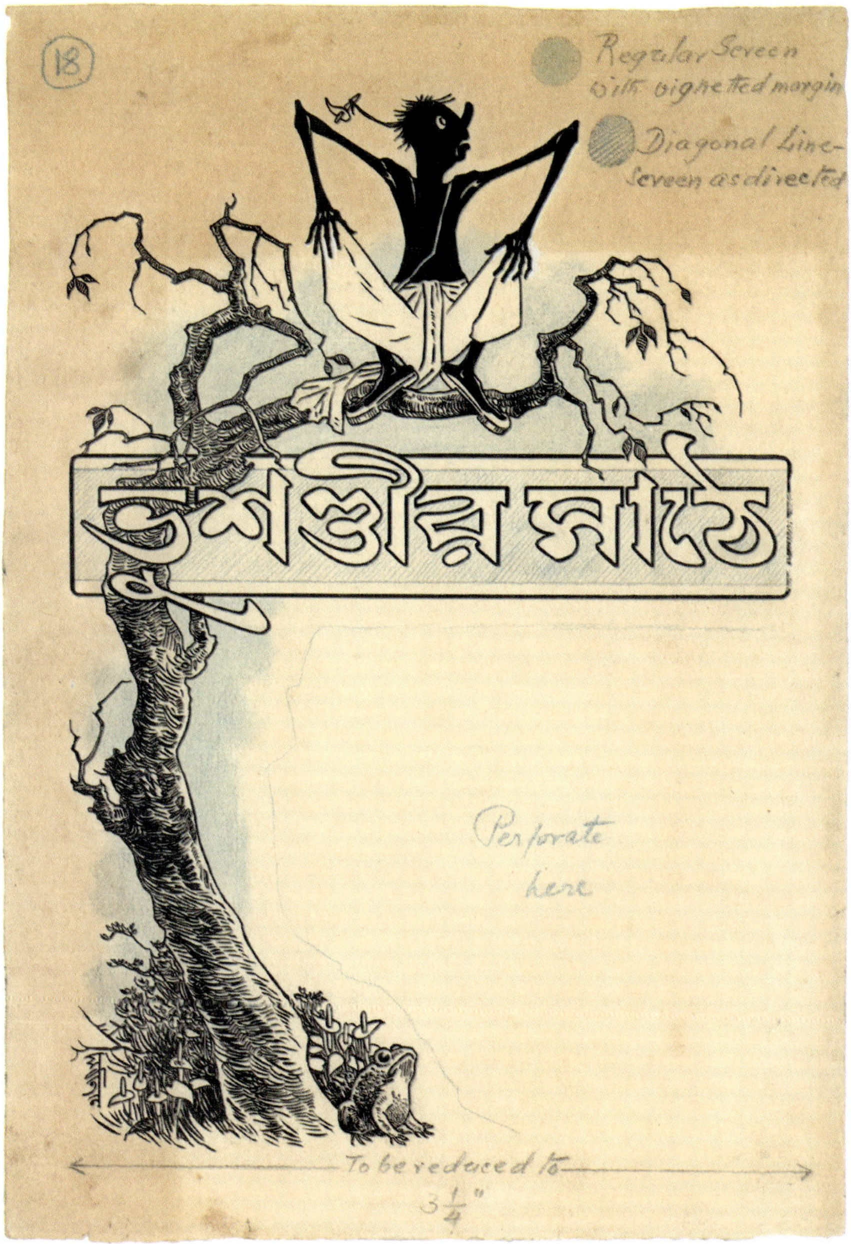

Illustration and title design for the opening page of *Bhushandir Mathe* (published in the collection *Gaddalika*, 1924)

Character: Shibu Bhattacharya.

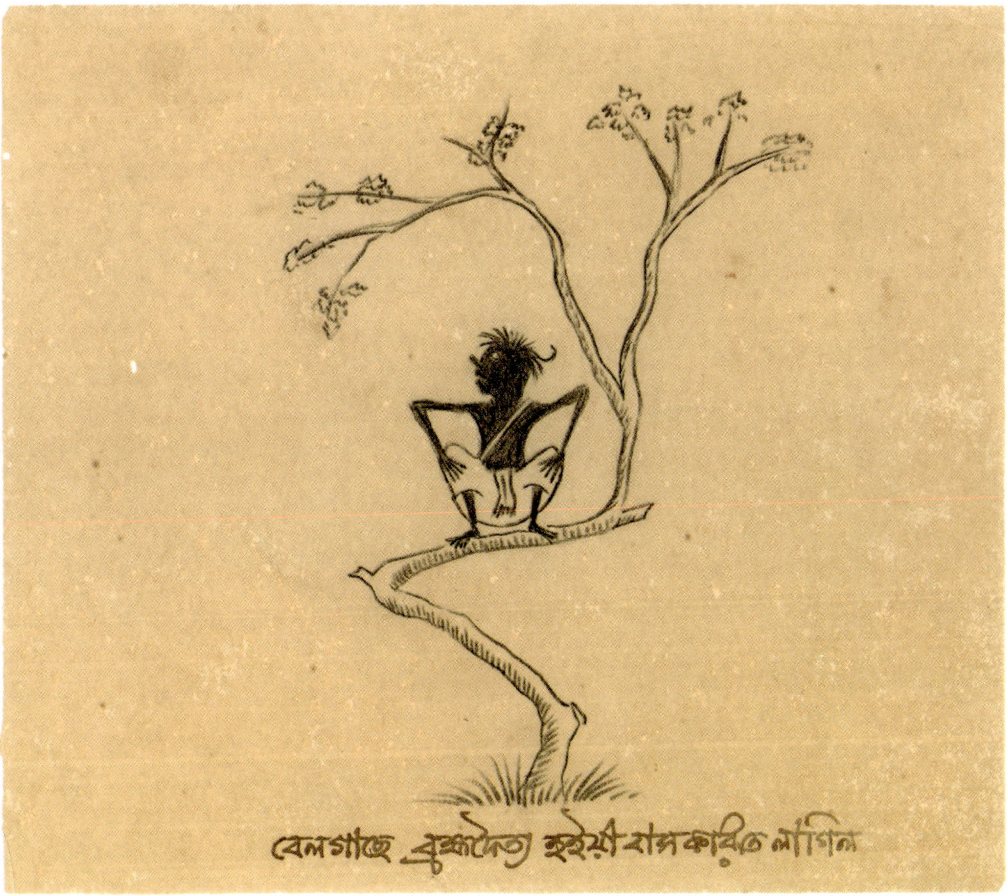

Parashuram's sketch for Shibu in *Bhushandir Mathe* (*Gaddalika*, 1924)

Bangla text: "Began living in the bael tree as a Brahmadaitya (Brahman turned ghost)".
Character: Shibu Bhattacharya.

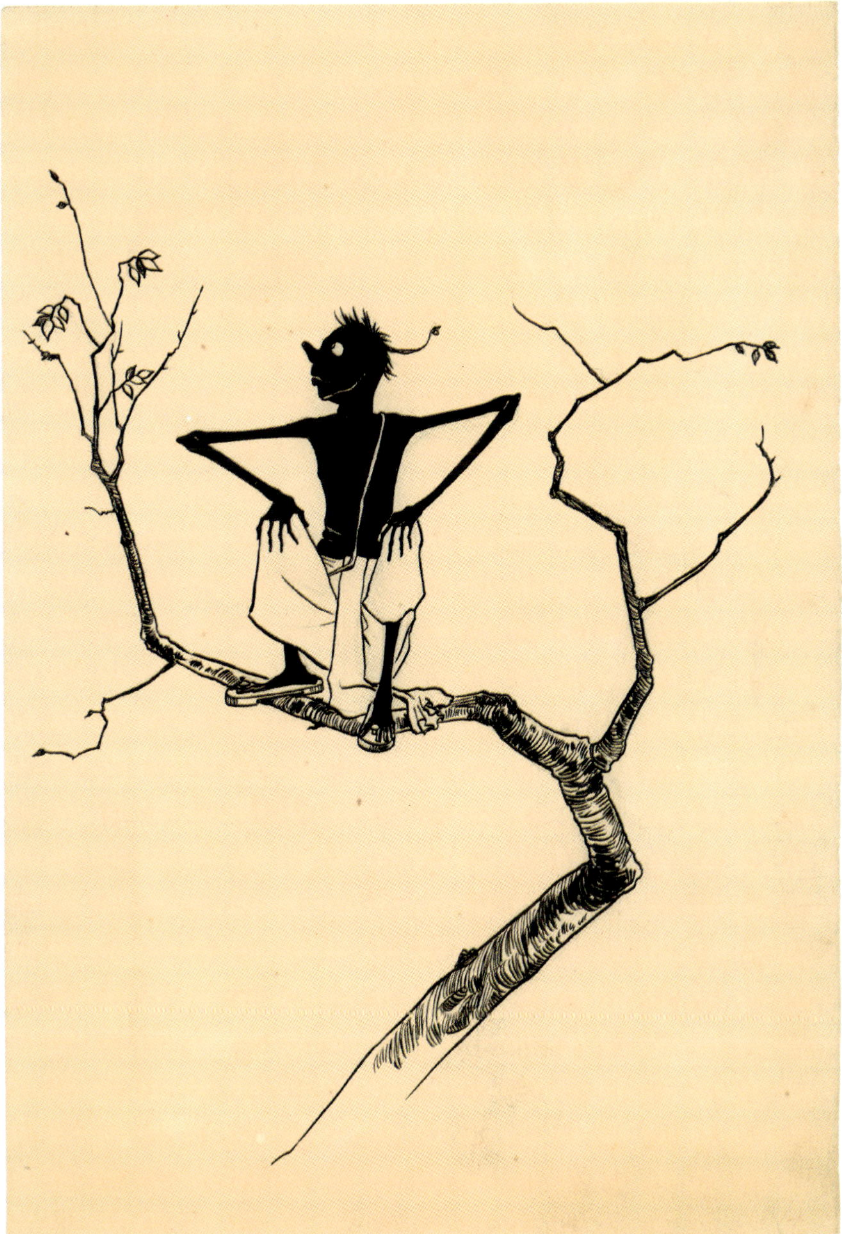

Jatindrakumar Sen's draft sketch for Shibu in *Bhushandir Mathe* (*Gaddalika*, 1924)

Character: Shibu Bhattacharya.

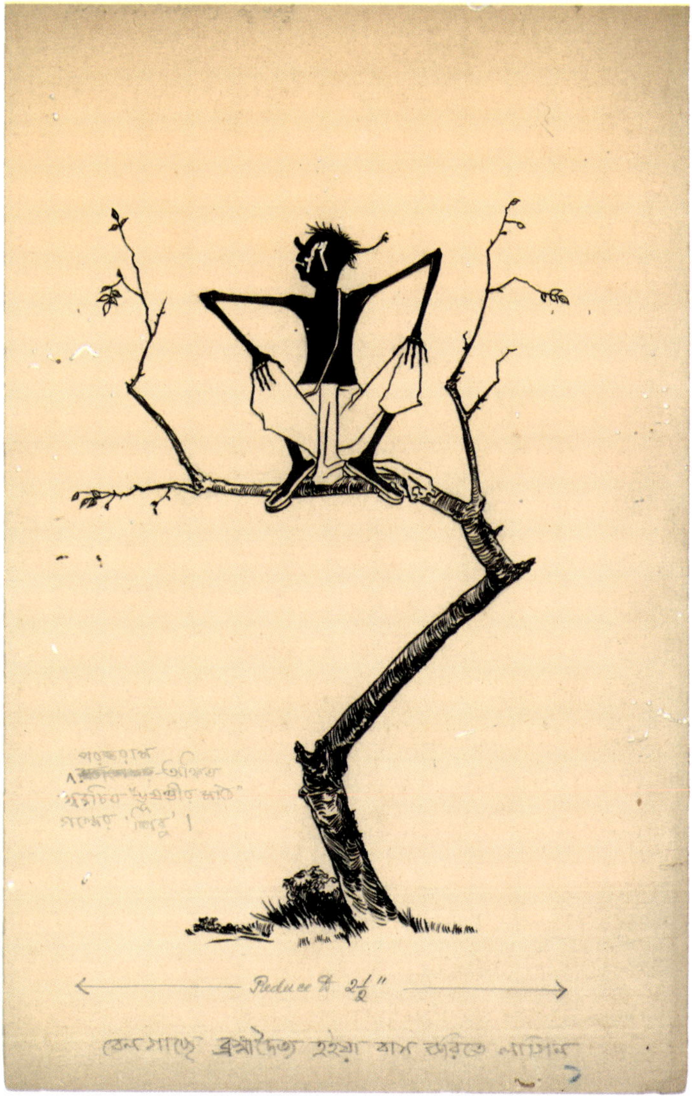

Jatindrakumar Sen's final illustration for Shibu in *Bhushandir Mathe* (*Gaddalika*, 1924)

Bangla text on the left: "Parashuram's design for Shibu, from Parashuram's story *Bhushandir Mathe*."
Bangla text at the bottom: "Began living in the bael tree as a Brahmadaitya (Brahman turned ghost)".
Character: Shibu Bhattacharya.

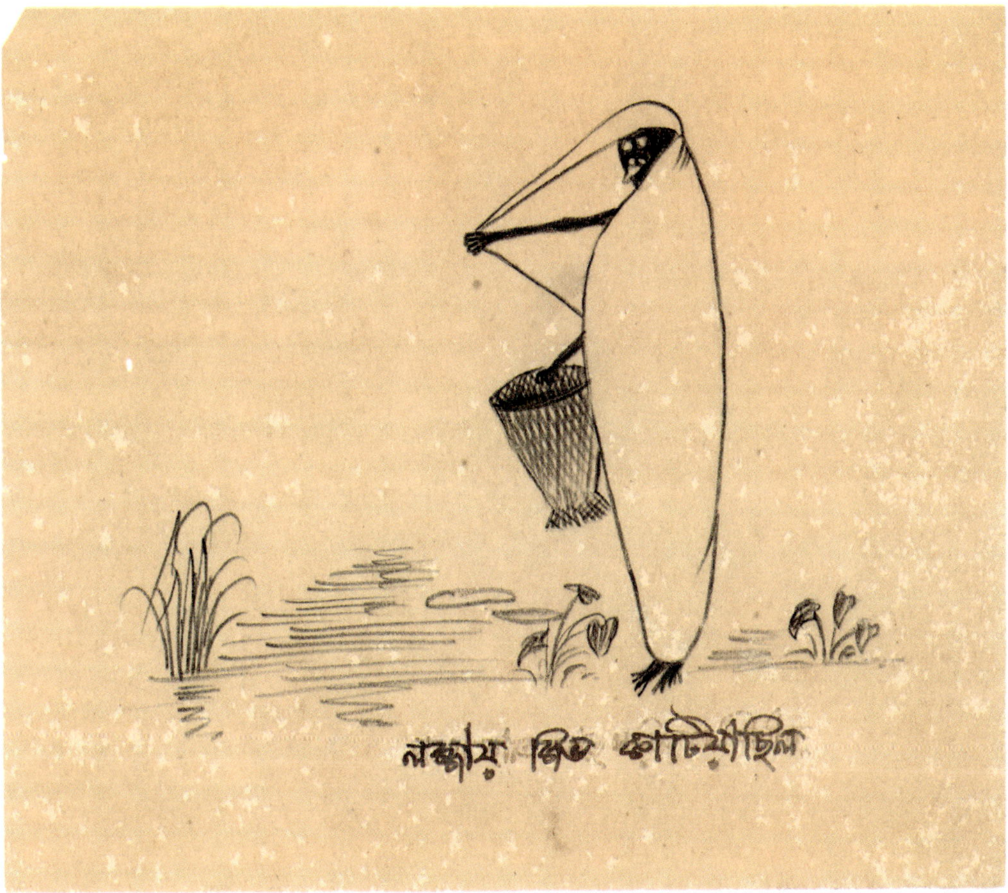

Parashuram's sketch for Petni, the old hag in *Bhushandir Mathe* (*Gaddalika*, 1924)

Bangla text: "She shyly stuck out her tongue".
Character: Petni.

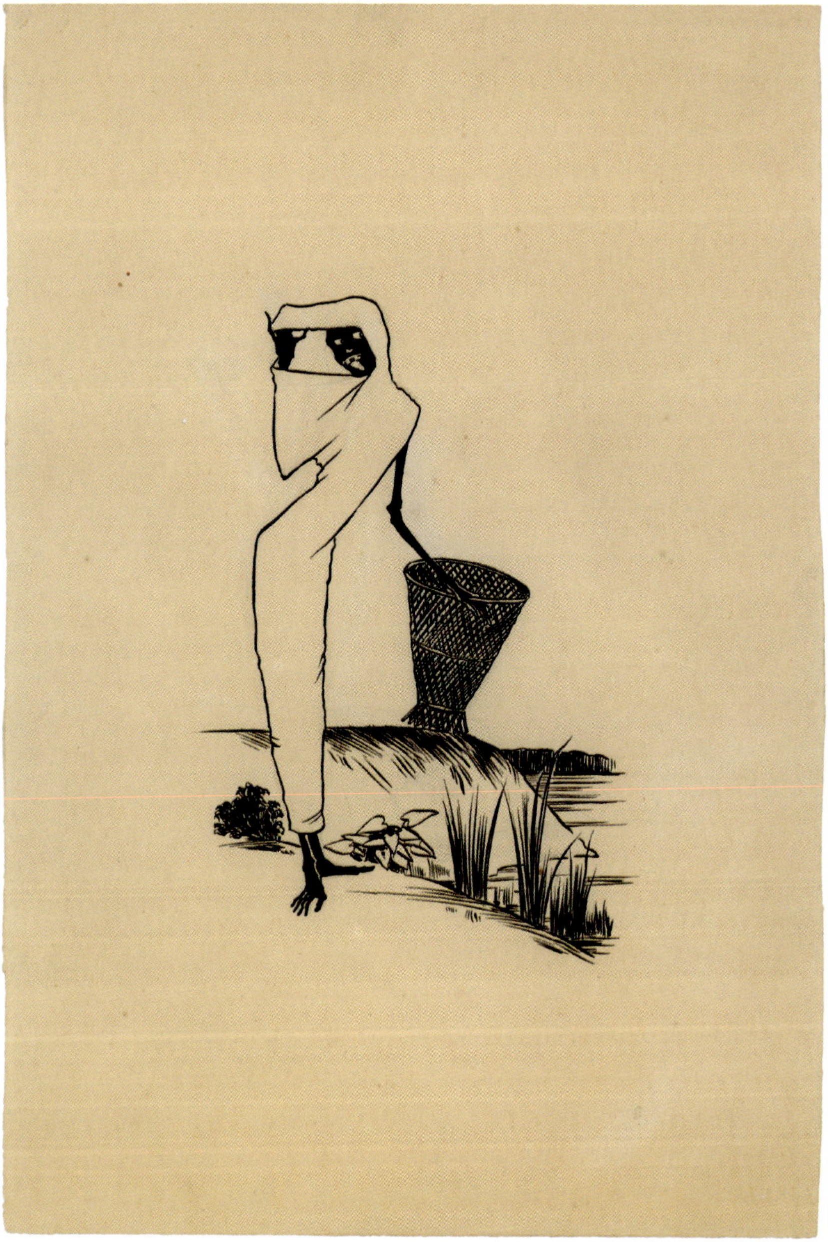

Jatindrakumar Sen's draft sketch for Petni, the old hag in *Bhushandir Mathe* (*Gaddalika*, 1924)

Character: Petni.

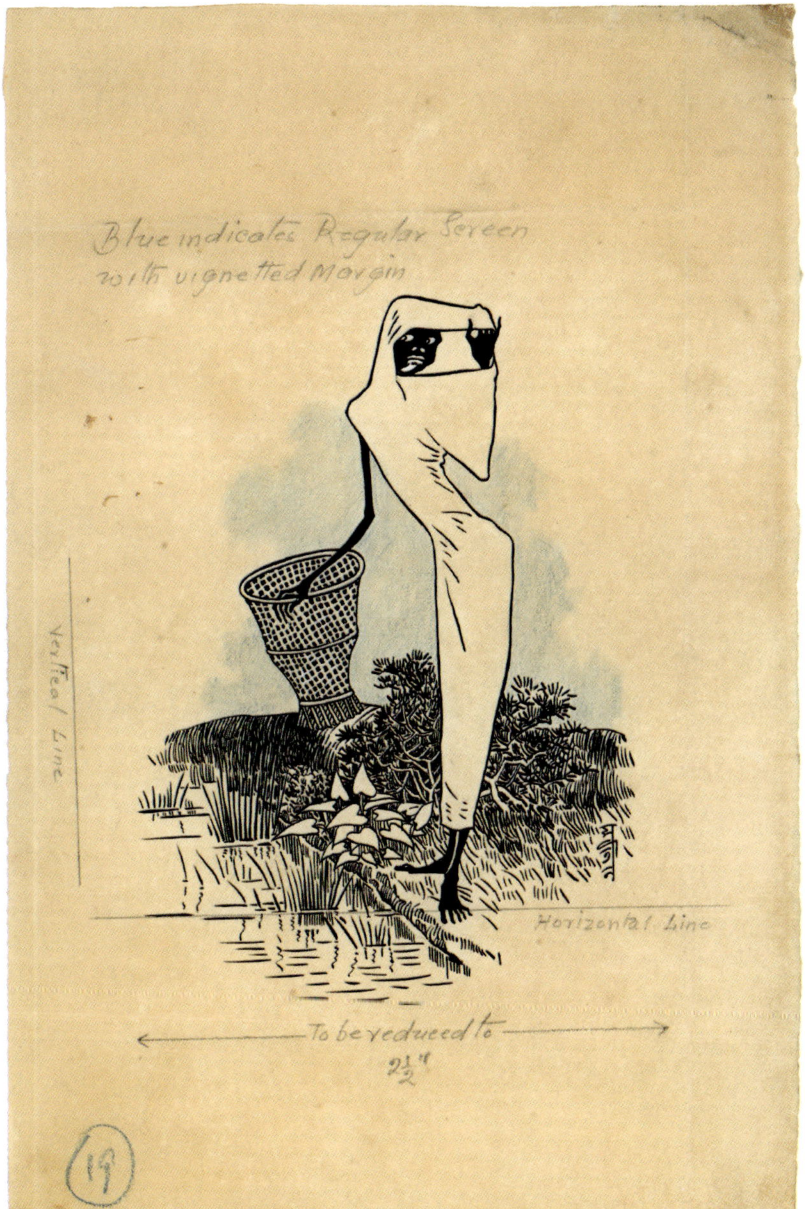

Jatindrakumar Sen's final illustration for Petni, the old hag in *Bhushandir Mathe* (*Gaddalika*, 1924)

Character: Petni.

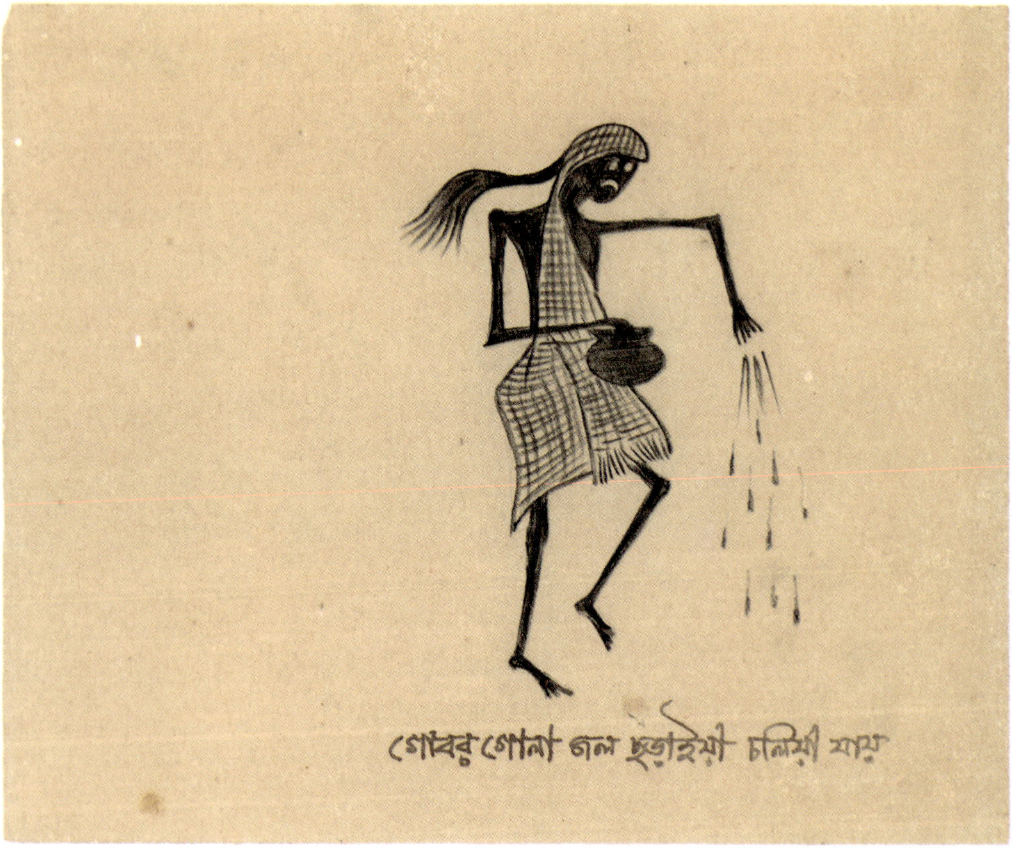

Parashuram's sketch for Shankchunni, the housewife-ghost in *Bhushandir Mathe* (*Gaddalika*, 1924)

Bangla text: "Sprinkling cowdung-water as she went".
Character: Shankchunni.

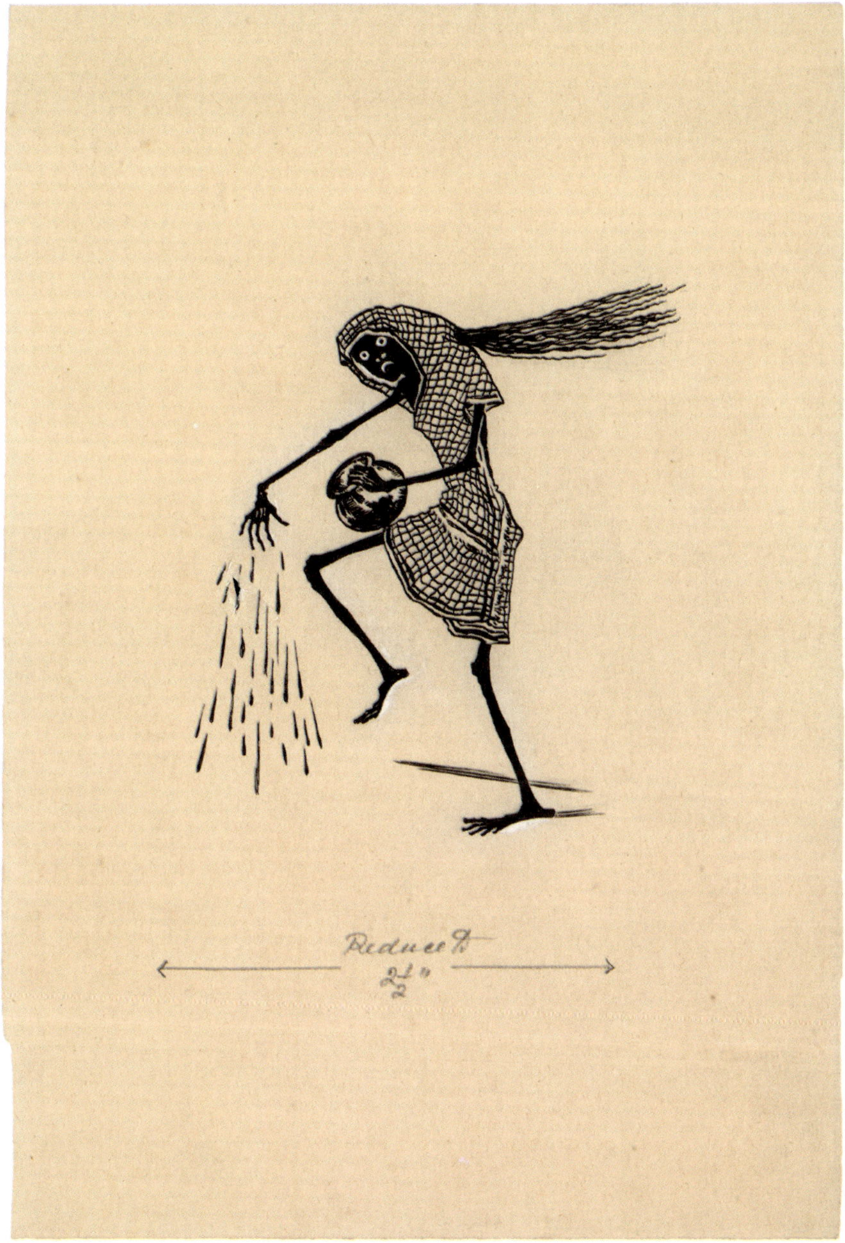

Jatindrakumar Sen's draft sketch for Shankchunni, the housewife-ghost in *Bhushandir Mathe* (*Gaddalika*, 1924)

Character: Shankchunni.

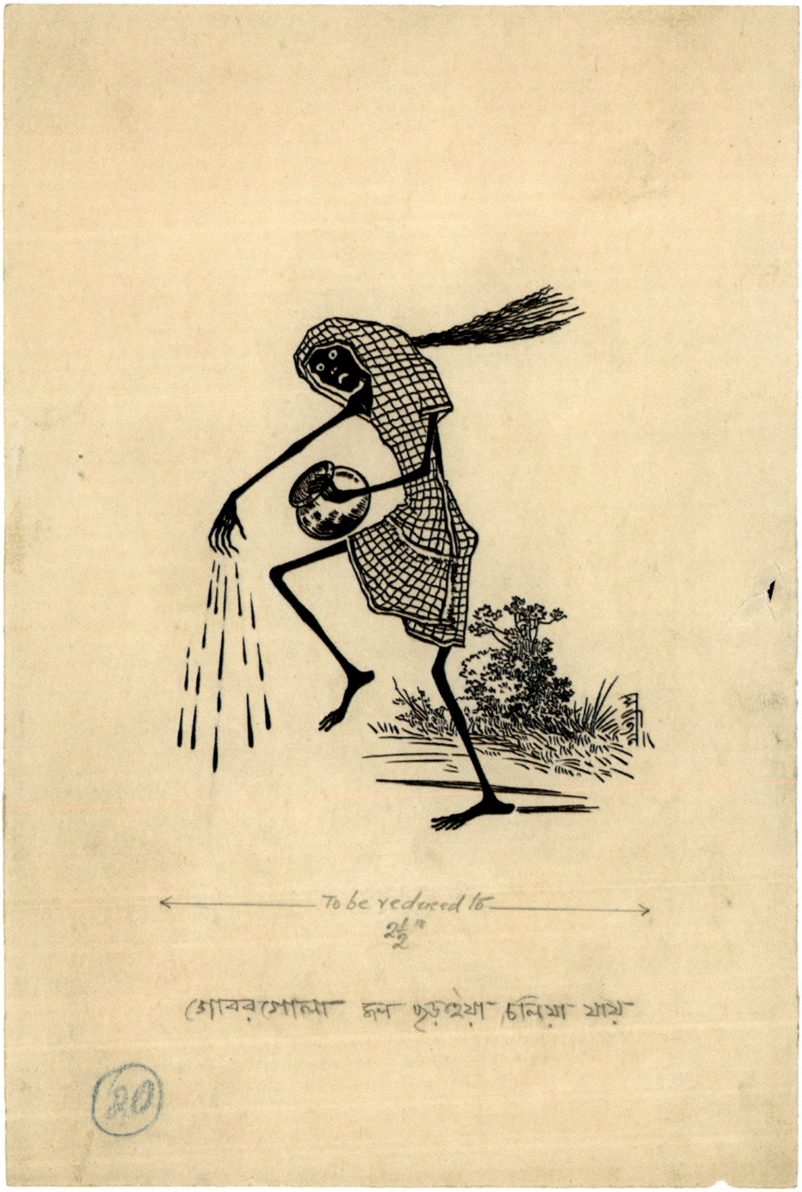

Jatindrakumar Sen's final illustration for Shankchunni, the housewife-ghost in *Bhushandir Mathe* (*Gaddalika*, 1924)

Bangla text: "Sprinkling cowdung-water as she went".
Character: Shankchunni.

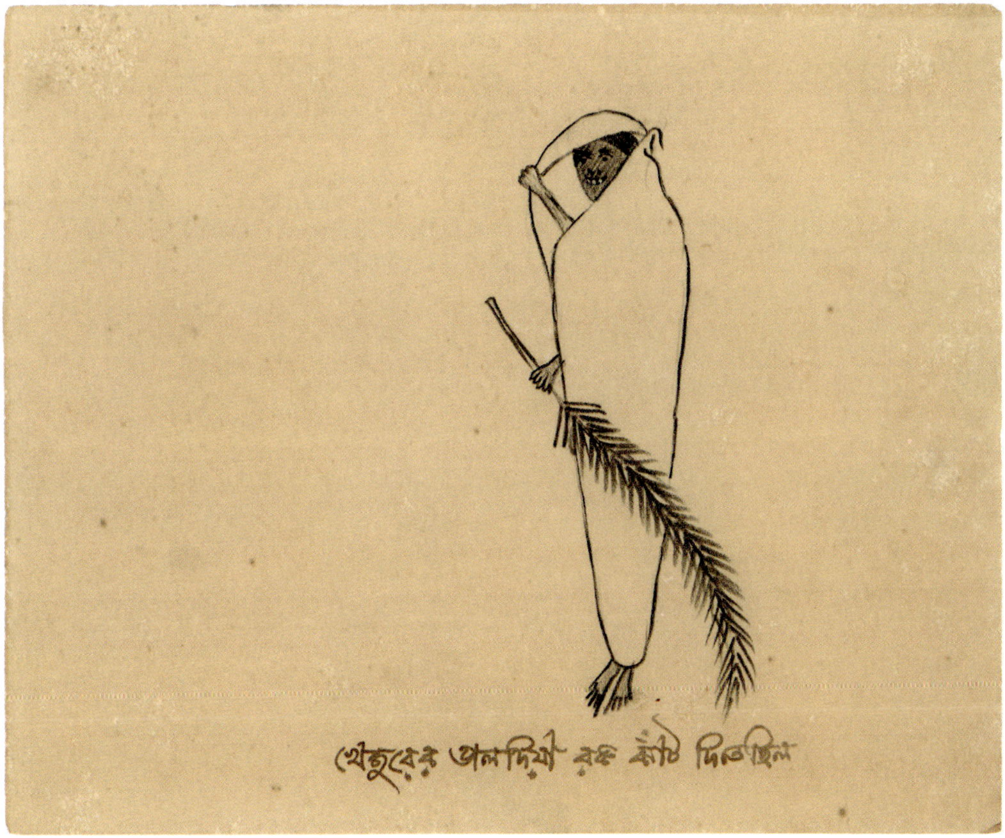

Parashuram's sketch for Dakini, the Ogress in *Bhushandir Mathe* (*Gaddalika*, 1924)

Bangla text: "Sweeping the porch with a date-palm branch".
Character: Dakini.

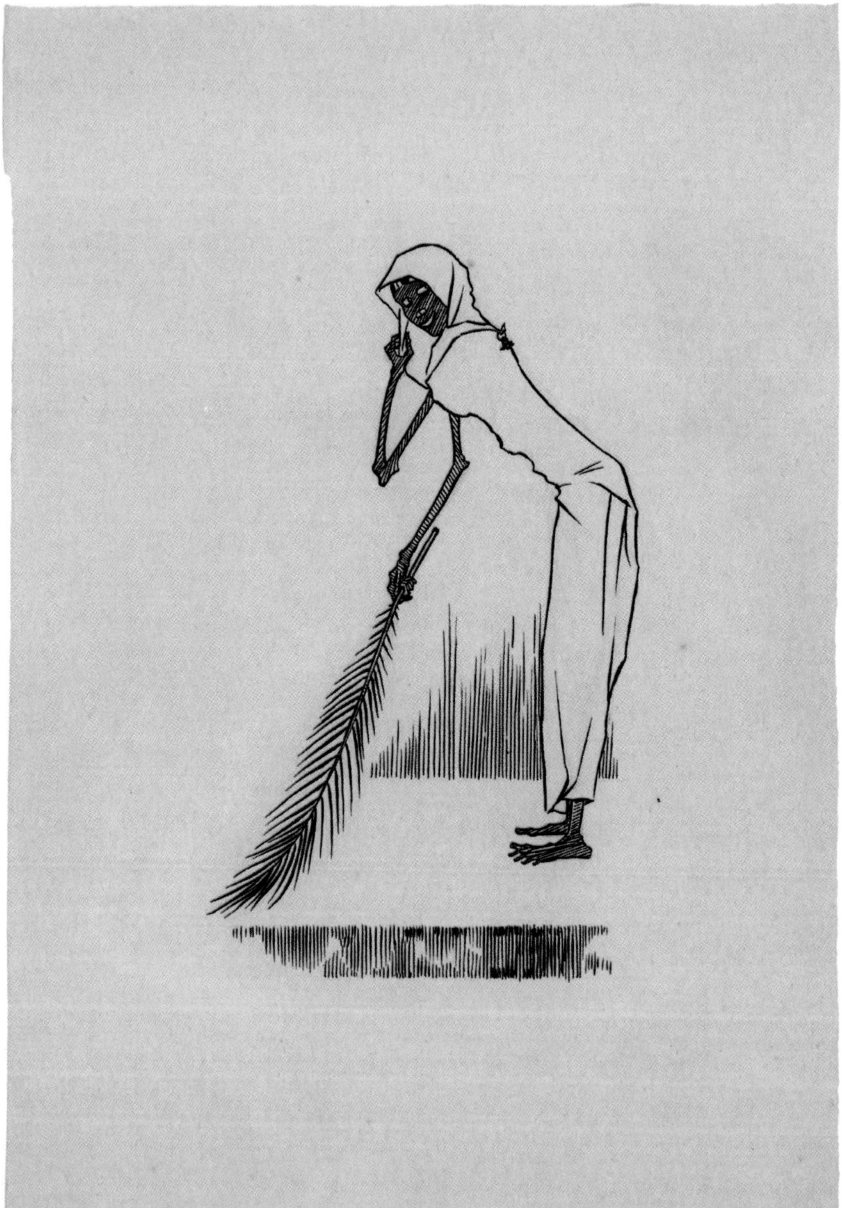

Jatindrakumar Sen's draft sketch for Dakini, the Ogress in *Bhushandir Mathe* (*Gaddalika*, 1924)

Character: Dakini.

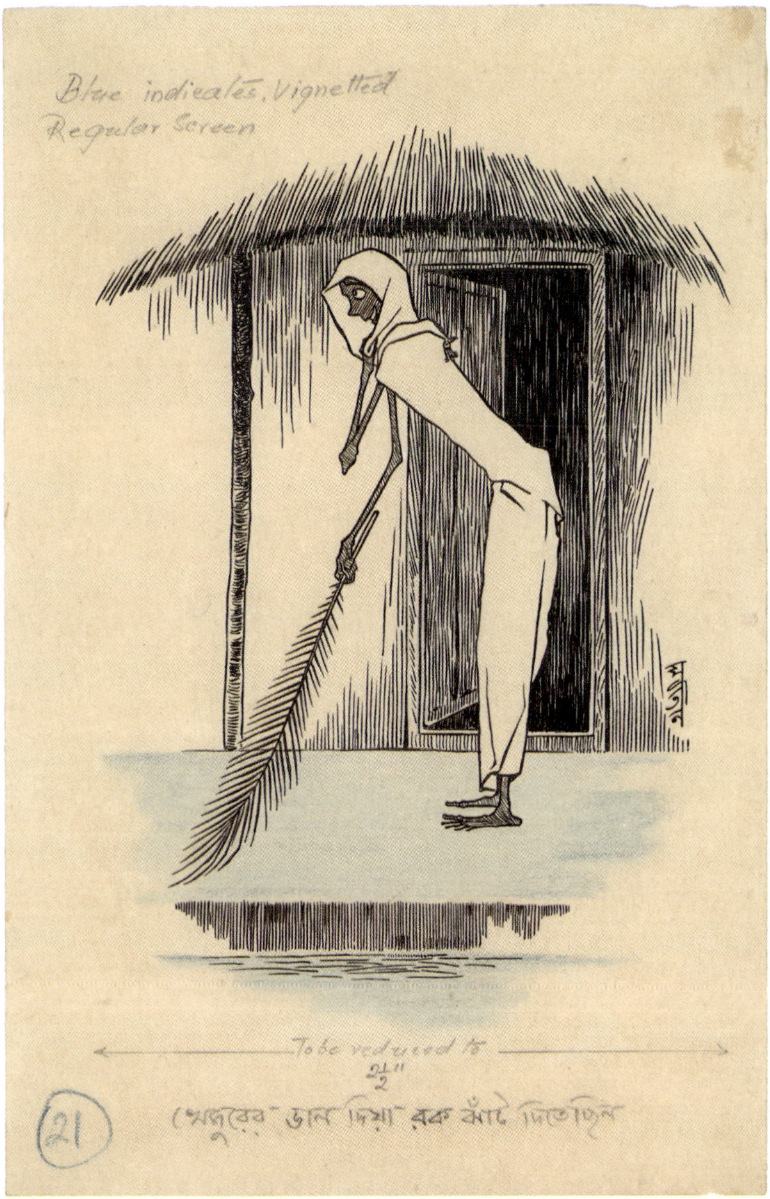

Jatindrakumar Sen's final illustration for Dakini, the Ogress in *Bhushandir Mathe* (*Gaddalika*, 1924)

Bangla text: "Sweeping the porch with a date-palm branch".
Character: Dakini.

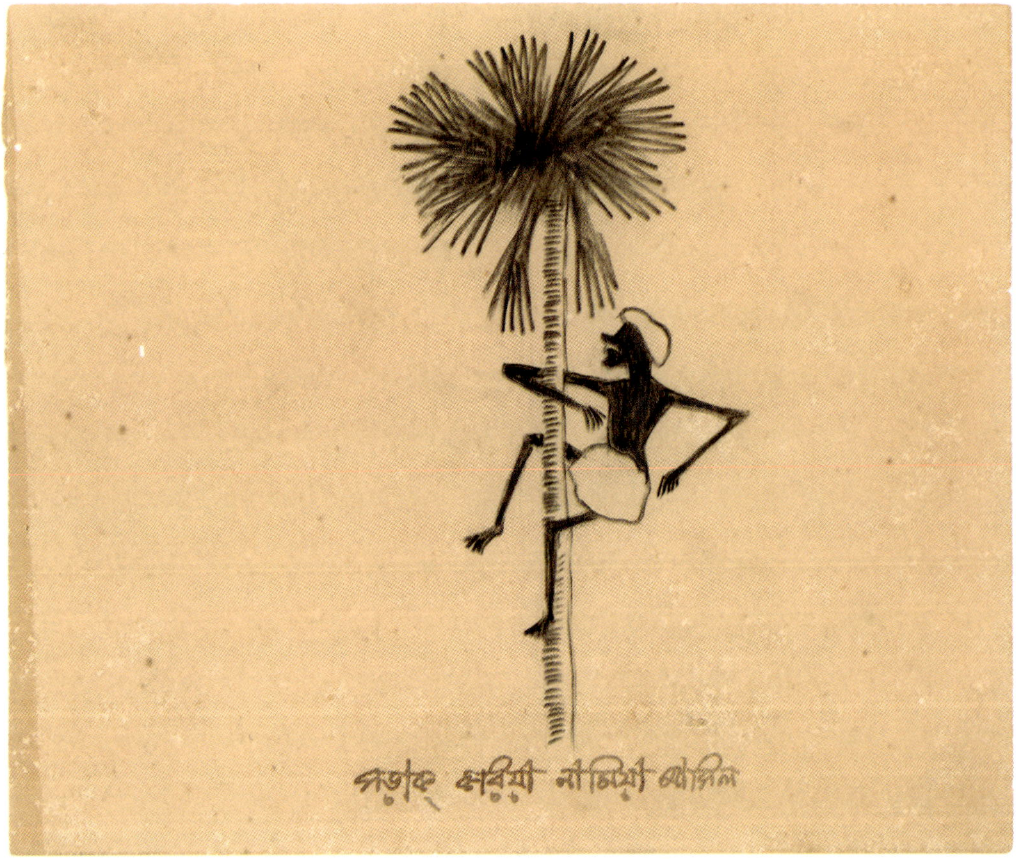

Parashuram's sketch for Kele bhoot (the black ghost) in *Bhushandir Mathe* (*Gaddalika*, 1924)

Bangla text: "He slid down the toddy-palm".
Character: Kele bhoot or Kariya Piret.

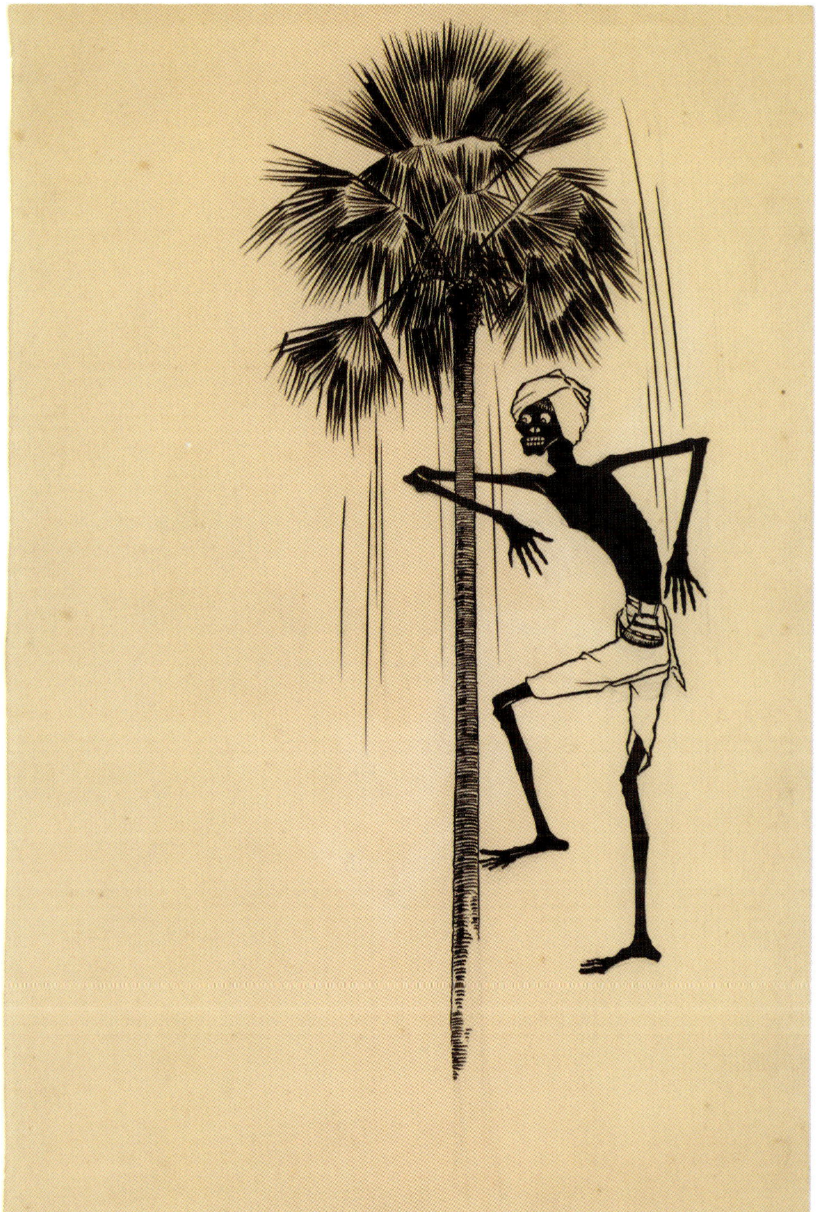

Jatindrakumar Sen's draft sketch for Kele bhoot (the black ghost) in *Bhushandir Mathe* (*Gaddalika*, 1924)

Character: Kele bhoot or Kariya Piret.

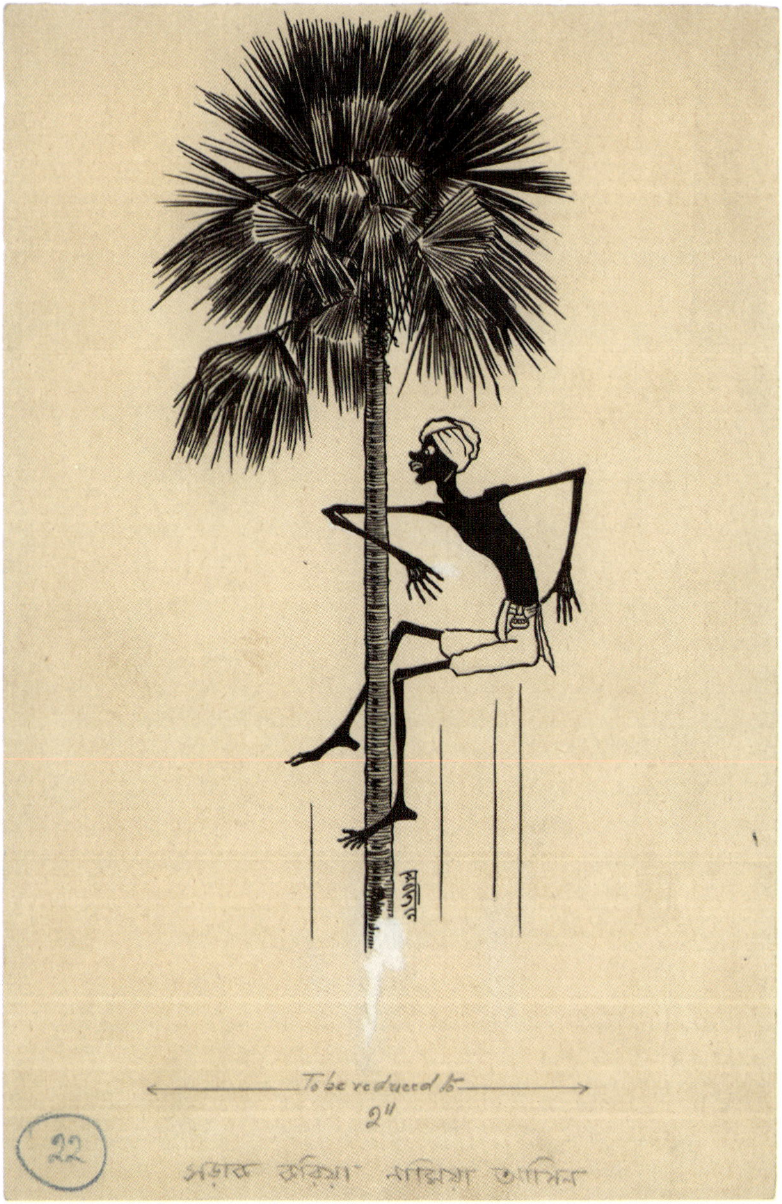

Jatindrakumar Sen's final illustration for Kele bhoot (the black ghost) in *Bhushandir Mathe* (*Gaddalika*, 1924)

Bangla text: "He slid down the toddy-palm".
Character: Kele bhoot or Kariya Piret.

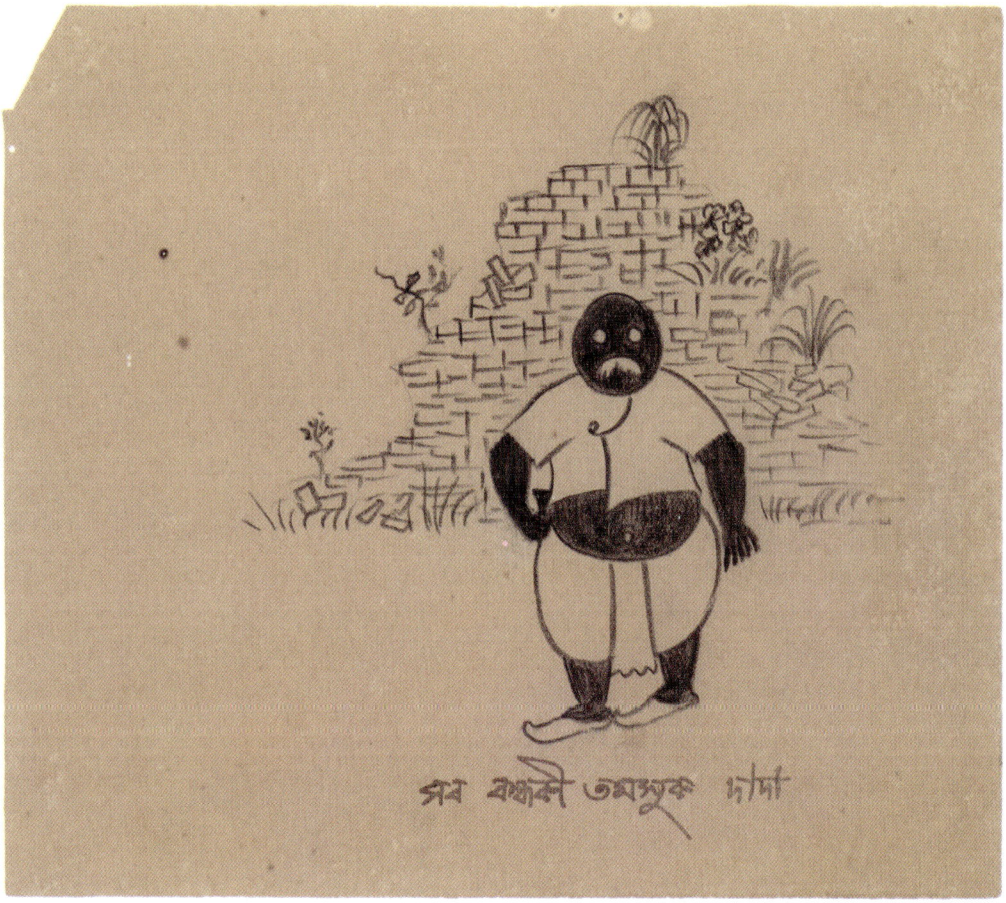

Parashuram's sketch for the Yaksha in *Bhushandir Mathe* (*Gaddalika*, 1924)

Bangla text: "It's all paper securities, brother".
Character: Yaksha (Naderchanda Mullick when he was alive).

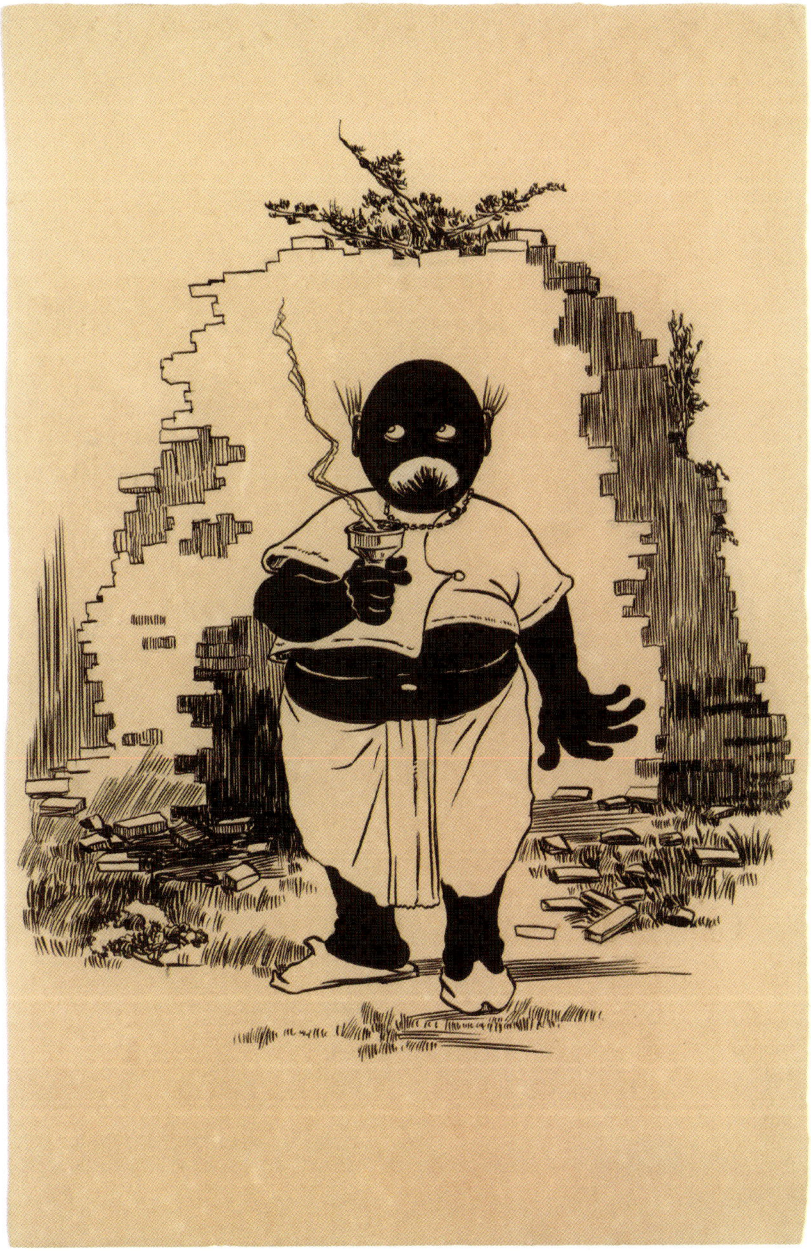

Jatindrakumar Sen's draft sketch for the Yaksha in *Bhushandir Mathe* (Gaddalika, 1924)

Character: Yaksha.

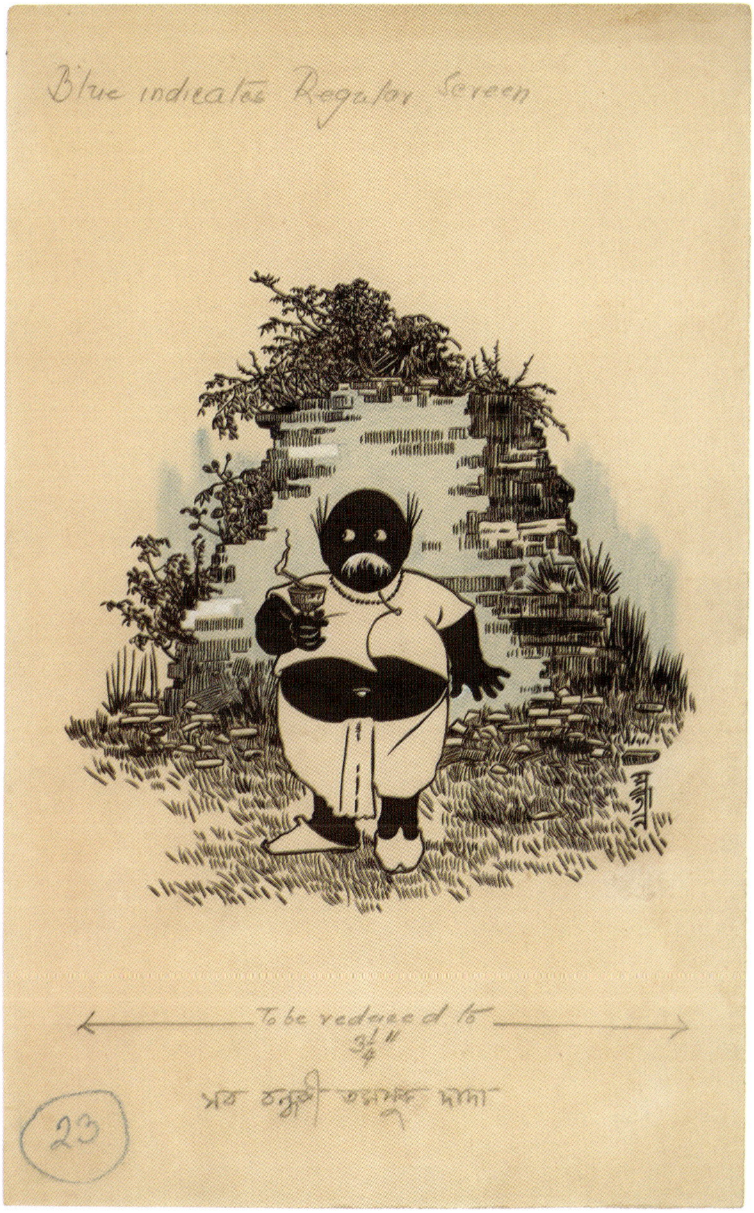

Jatindrakumar Sen's final illustration for the Yaksha in *Bhushandir Mathe* (*Gaddalika*, 1924)

Character: Yaksha.
Bangla text: "It's all paper securities, brother".

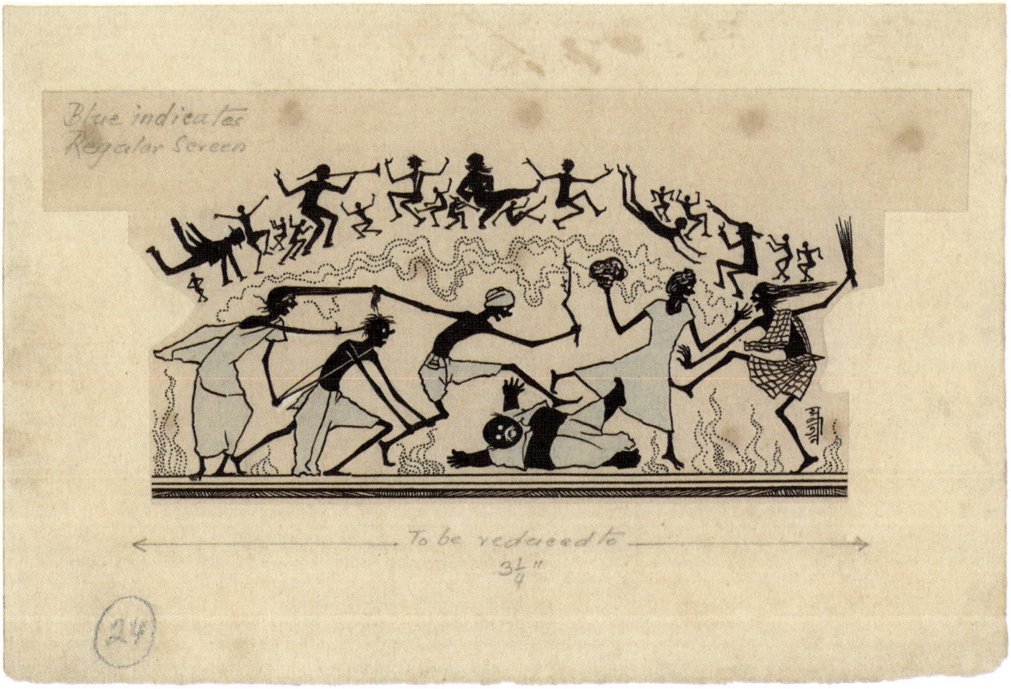

Jatindrakumar Sen's illustration for the end of *Bhushandir Mathe* (*Gaddalika*, 1924)

Characters: Dance of the ghosts, with many Indian, European, Middle Eastern and Chinese ghosts!

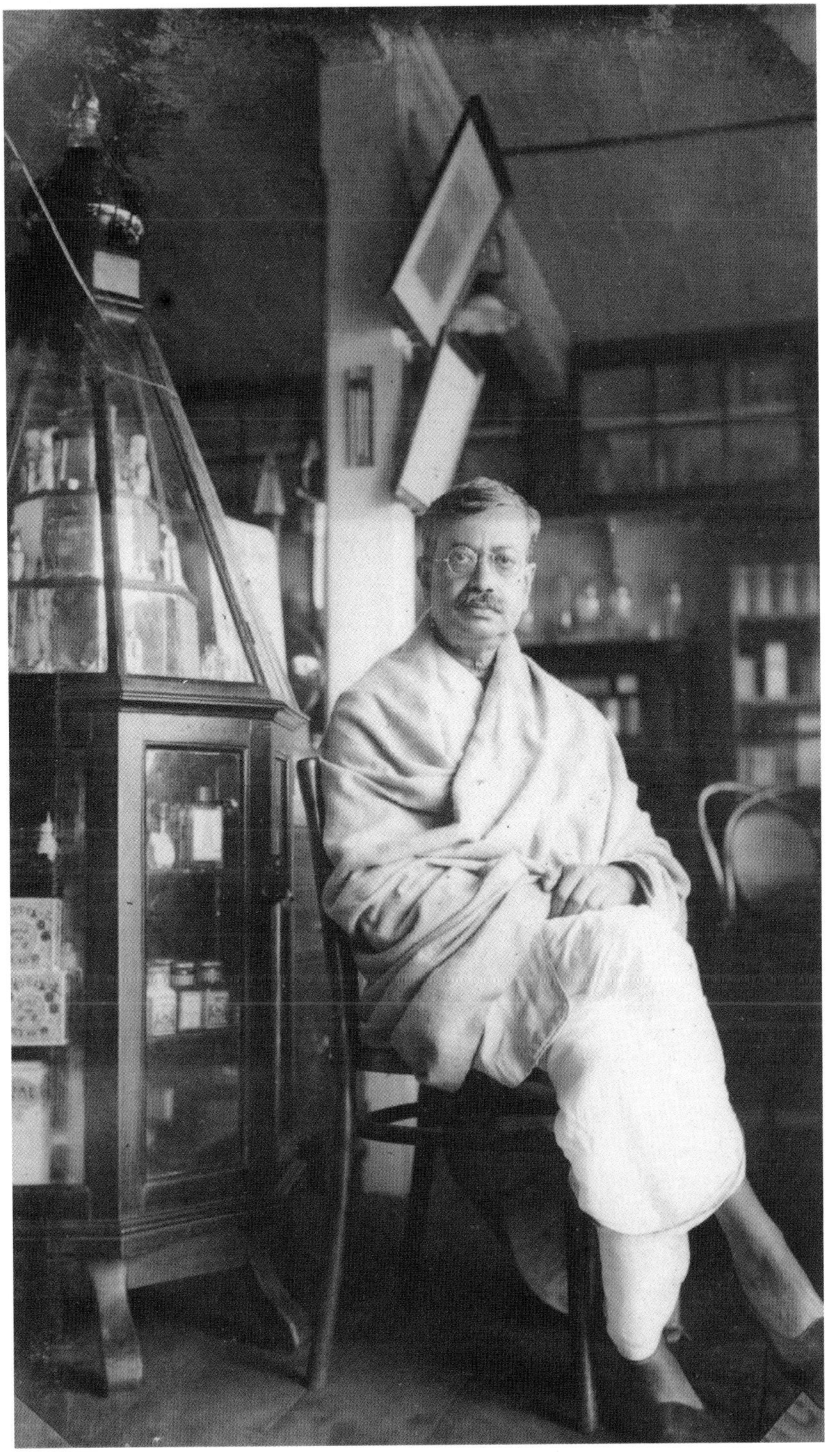

Rajshekhar Basu

STORIES FROM *KAJJALI*

ILLUSTRATIONS AND TRIAL SKETCHES
FOR THE COVER OF *KAJJALI*, 1928

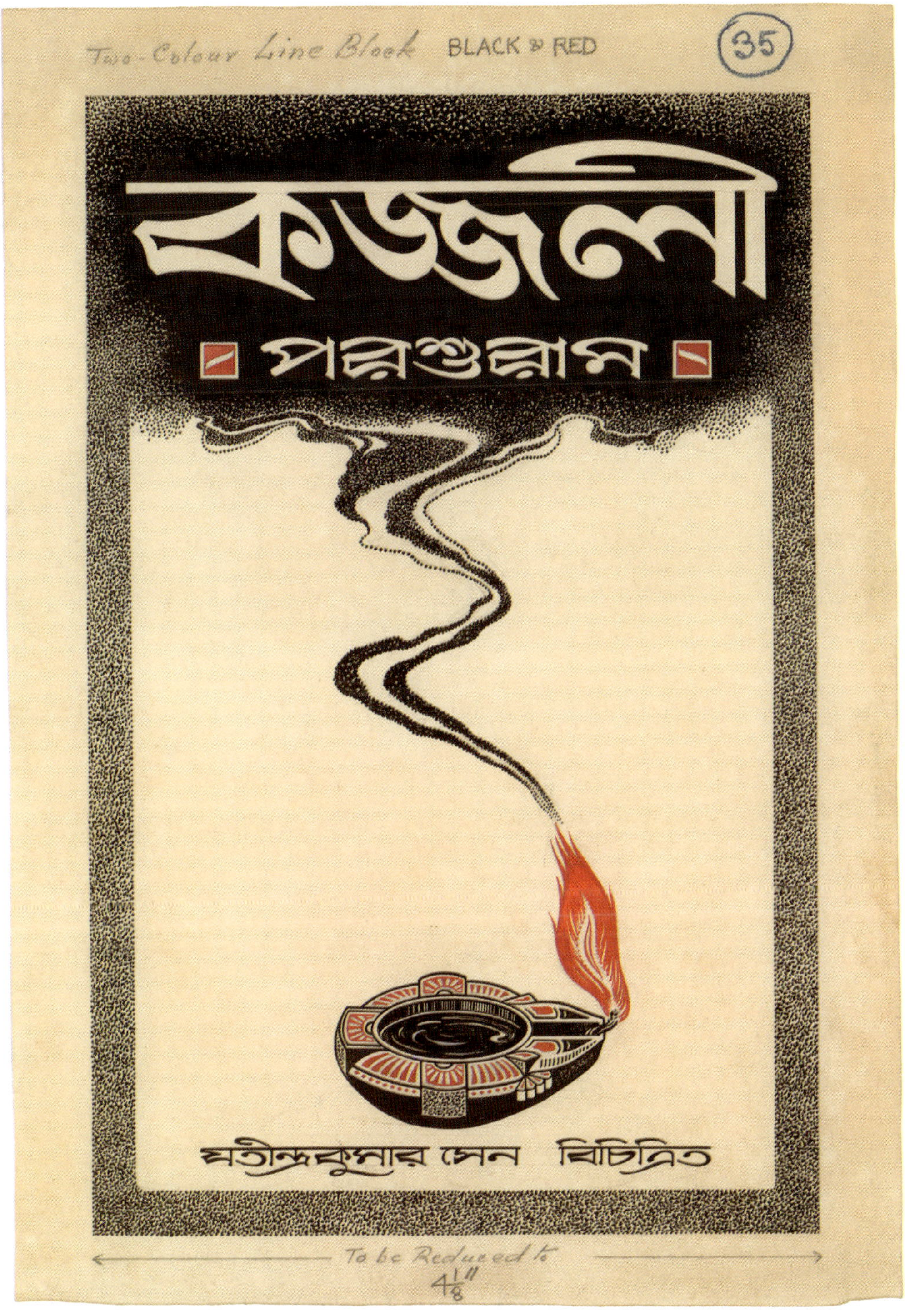
Two-Colour Line Block BLACK & RED
35
কজ্জলী
পরশুরাম
যতীন্দ্রকুমার সেন বিচিত্রিত
To be Reduced to
4 1/8"

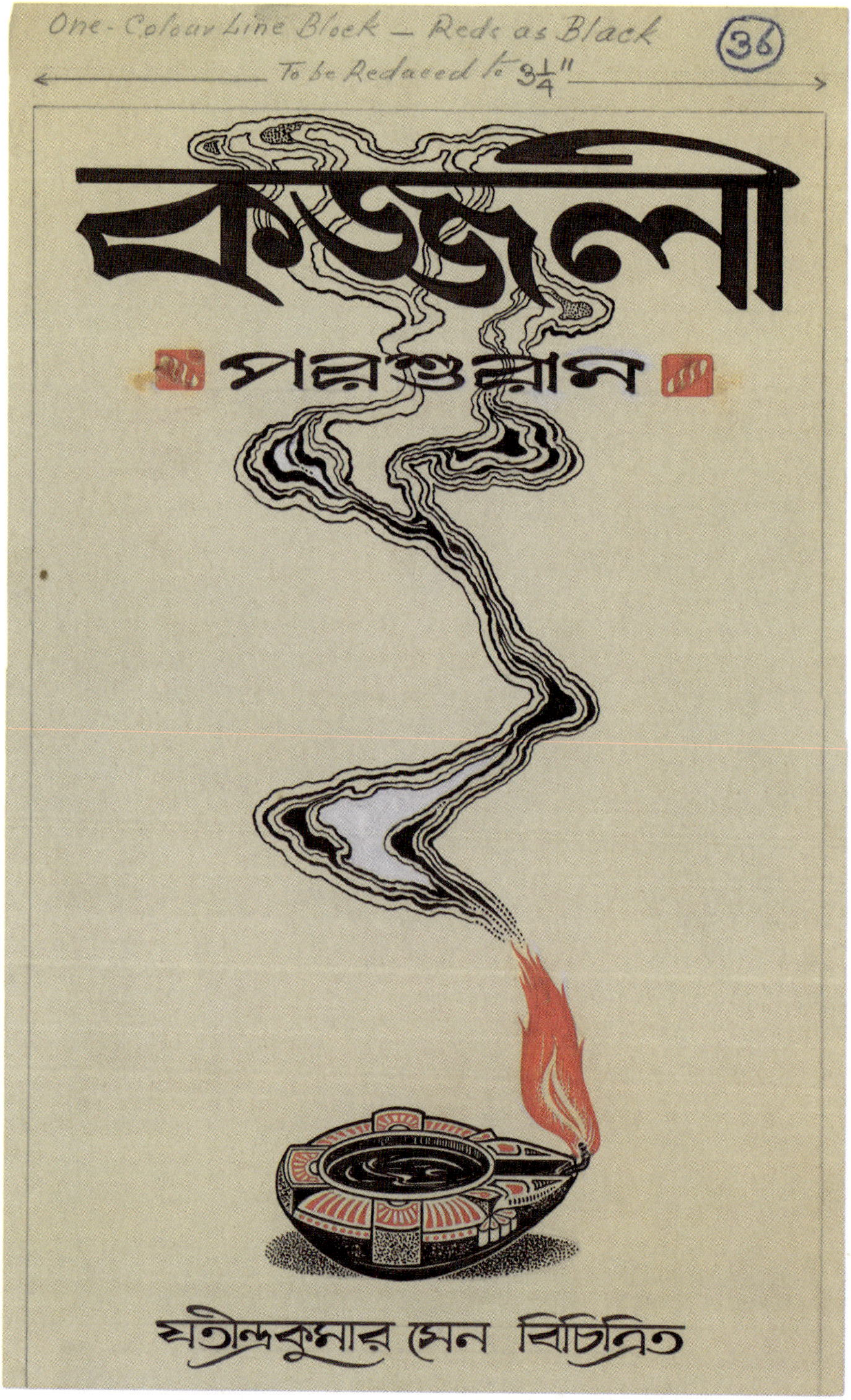

One-Colour Line Block — Reds as Black
36
To be Reduced to 3 1/4"
কজ্জলী
পরশুরাম
যতীন্দ্রকুমার সেন বিচিত্রিত

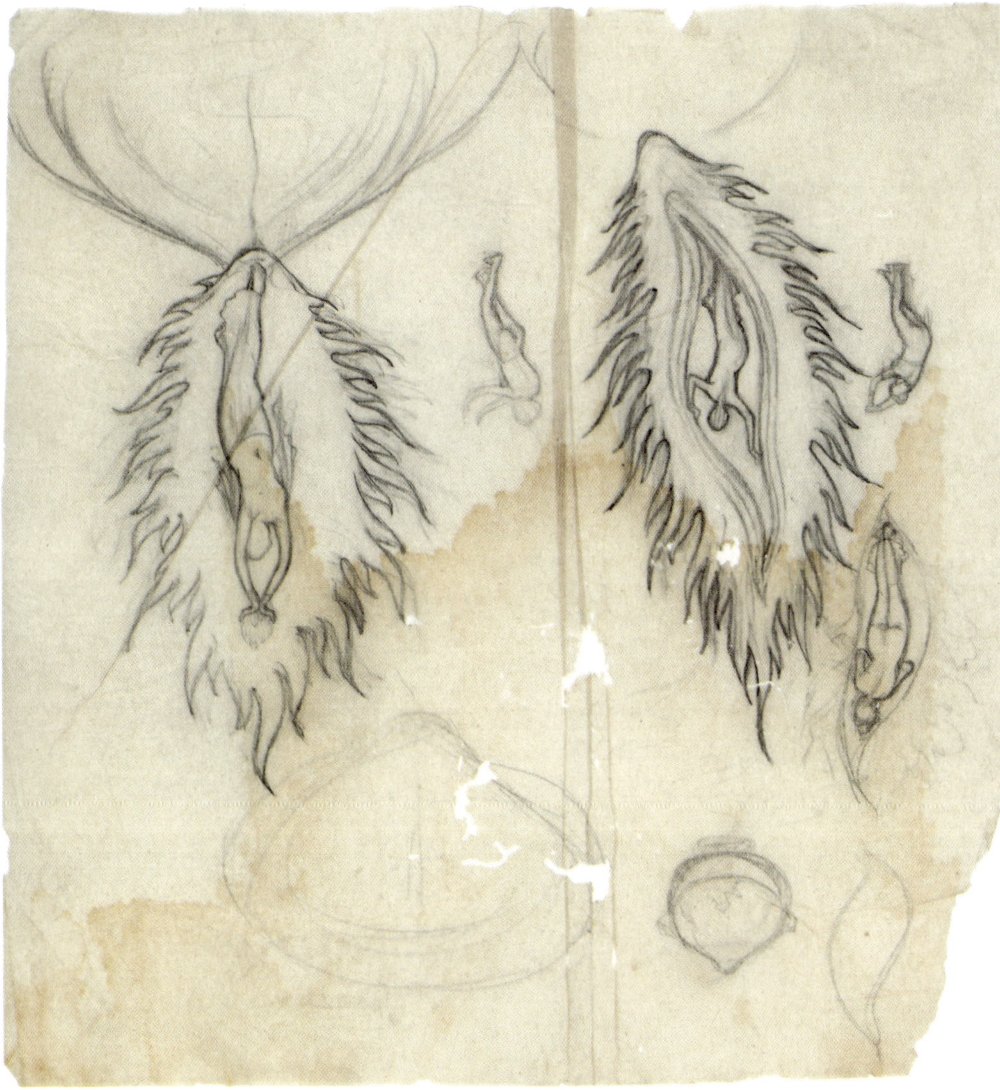

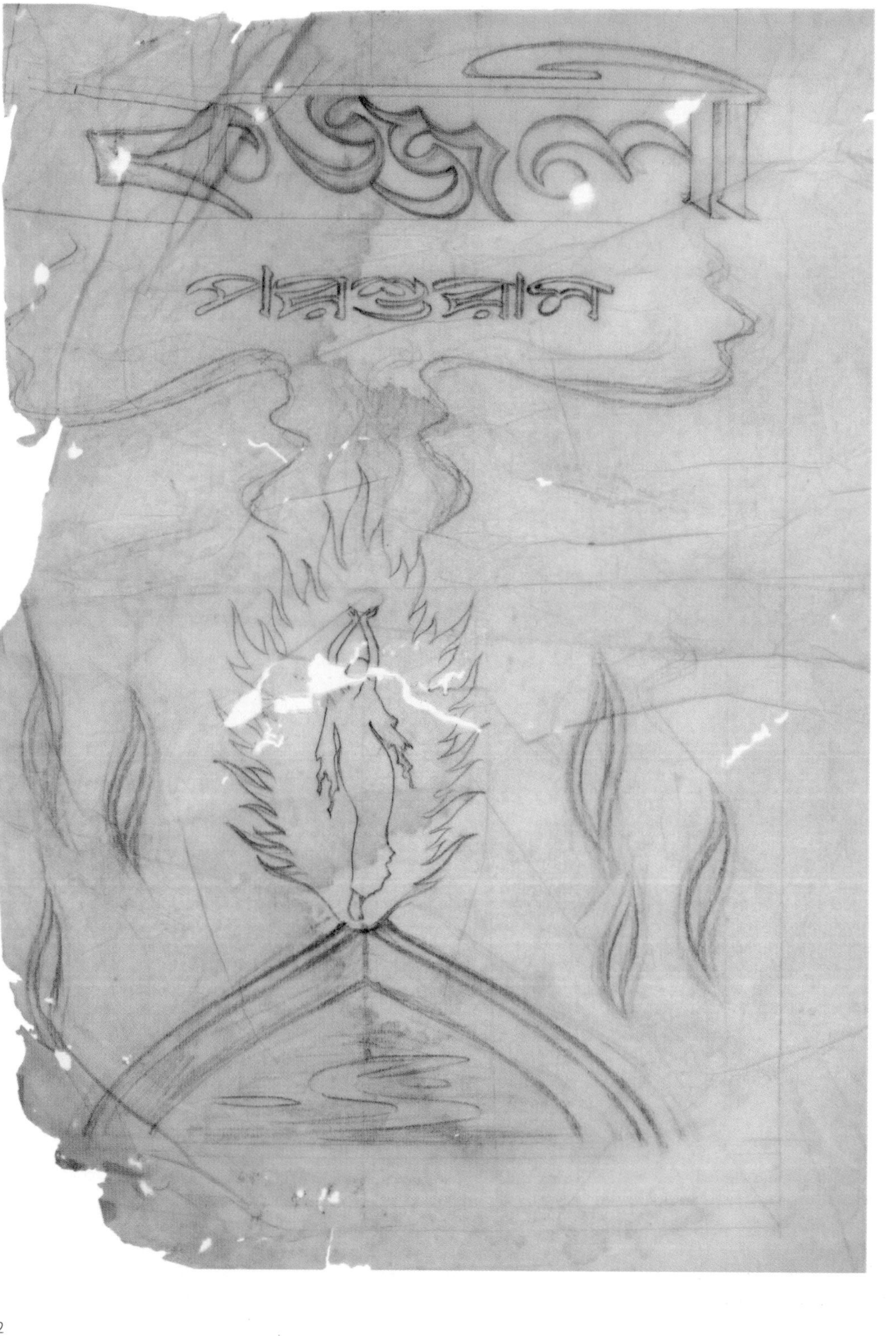
কজ্জলী
পরশুরাম

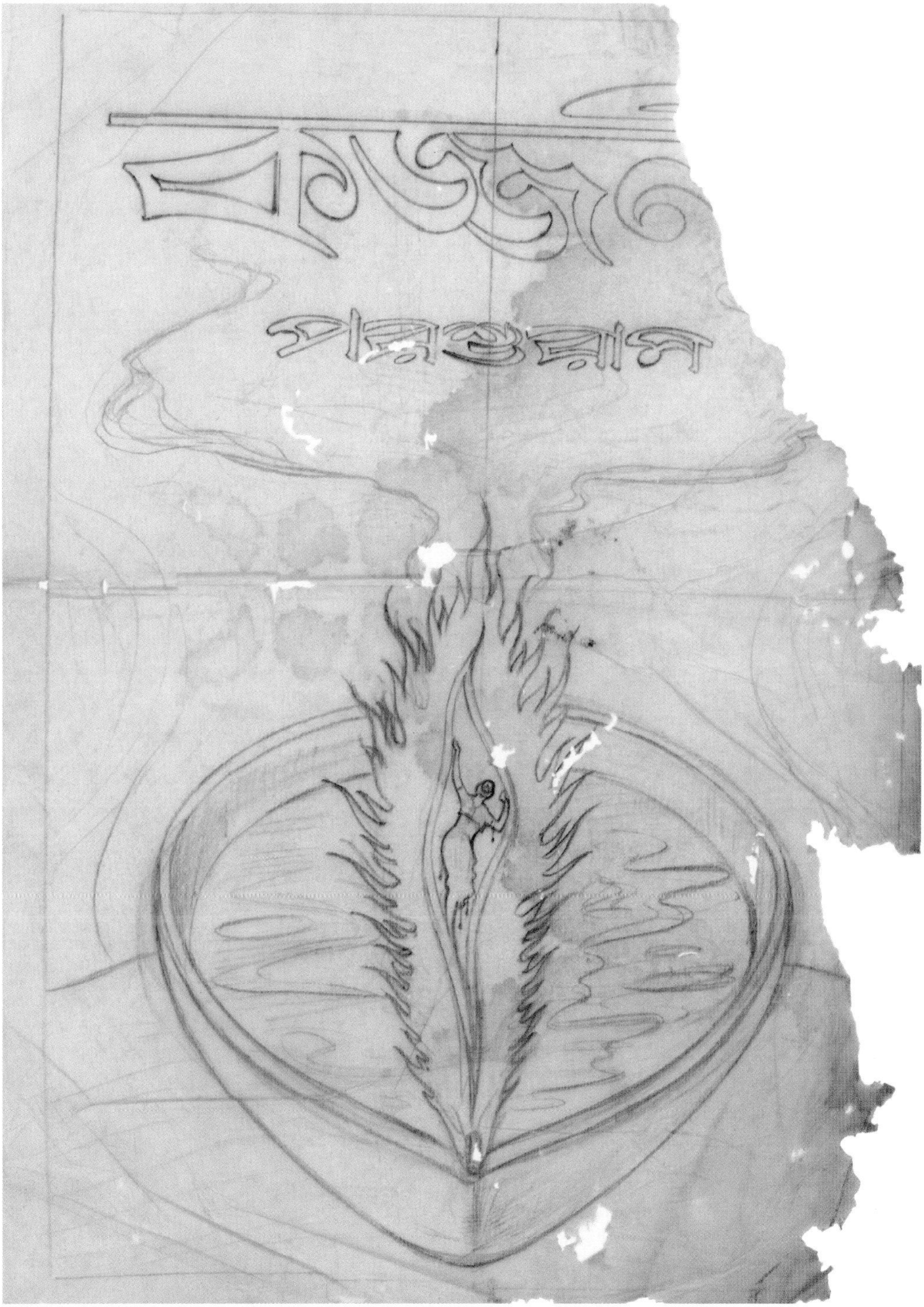
পরশুরাম

BIRINCHI BABA

Nibaran, Satya and Paramartha are friends who stay in a mess in Calcutta. They come to know that their friend Prof Noni's father-in-law, Gurupada Mitra, has fallen under the spell of a holy man and is planning to leave all his property to the baba. This Birinchi Baba claims to be ageless and frequently mentions the good advice he had given to the likes of Tulsidas and Jesus! Gurupadababu's younger daughter Bunchki is Satya's love interest. Nibaran and his companions expose the fraud baba and Satya's love story finds a happy ending. (Satyjit Ray's film *Mahapurush* [1965] was based on this story.)

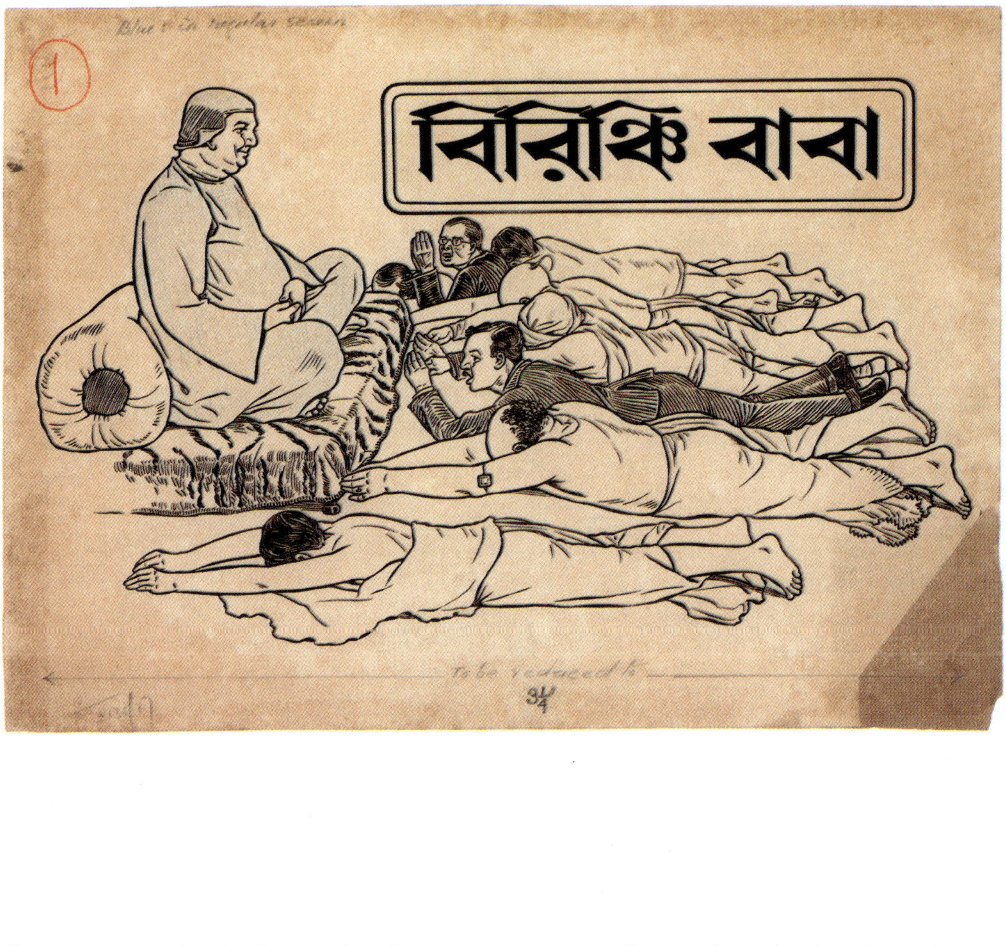

Illustration and title design for the opening page of *Birinchi Baba* (published in the collection *Kajjali*, 1928)

Characters: Birinchi Baba and his disciples.

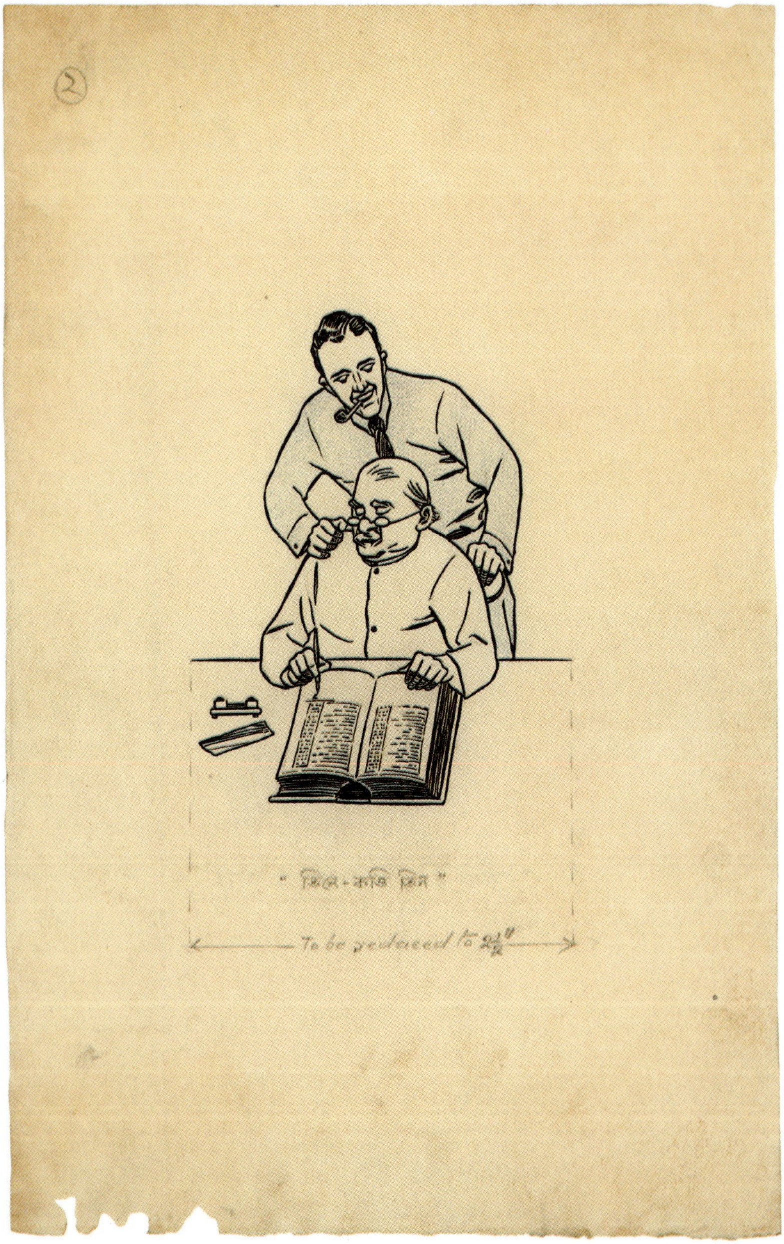

Illustration for *Birinchi Baba* (*Kajjali*, 1928)

Bangla text: "Carry three".
Characters: Mackenzie Sahib and Uncle Barada (Barada Mukherjee).

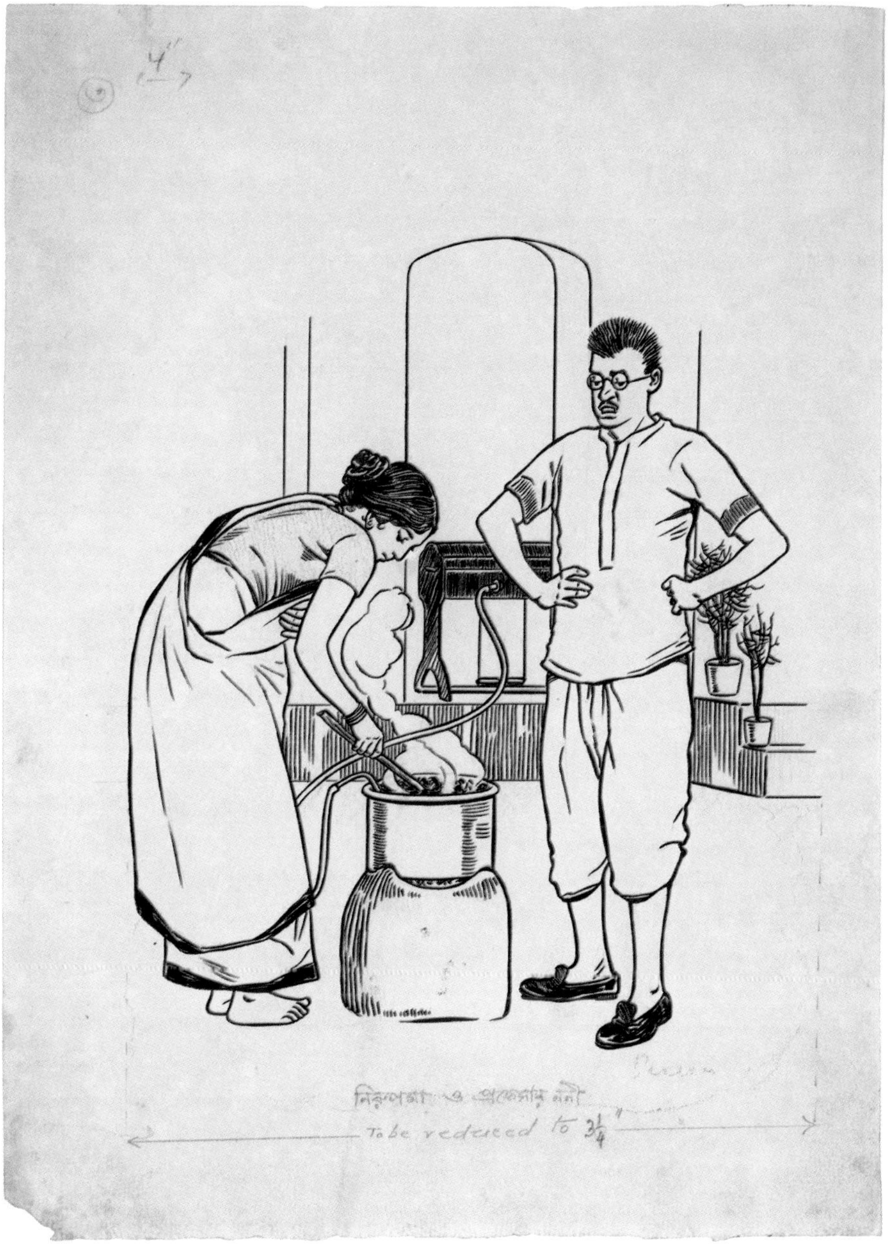

Illustration for *Birinchi Baba* (*Kajjali*, 1928)

Bangla text: "Nirupama and Professor Nani".
Characters: Nirupama and Professor Nani.

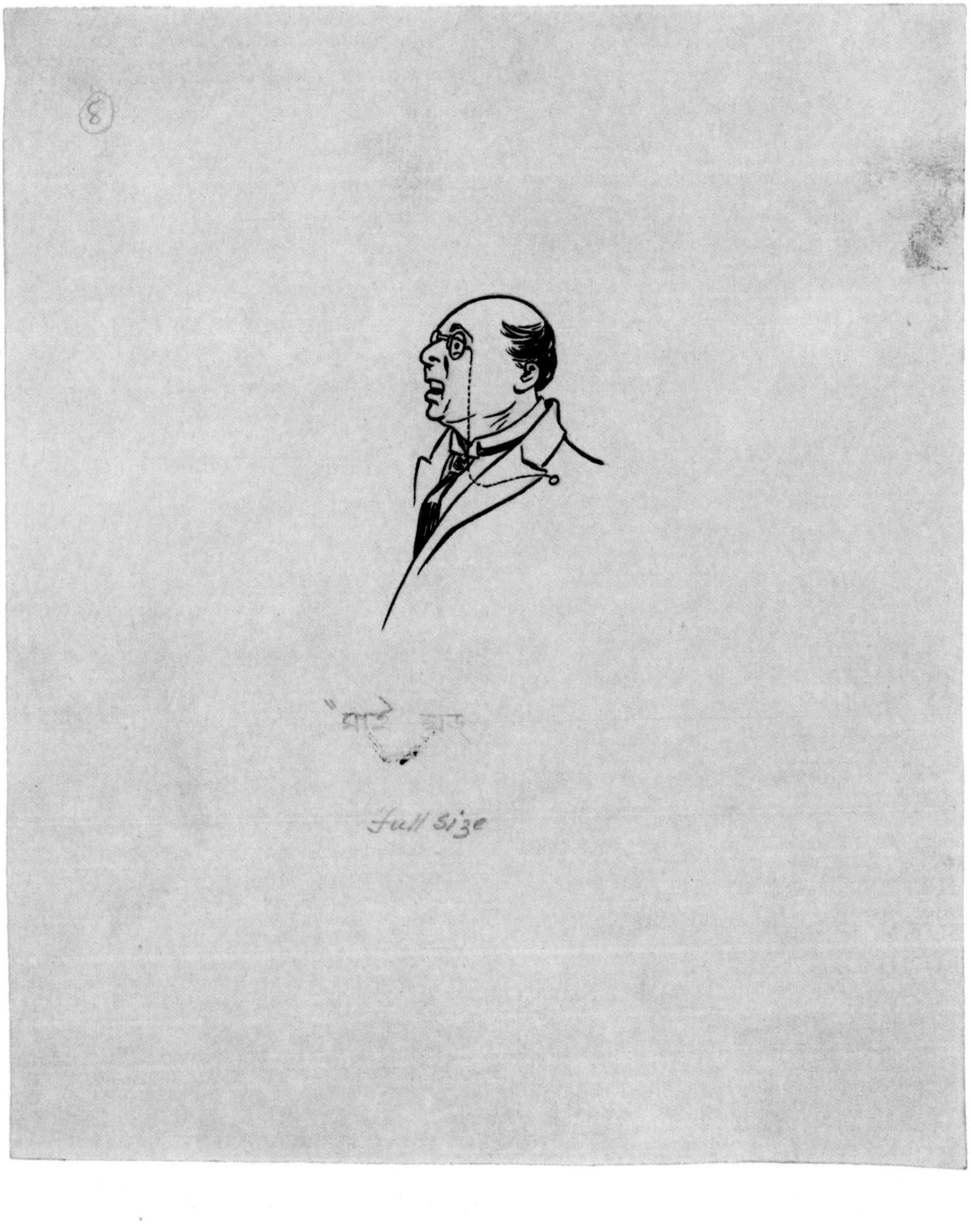

Illustration for *Birinchi Baba* (*Kajjali*, 1928)

Bangla text: "My god".
Character: Mr Sen.

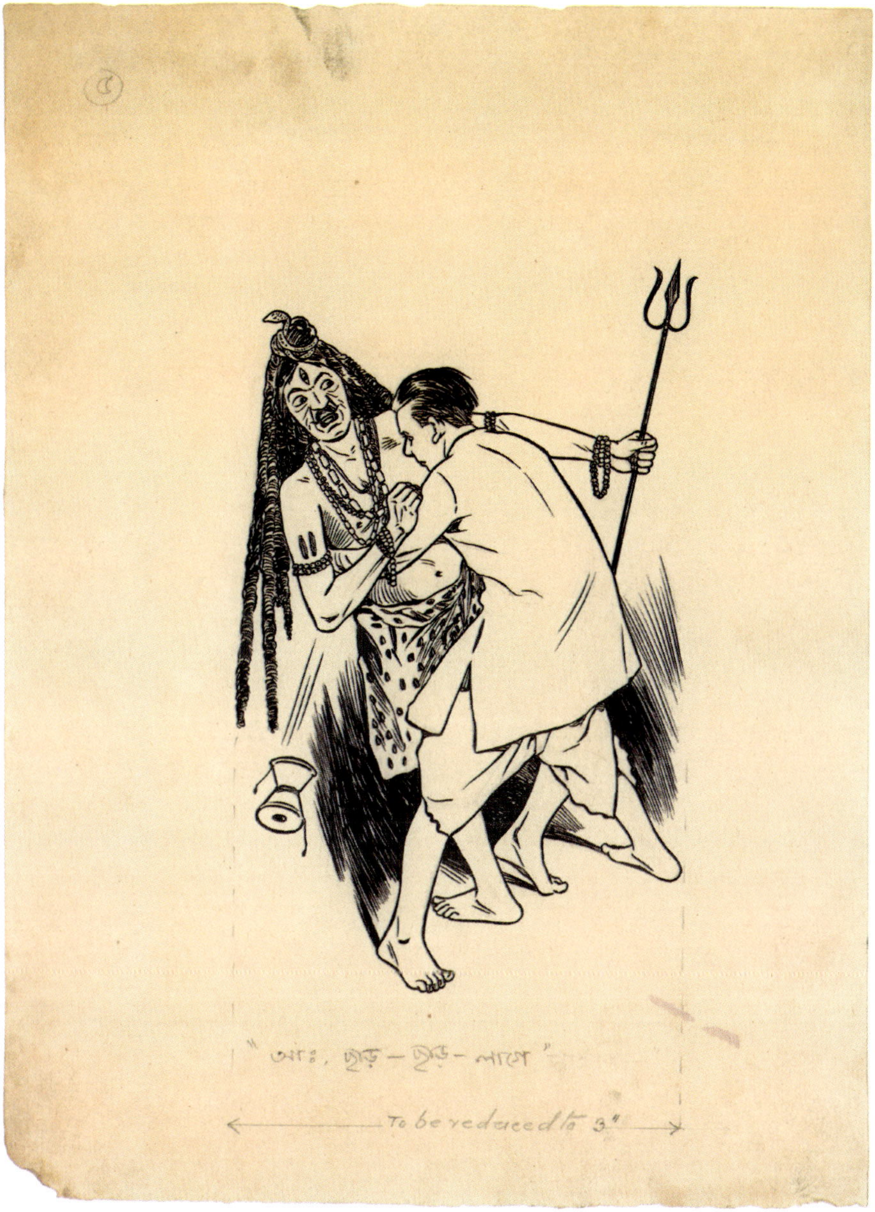

Illustration for *Birinchi Baba* (*Kajjali*, 1928)

Bangla text: "Let me go, you are hurting me".
Characters: Kebalananda (Birinchi baba's right-hand man) and Satyabrata.

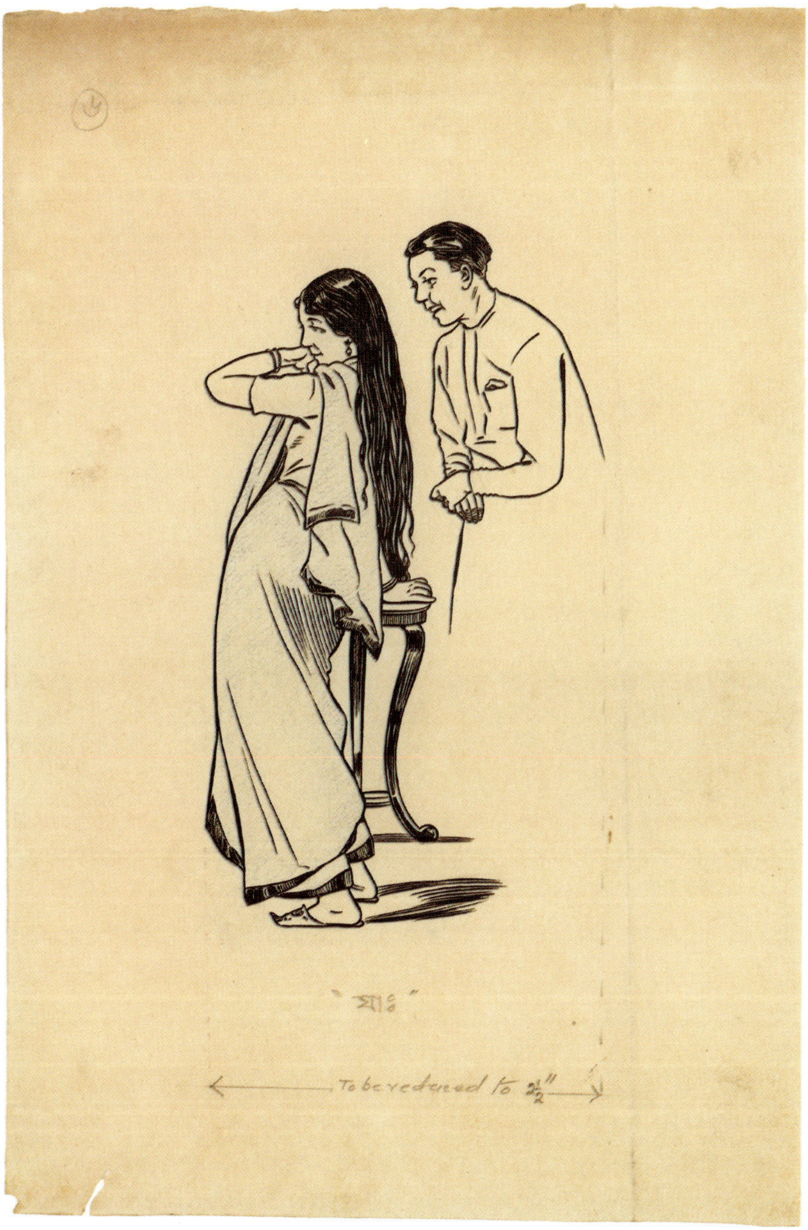

Illustration for *Birinchi Baba* (*Kajjali*, 1928)

Bangla text: "Go away".
Characters: Buchki and Satyabrata.

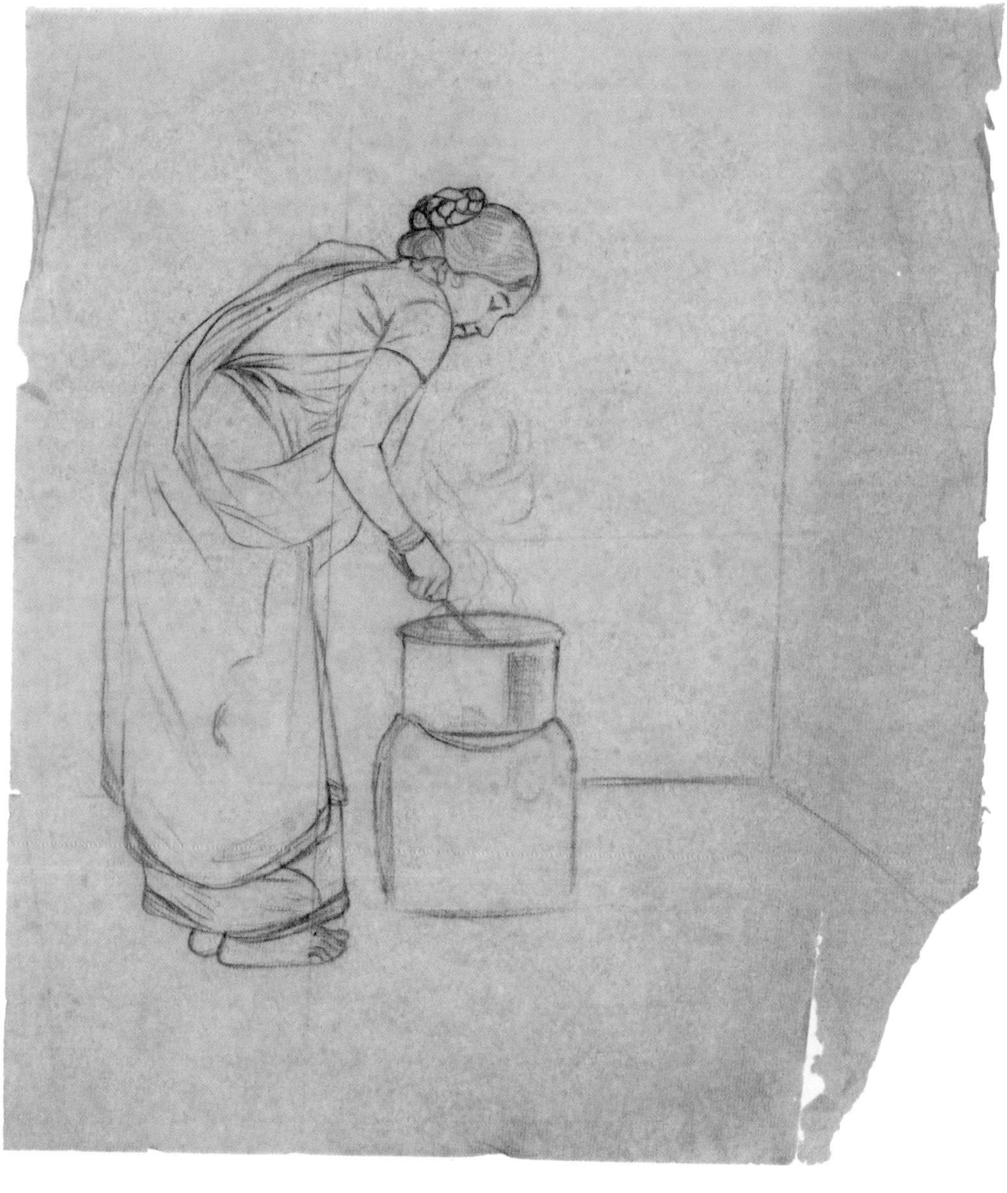

Draft sketch for *Birinchi Baba* (*Kajjali*, 1928)

Character: Nirupama.

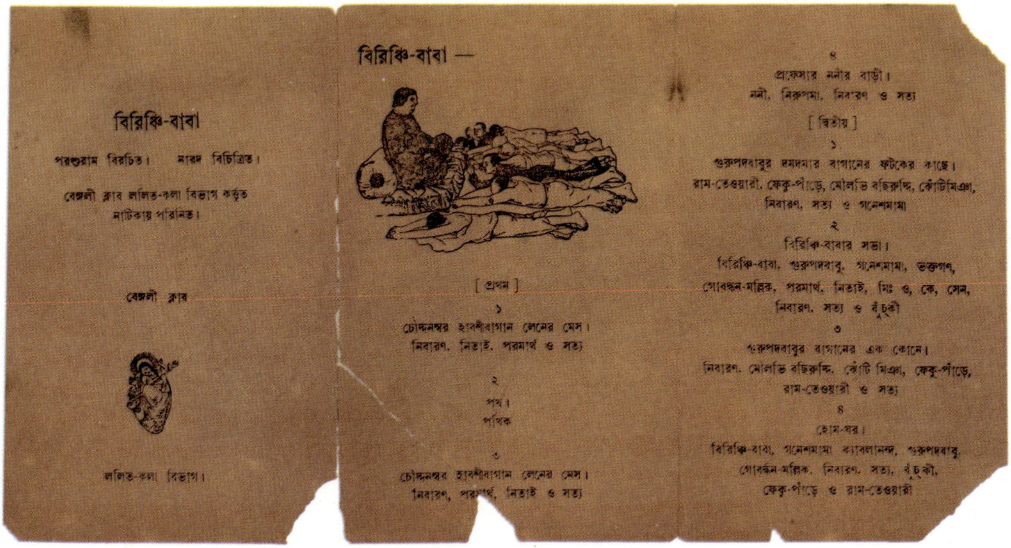

বিরিঞ্চি-বাবা

পরশুরাম বিরচিত। নারদ বিচিত্রিত।

বেঙ্গলী ক্লাব ললিত-কলা বিভাগ কর্ত্তৃক
নাটিকায় পরিনত।

বেঙ্গলী ক্লাব

ললিত-কলা বিভাগ।

বিরিঞ্চি-বাবা —

[প্রথম]

১

চৌদ্দনম্বর হাবশীবাগান লেনের মেস।
নিবারণ, নিতাই, পরমার্থ ও সত্য

২

পথ।
পথিক

৩

চৌদ্দনম্বর হাবশীবাগান লেনের মেস।
নিবারণ, পরমার্থ, নিতাই ও সত্য

৪

প্রফেসার ননীর বাড়ী।
ননী, নিরুপমা, নিবারণ ও সত্য

[দ্বিতীয়]

১

গুরুপদবাবুর দমদমার বাগানের ফটকের কাছে।
রাম-তেওয়ারী, ফেকু-পাঁড়ে, মৌলভি বছিরুদ্দি, কোঁটিমিশ্রা,
নিবারণ, সত্য ও গনেশমামা

২

বিরিঞ্চি-বাবার সভা।
বিরিঞ্চি-বাবা, গুরুপদবাবু, গনেশমামা, ভক্তগণ,
গোবৰ্দ্ধন-মল্লিক, পরমার্থ, নিতাই, মিঃ ও, কে, সেন,
নিবারণ, সত্য ও বুঁচকী

৩

গুরুপদবাবুর বাগানের এক কোনে।
নিবারণ, মৌলভি বছিরুদ্দি, ঝোঁটি মিশ্রা, ফেকু-পাঁড়ে,
রাম-তেওয়ারী ও সত্য

৪

হোম-ঘর।
বিরিঞ্চি-বাবা, গনেশমামা ক্যাবলানন্দ, গুরুপদবাবু,
গোবৰ্দ্ধন-মল্লিক, নিবারণ, সত্য, বুঁচকী,
ফেকু-পাঁড়ে ও রাম-তেওয়ারী

A dramatisation of *Birinchi Baba* by Bengali Club, presented by Lalit Kala Vibhag (Fine Arts Department).

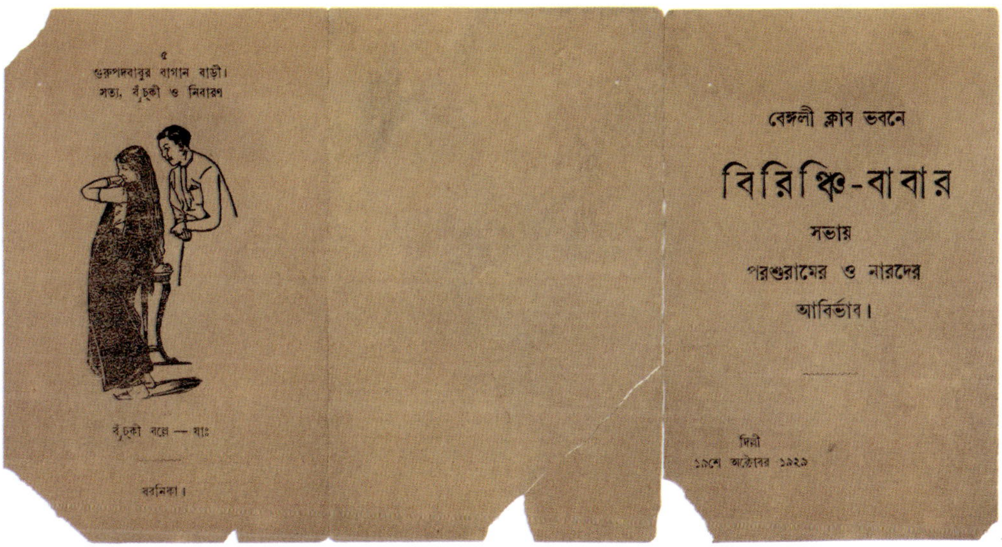

A humorous announcement of an appearance by Parashuram and Narad (Jatindrakumar Sen's pseudonym) at the Bengali Club Bhavan "in Birinchi Baba's meeting hall"! Delhi, 19th October 1929.

JABALI

Rishi Jabali was a sage and an advisor to King Dasharatha. In Valmiki's *Ramayana*, he accompanied Bharat, Rishi Vashishtha and others to the forest to persuade Ram to stay on in Ayodhya and give up the idea of exile. Ram became angry with Jabali's apparently anti-dharma reasoning. In Parashuram's story, after Ram goes on exile, Jabali is shunned by his peers and goes away to live in the forest with his wife Hindralini. A free-thinking ascetic, he is repeatedly denounced by petty hermits, while an insecure Indra tries to disturb his meditation. Once he pays for his unwitting sin at the hands of Yama, Brahma appears and tells him to go and preach among people, freeing them from worldliness.

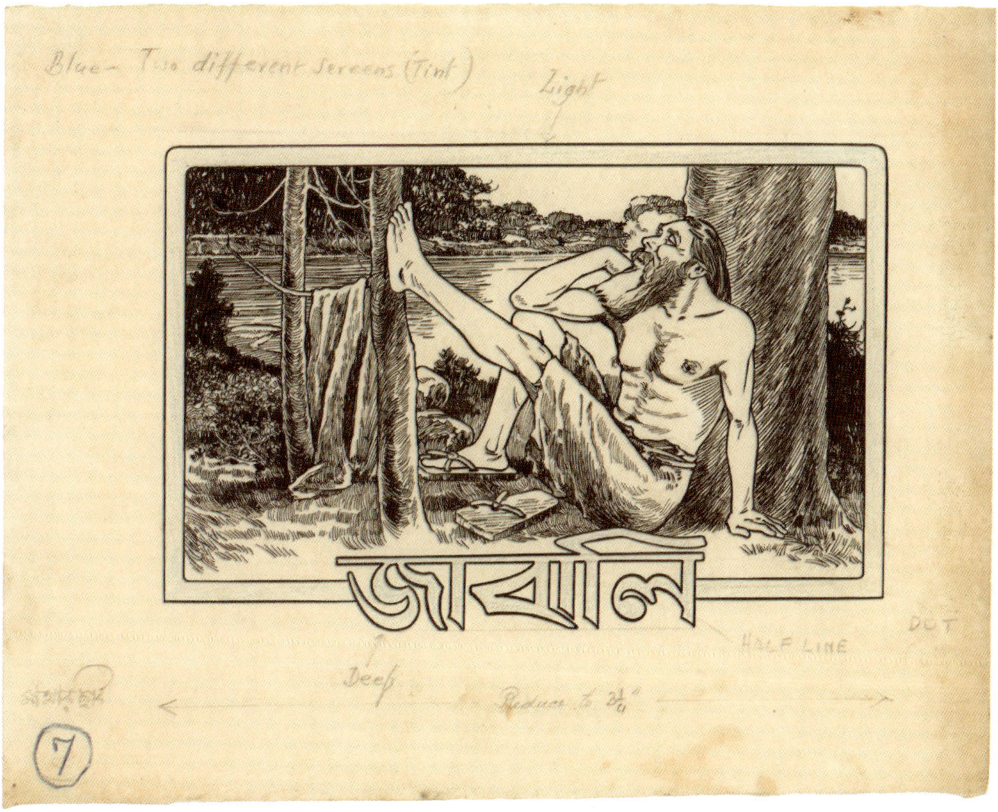

Illustration and title design for the opening page of *Jabali* (published in the collection *Kajjali*,1928)

Character: Jabali.
Small Bangla text on the left: “Illustration on top”.

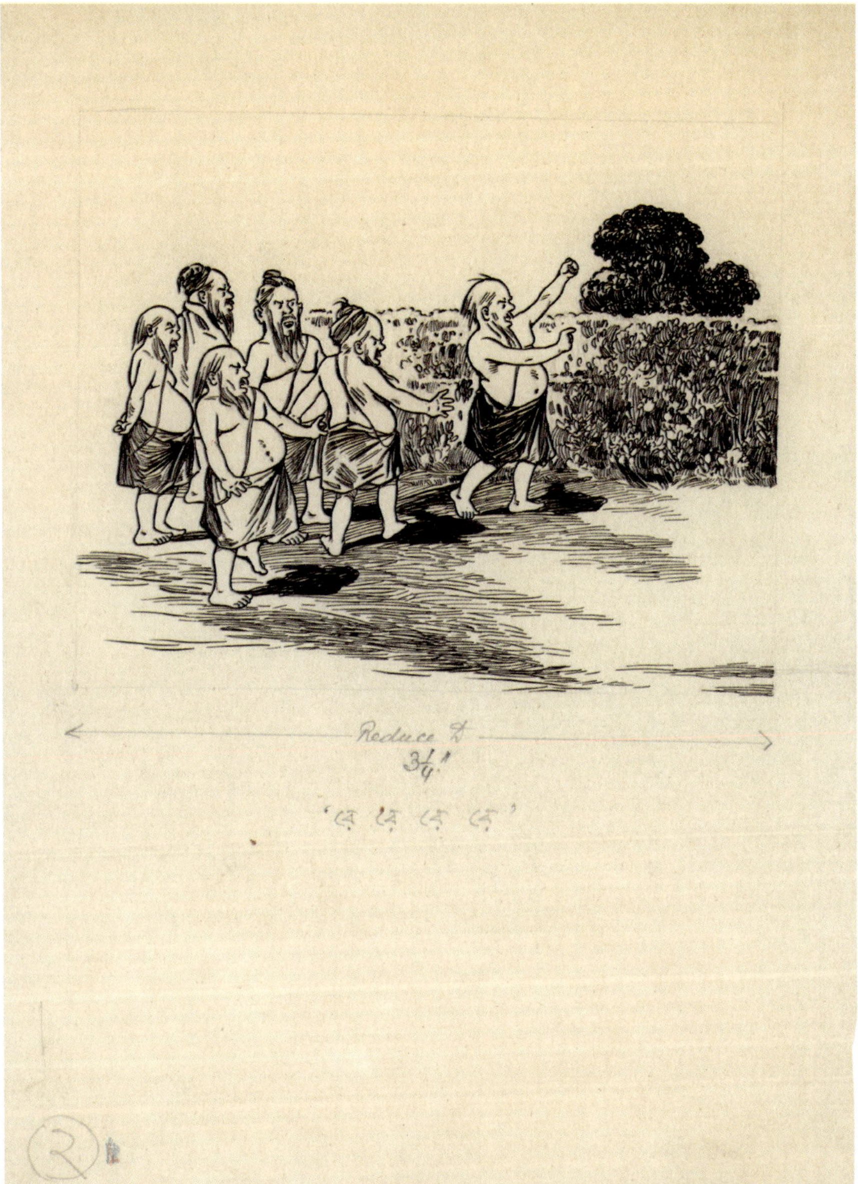

Illustration for *Jabali* (*Kajjali*, 1928)

Bangla text: "Re re re re" (*making an aggressive noise*).
Characters: Balkhillo Muni – dwarf sages.

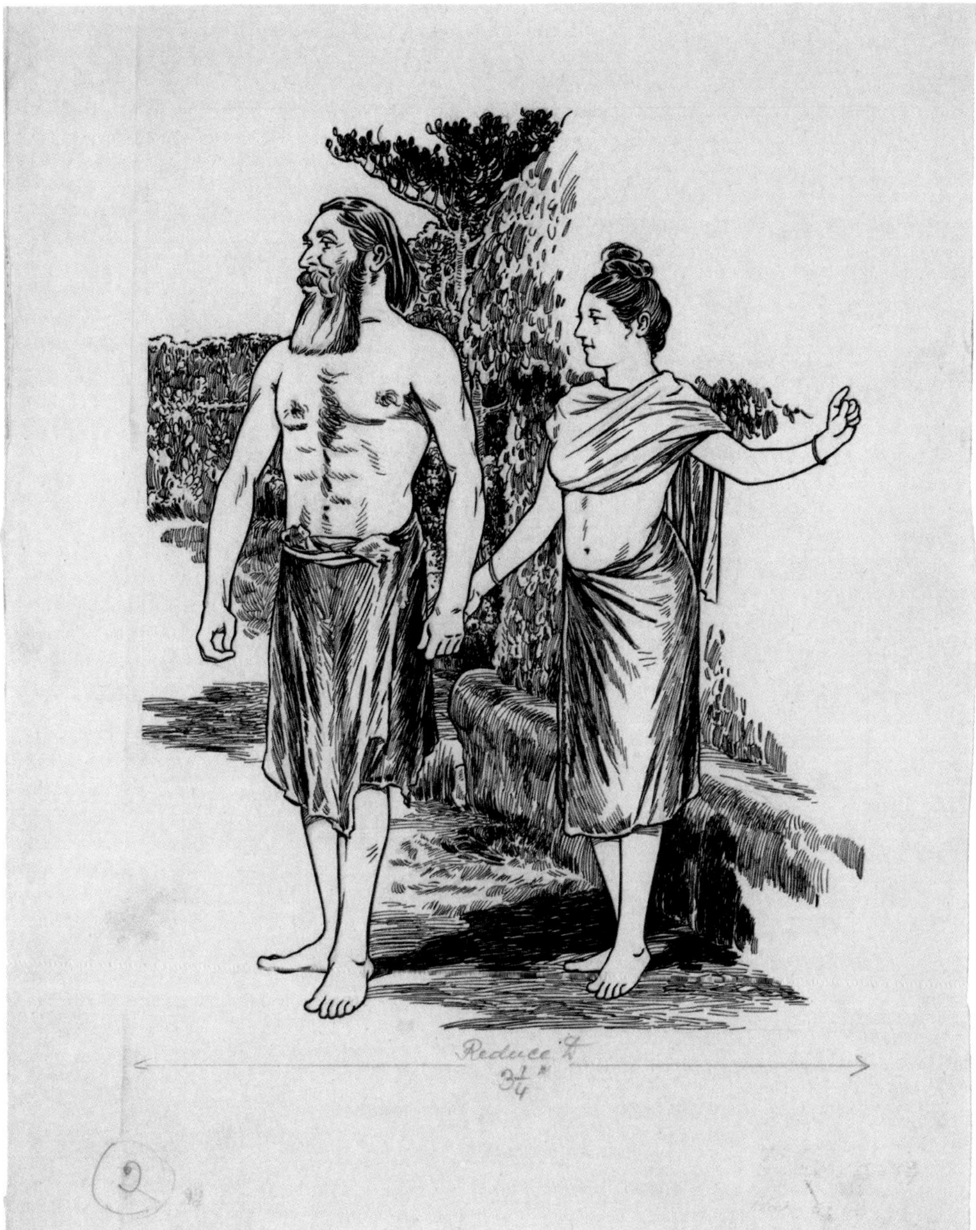

Illustration for *Jabali* (*Kajjali*, 1928)

Characters: Jabali and his wife Hindralini.

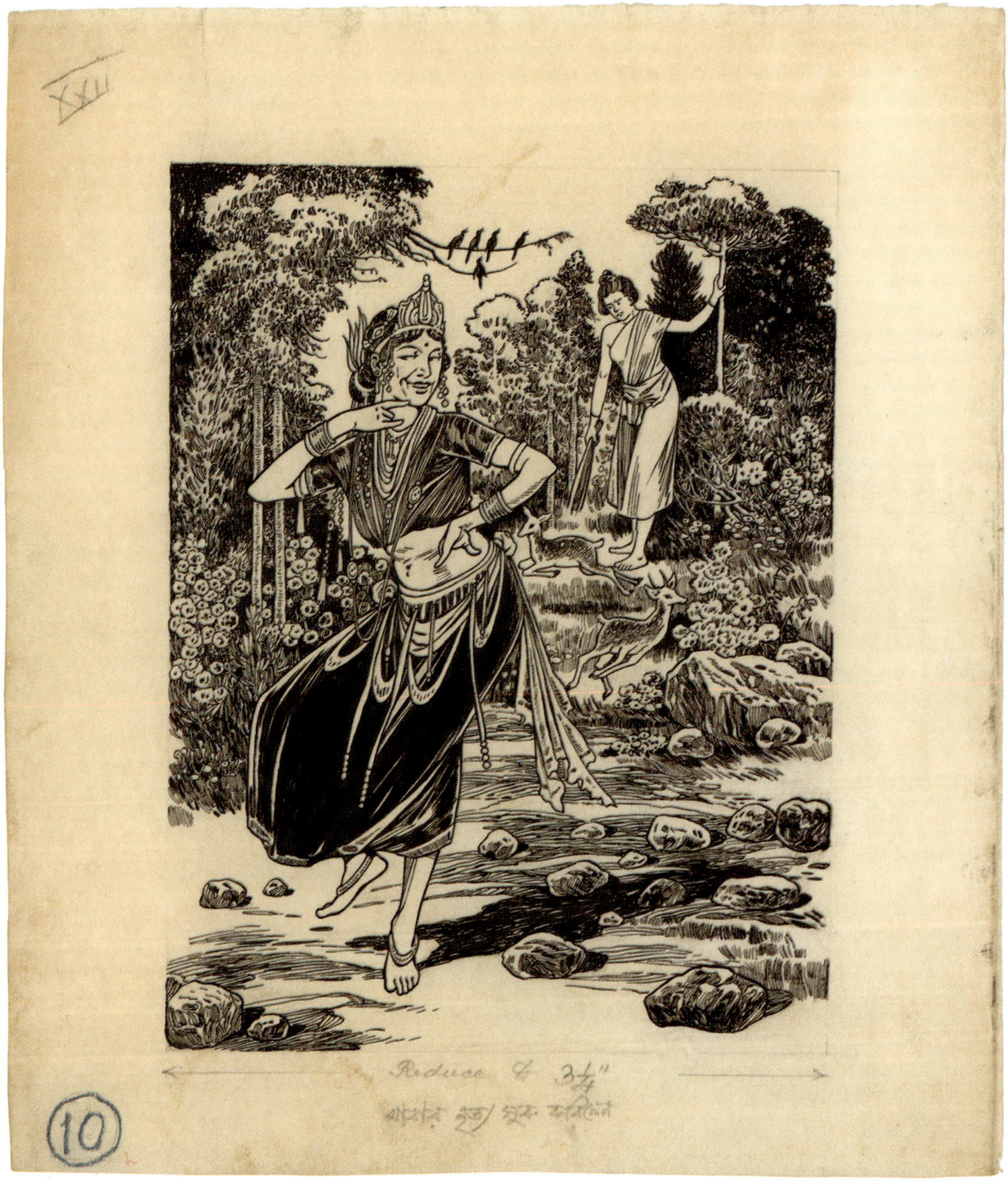

Illustration for *Jabali* (*Kajjali*, 1928)

Bangla text: "Started dancing again".
Characters: Ghritachi (dancing) and Hindralini.

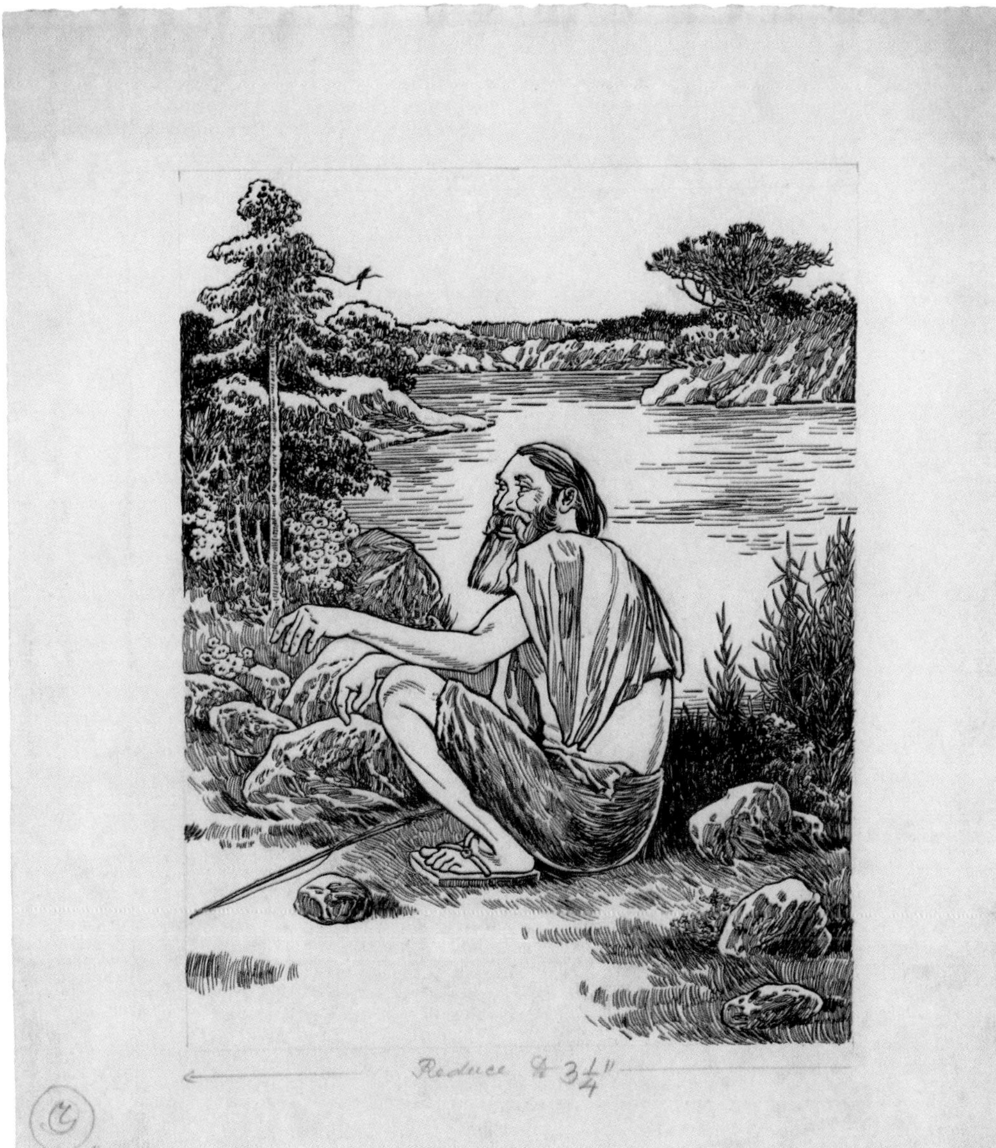

Illustration for *Jabali* (*Kajjali*, 1928)

Character: Jabali.

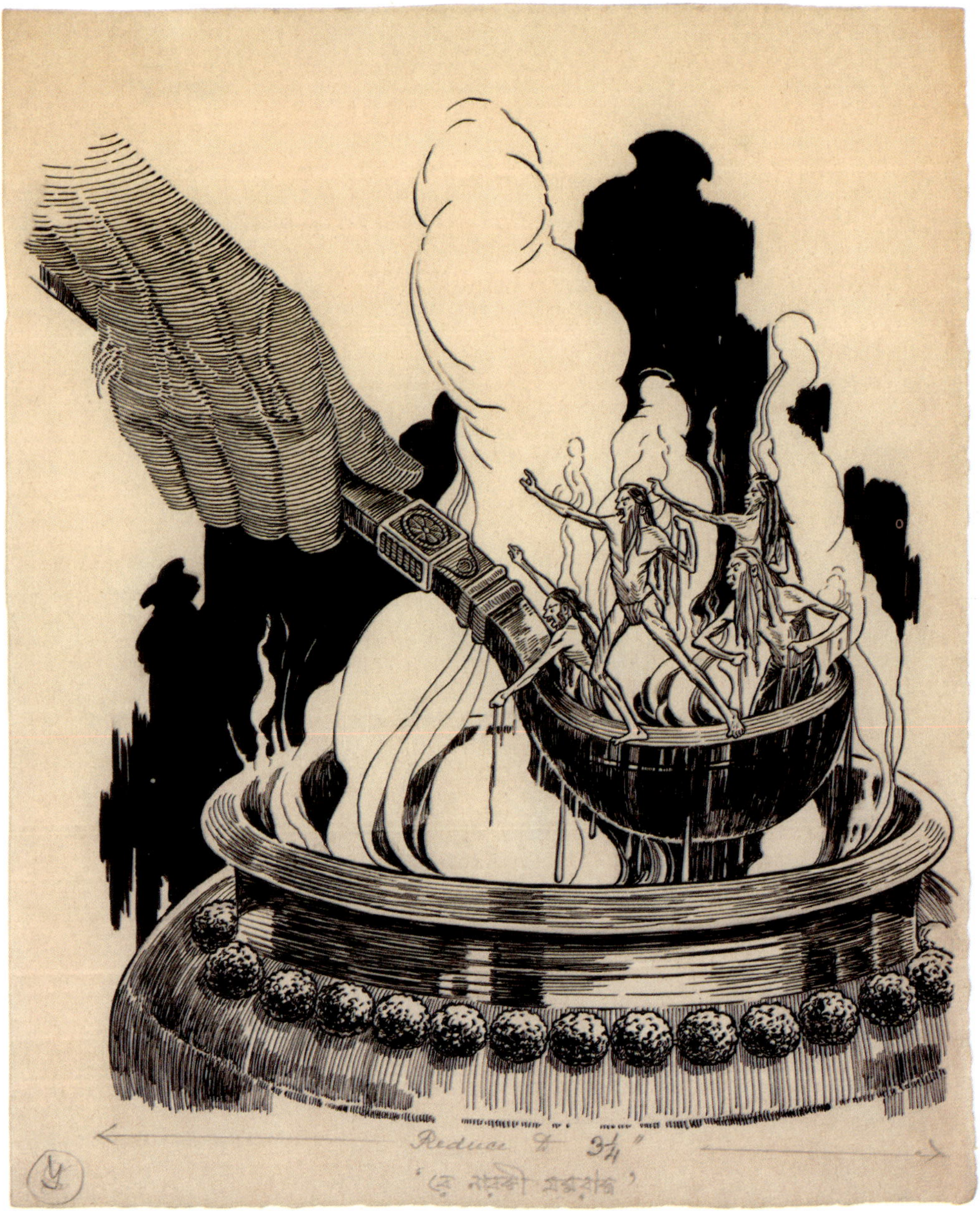

Illustration for *Jabali* (*Kajjali*, 1928)

"O king of hell, Yamraj".
Characters: Rishis (sages) being burnt in hell.

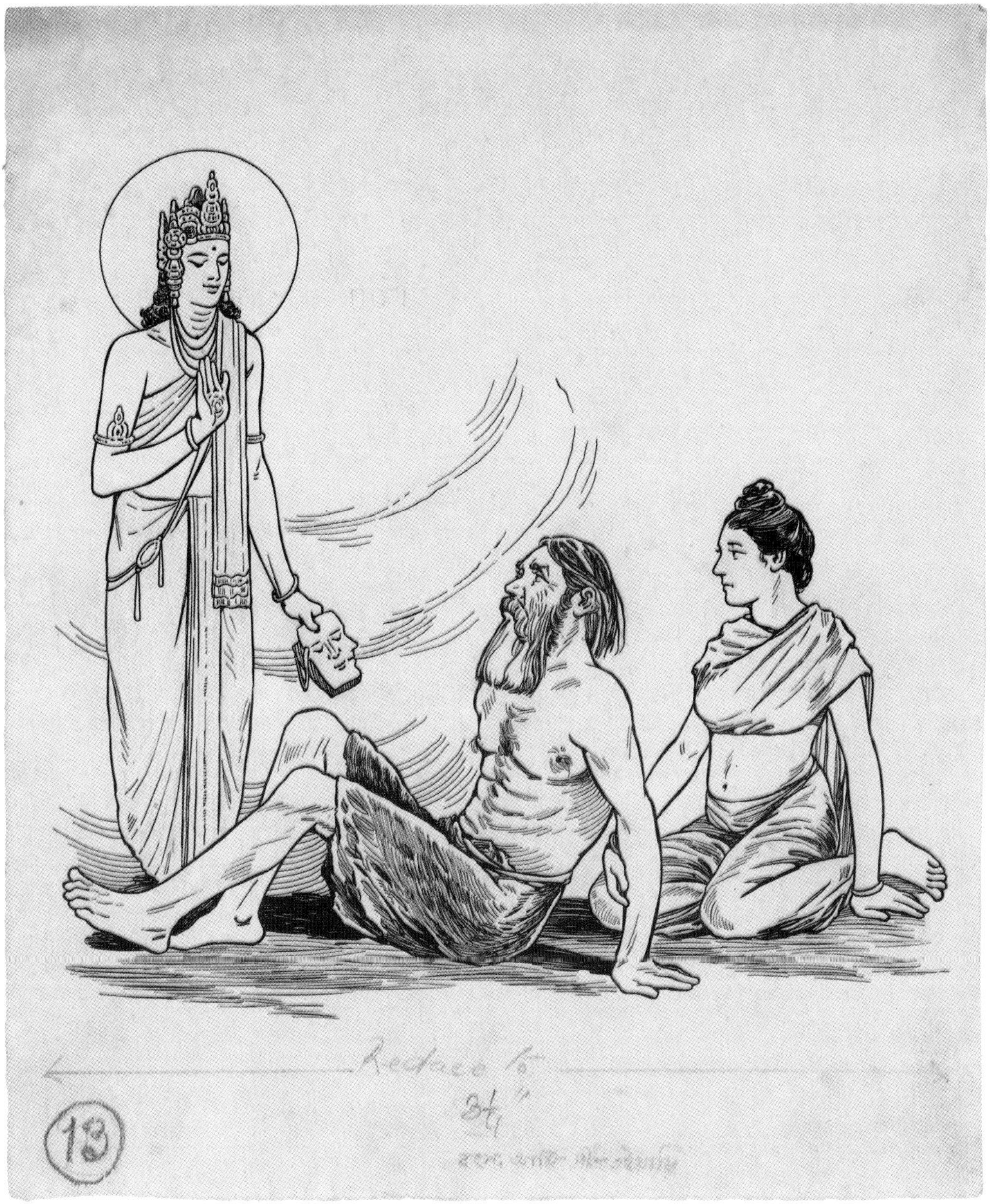

Illustration for *Jabali* (*Kajjali*, 1928)

Bangla text: “Son, I am satisfied”.
Characters: Brahma, Jabali and his wife Hindralini.

DAKKHIN RAI

Dakkhin Rai is a tiger deity who is worshipped in the Sunderbans. In the story, Parashuram satirises both the oppressive British rulers and their treacherous Bengali allies. In the drawing room of Rai Bahadur Banshalochan Banerjee, a typically Bengali *adda* with much chatting and storytelling is in full flow. Tigers are the subject. Ace storyteller Kedar Chatterjee narrates the tale of the corrupt, vengeful and ambitious Bakul Dutta who badly wants to win a seat in the Sunderbans council elections. He is hardly likely to win on his reputation so he desperately prays to Dakkhin Rai. Hearing his selfish request, the deity turns him into an old diseased tiger, who is then sent to Alipore zoo. The *adda* participants also joke about how patriotic Bengal tigers have developed a taste for British flesh and whether this could solve the problem of gaining Swaraj!

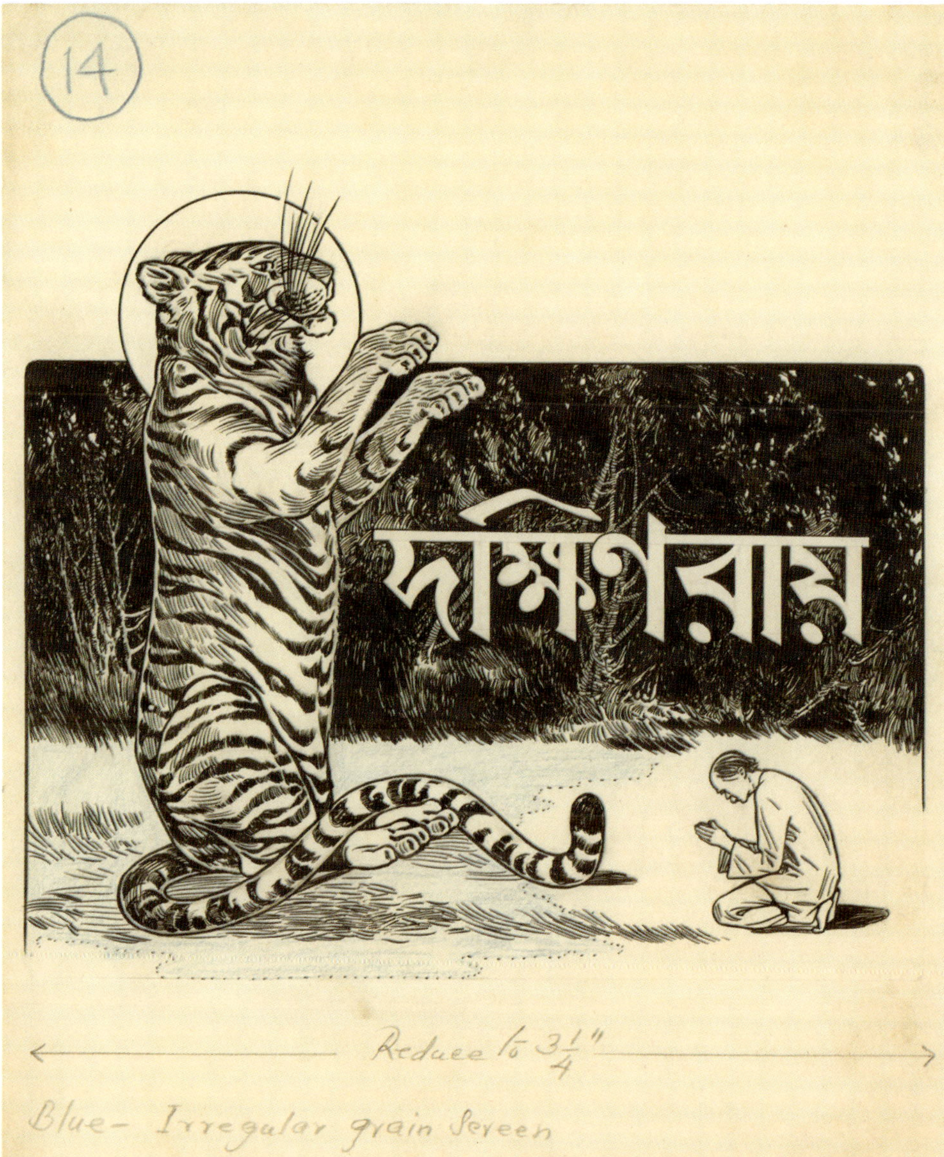

Illustration and title design for *Dakkhin Rai* (published in the collection *Kajjali*, 1928)

Character: Dakkhin Rai, the tiger

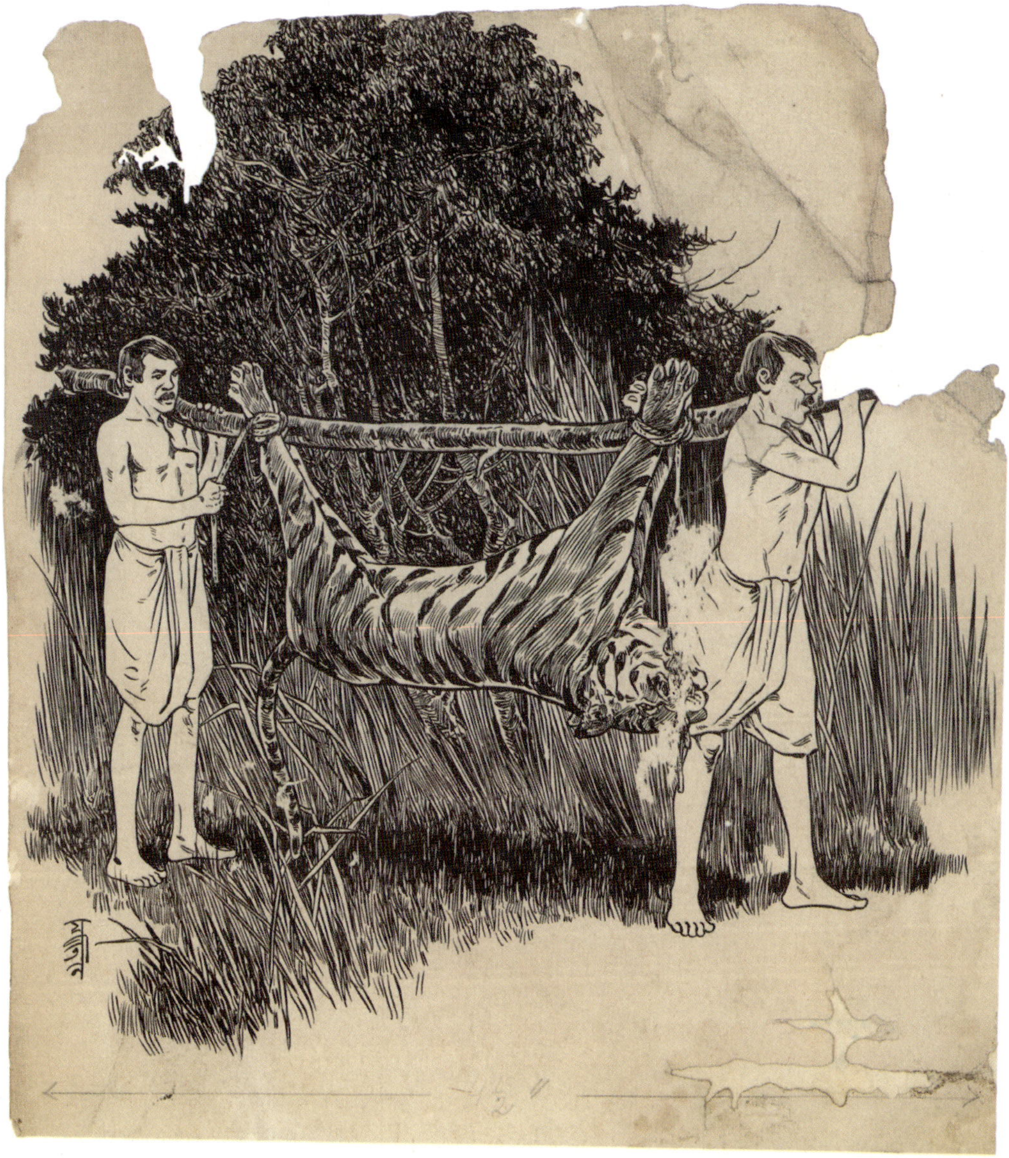

Draft illustration for *Dakkhin Rai* (*Kajjali*, 1928)

Characters: Baku babu being carried away after he turned into a tiger.

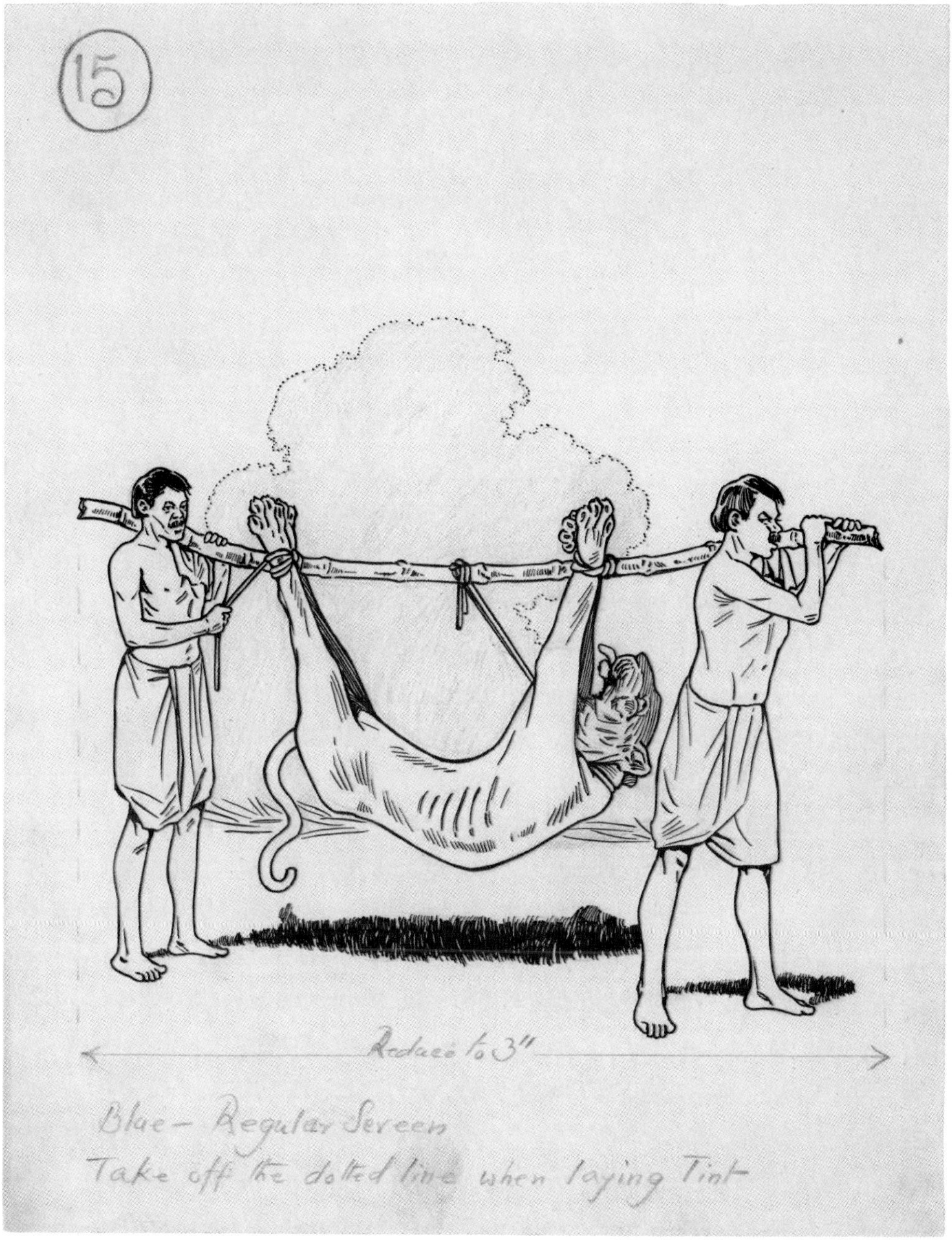

Final illustration for *Dakkhin Rai* (*Kajjali*, 1928)

Characters: Baku babu being carried away after he turned into a tiger.

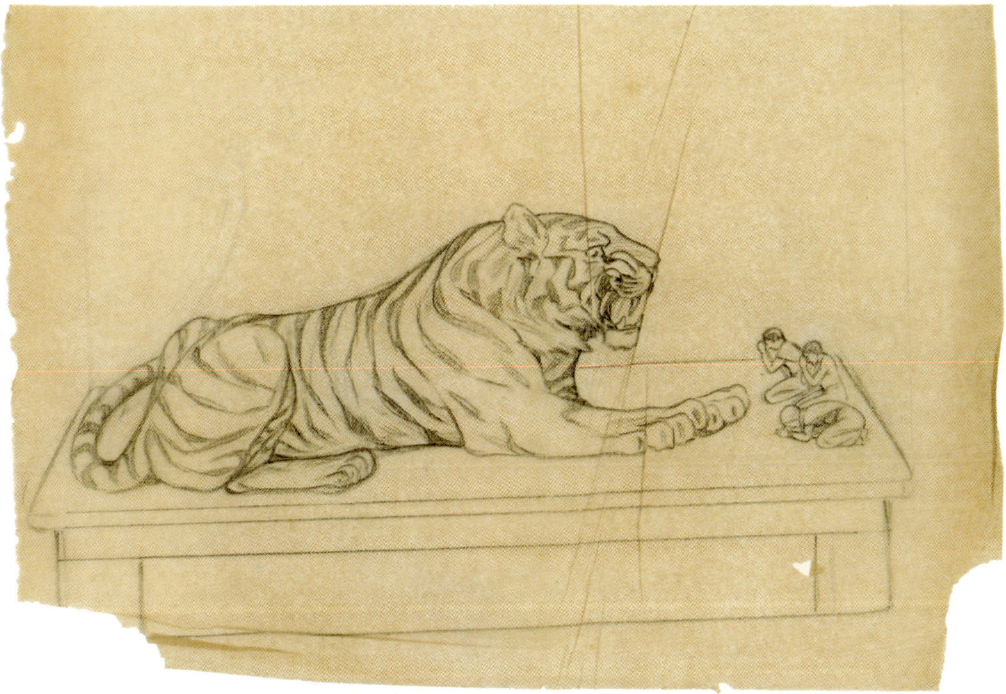

Draft sketch for *Dakkhin Rai* (*Kajjali*, 1928)

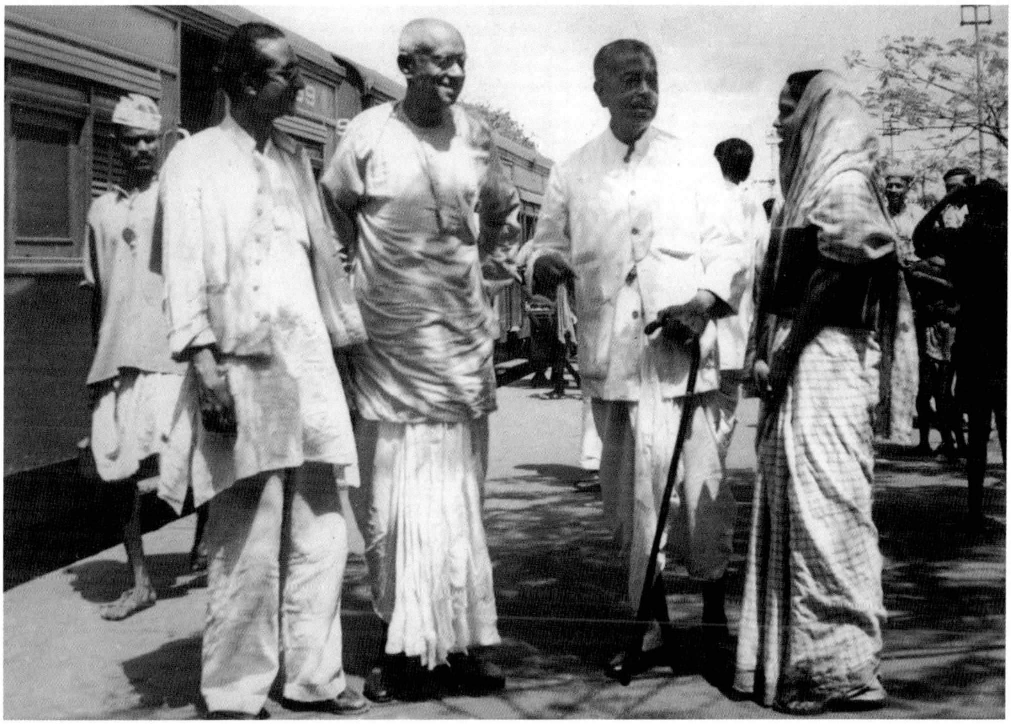

Rajshekhar Basu and Charuchandra Bhattacharya with others

SWAYAMBARAA

Parashuram's favourite raconteur, Kedar Chatterji, tells us another story. This one is about an American young woman, Joan Jilter, whom Kedar meets in a train compartment with her two suitors Timothy Topper and Christopher Columbus Blotto. (The names 'Jilter' and 'Blotto' are highly indicative.) The two men fight over Joan when Kedar brings Bill Bounder into the picture. Through Kedar's mediation Joan's wedding is arranged with Bill. But at the end of the story, Kedar finds that the bride had run away the day after the wedding and the groom is looking for her.

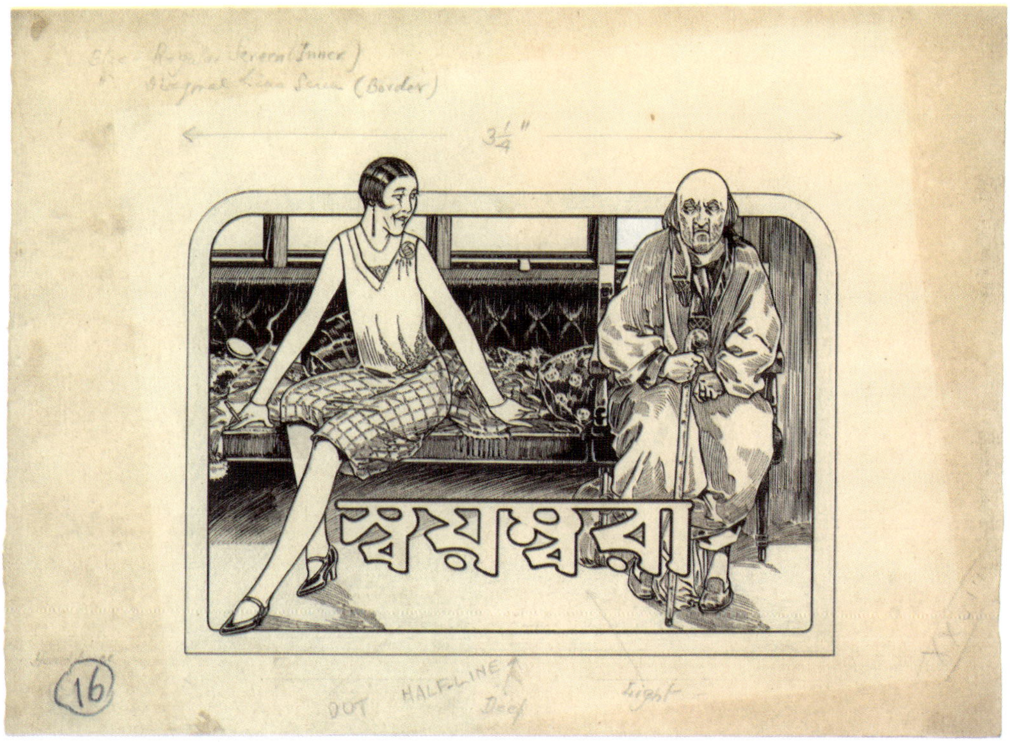

Illustration and title design for *Swayambaraa* (published in the collection *Kajjali*, 1928)

Characters: Joan Jilter ("memsahib") with Kedar Chatterjee.

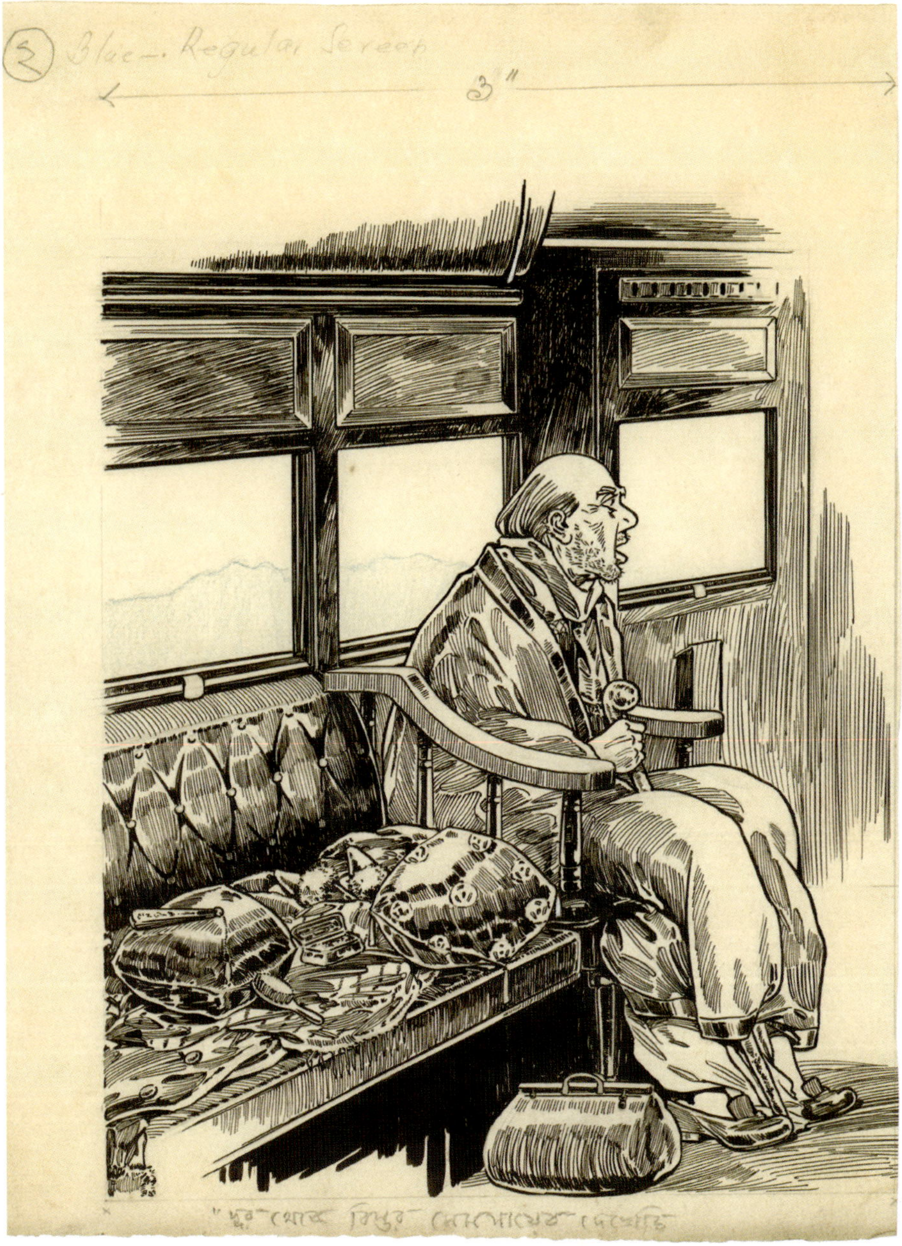

Illustration for *Swayambaraa* (*Kajjali*, 1928)

Bangla text: "I had seen many memsahibs from far off".
Character: Kedar Chatterjee.

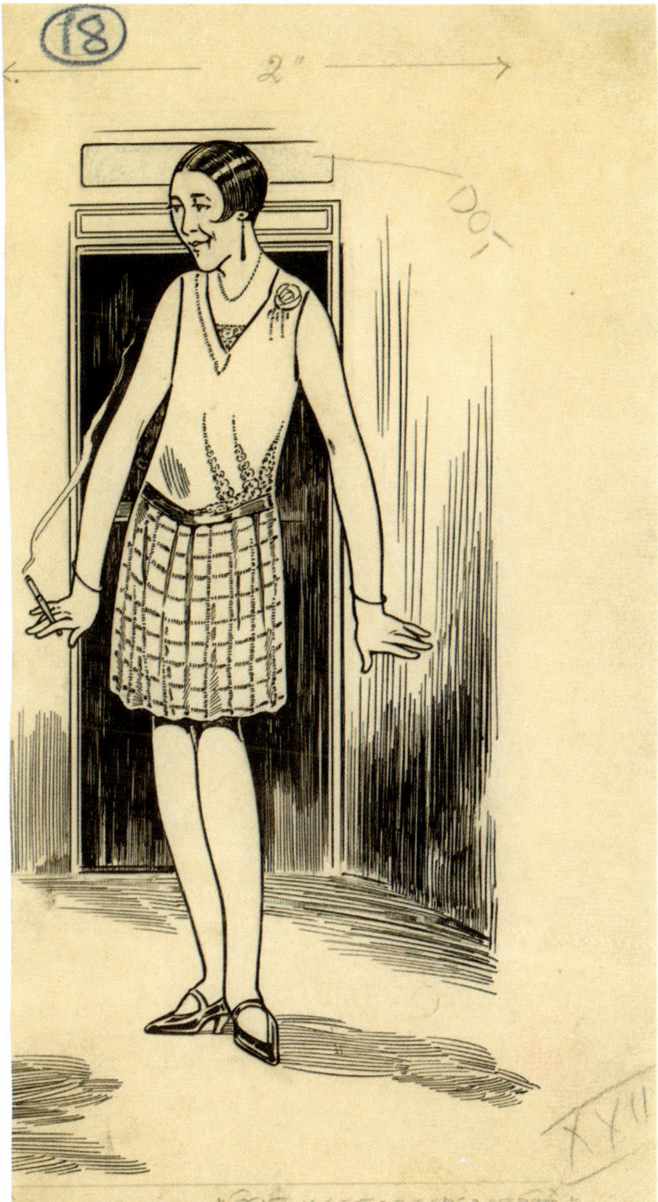

Illustration for *Swayambaraa* (*Kajjali*, 1928)

Bangla text: “But never at close quarters like this”.
Character: Joan Jilter (“memsahib”).

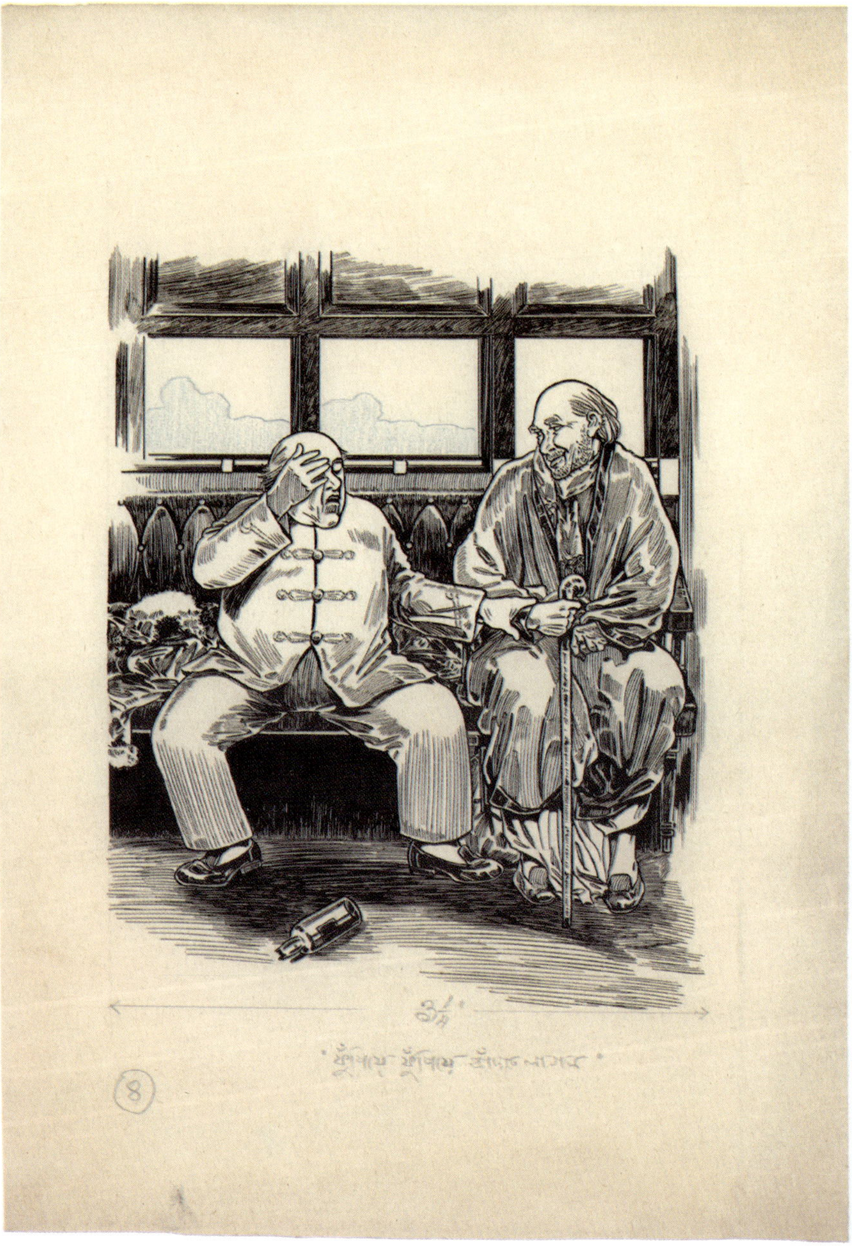

Illustration for *Swayambaraa* (*Kajjali*, 1928)

Bangla text: “Broke out into sobs”.
Characters: Christopher Columbus Blotto and Kedar Chatterjee.

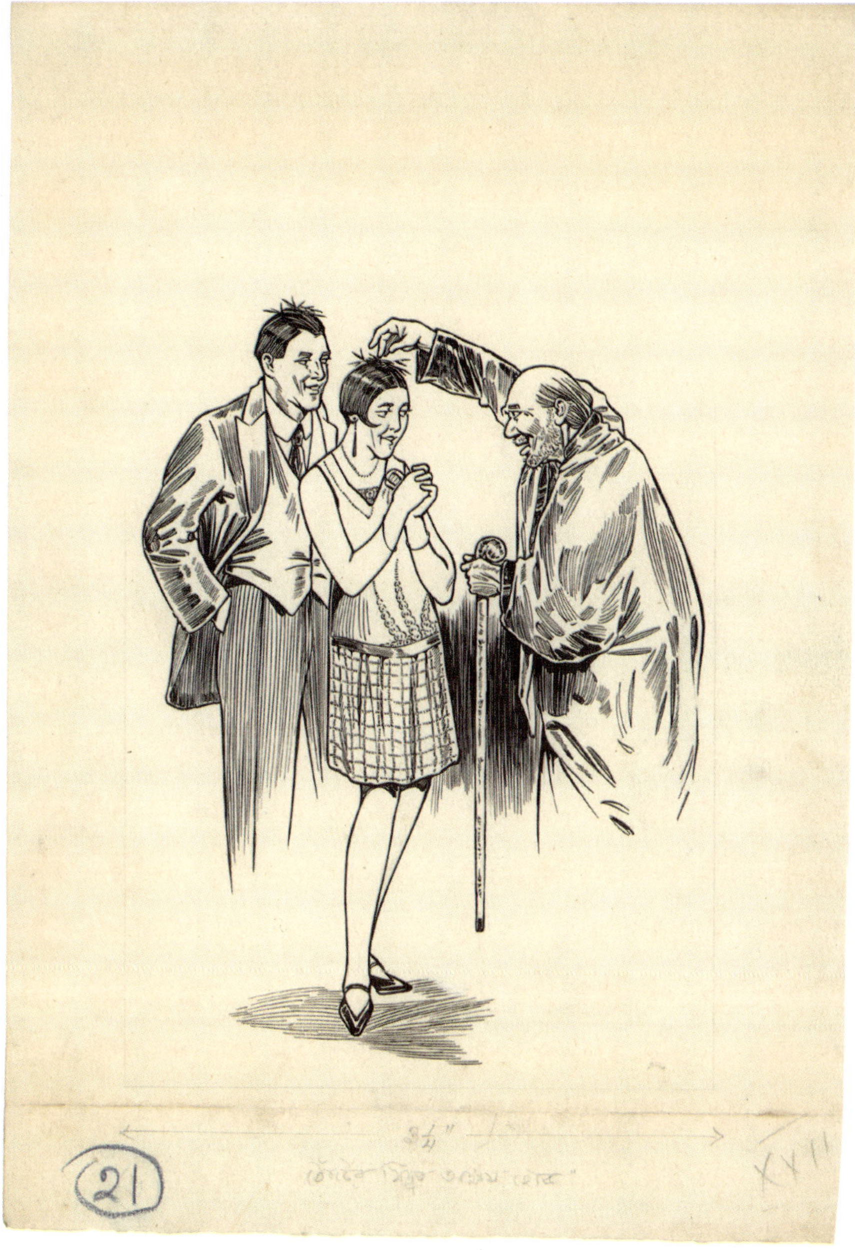

Illustration for *Swayambaraa* (*Kajjali*, 1928).

Bangla text: "May the *shindur* (marriage vermilion) on your lips never fade". Characters: Timothy Toper and Joan Jilter.

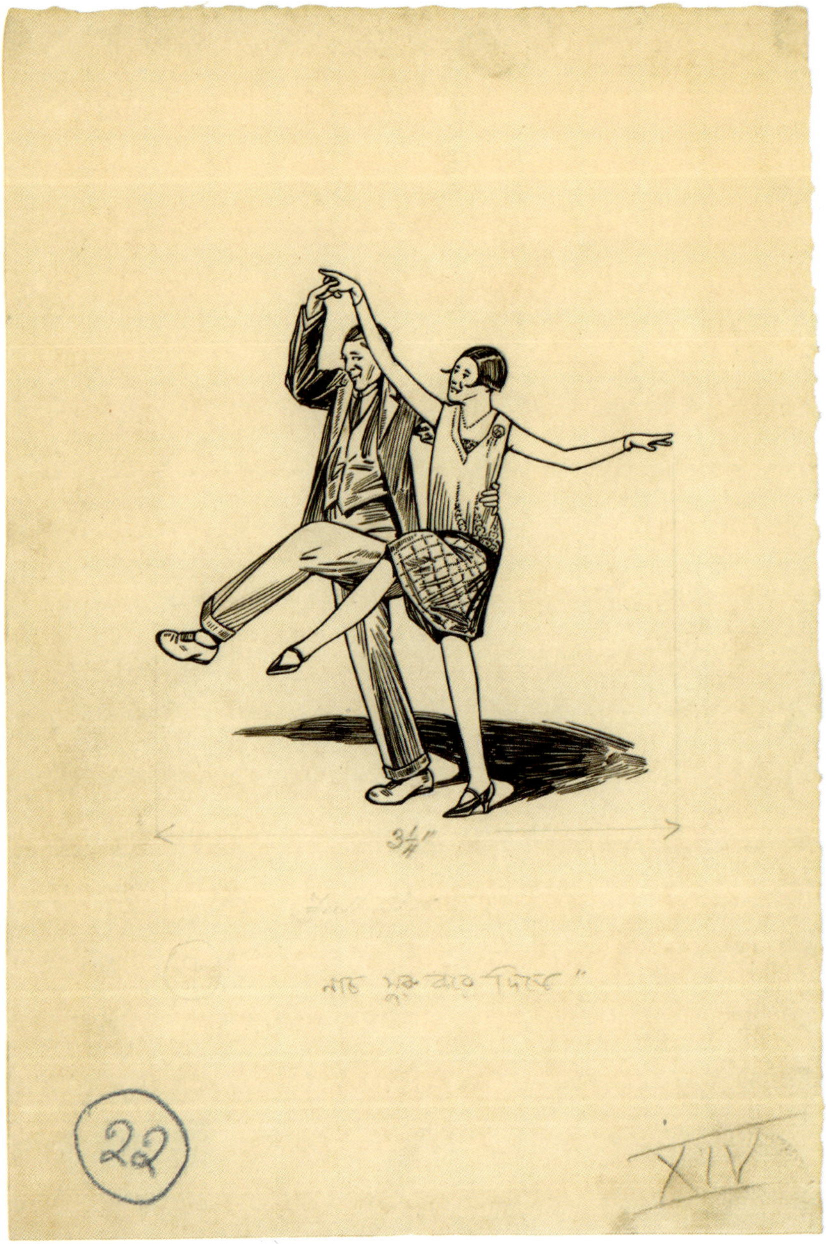

Illustration for *Swayambaraa* (*Kajjali*, 1928).

Bangla text: "They began to dance".
Characters: Timothy Toper and Joan Jilter.

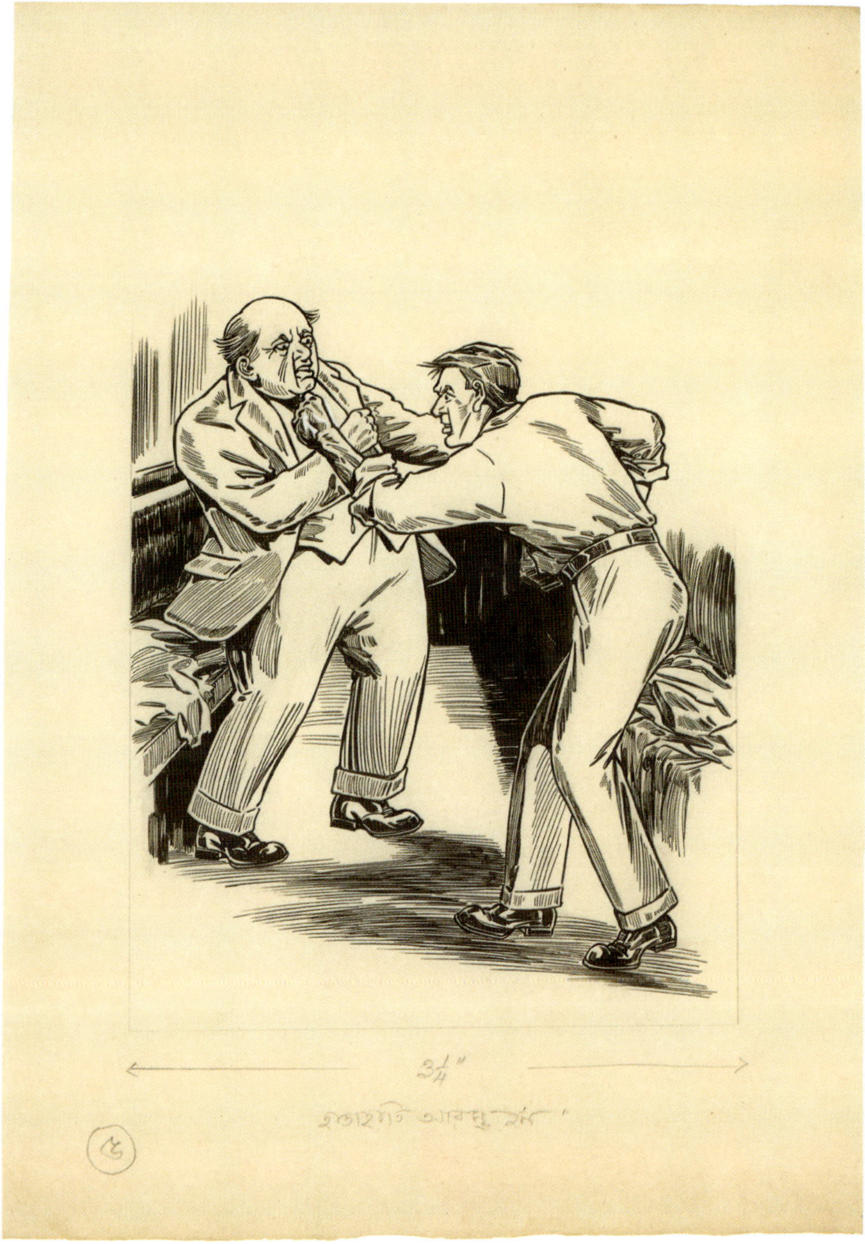

Illustration for *Swayambaraa* (*Kajjali*, 1928)

Bangla text: "They came to blows".
Characters: Christopher Columbus Blotto and Timothy Toper.

KOCHI-SANSAD

The story is set in Darjeeling and narrated by advocate Brajen who is here on holiday. Kochi-Sansad (the Club of Tender Spirits) has been formed by the rich and slightly eccentric young man Keshto. The club members, long-haired and soft-hearted young men called Pelab (soft) Ray, Shiharan (shivering) Sen, and Bigalito (melting) Bannerjee, moan about love and pain. Keshto, however, shocks them by changing his appearance radically and embracing a new philosophy. He will only go through a period of 'high-courtship' with a woman he feels no love for at all so they can rationally discuss their compatibility. Brajen moderates such a discussion between Keshto and the lovely Padma. However, Keshto actually falls in love...

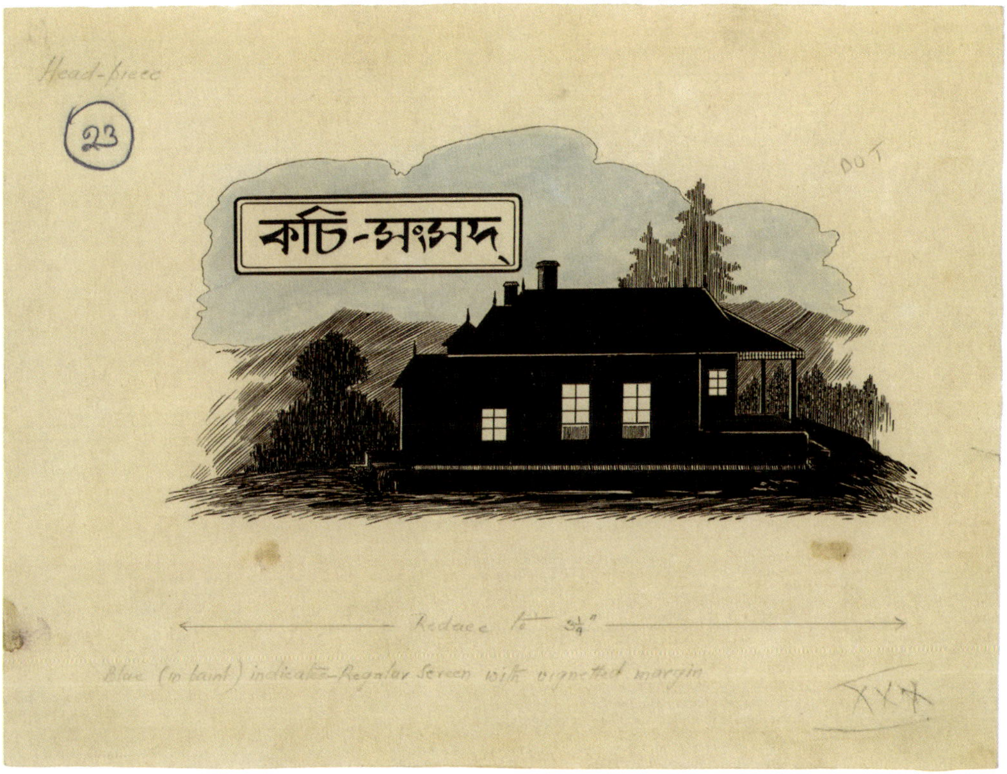

Illustration and title design for the opening page of *Kochi-Sansad* (published in the collection *Kajjali*, 1928).

Visual: Moonshine Villa, Darjeeling.

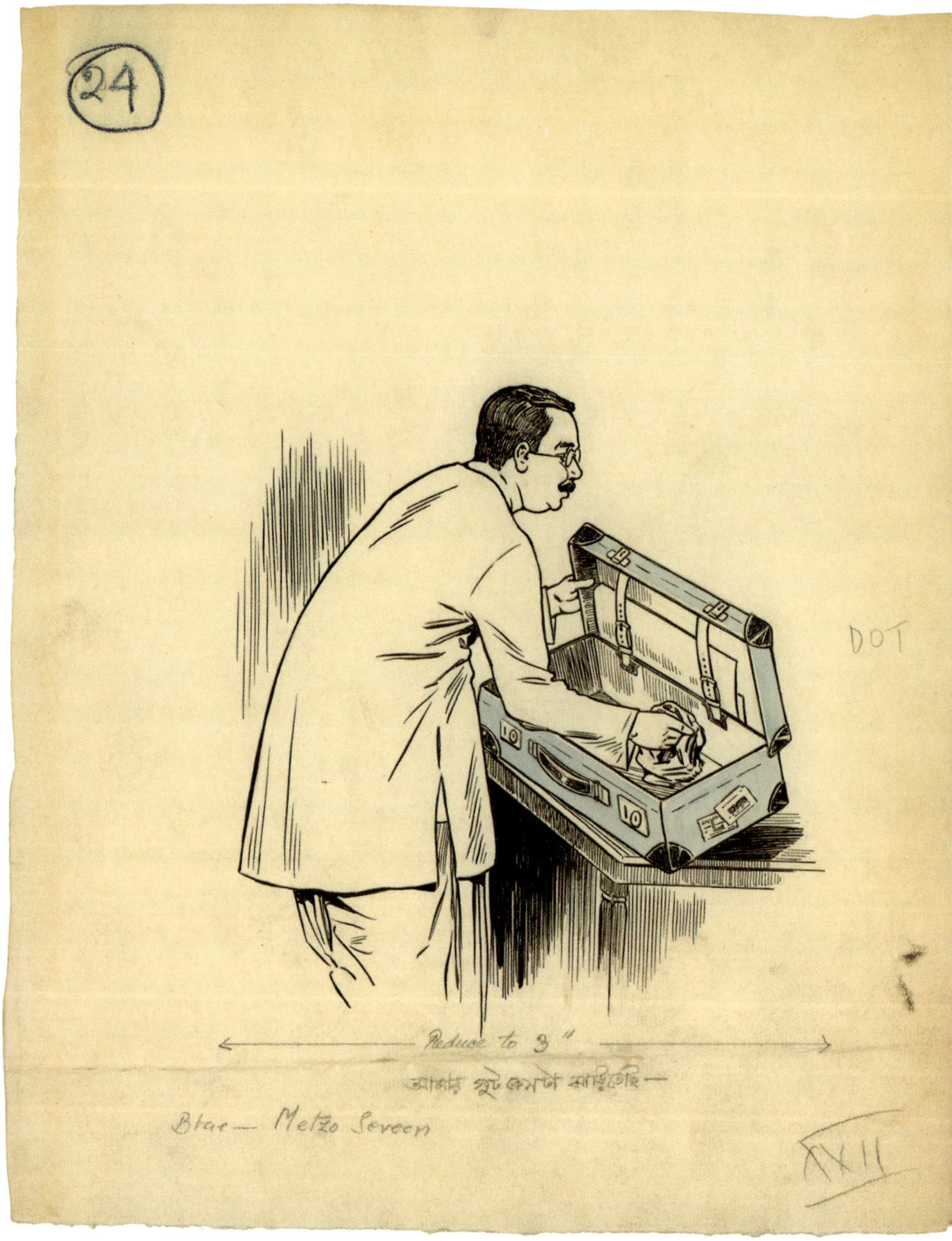

Illustration for *Kochi-Sansad* (*Kajjali*, 1928)

Bangla text: "I had just begun dusting my suitcase".
Character: Brajen, the narrator of the story.

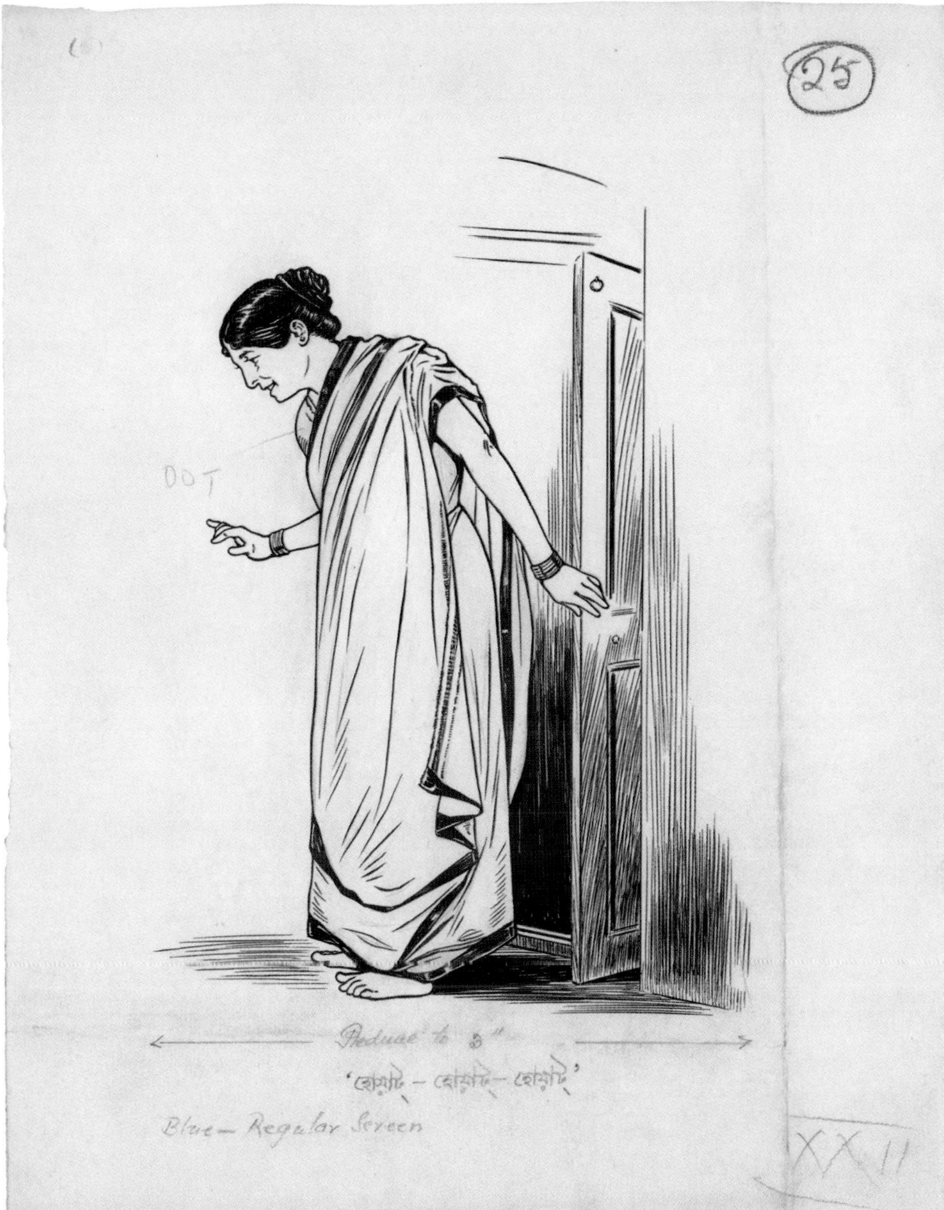

Illustration for *Kochi-Sansad* (*Kajjali*, 1928)

Bangla text: “What what what”.
Character: Brajen’s wife.

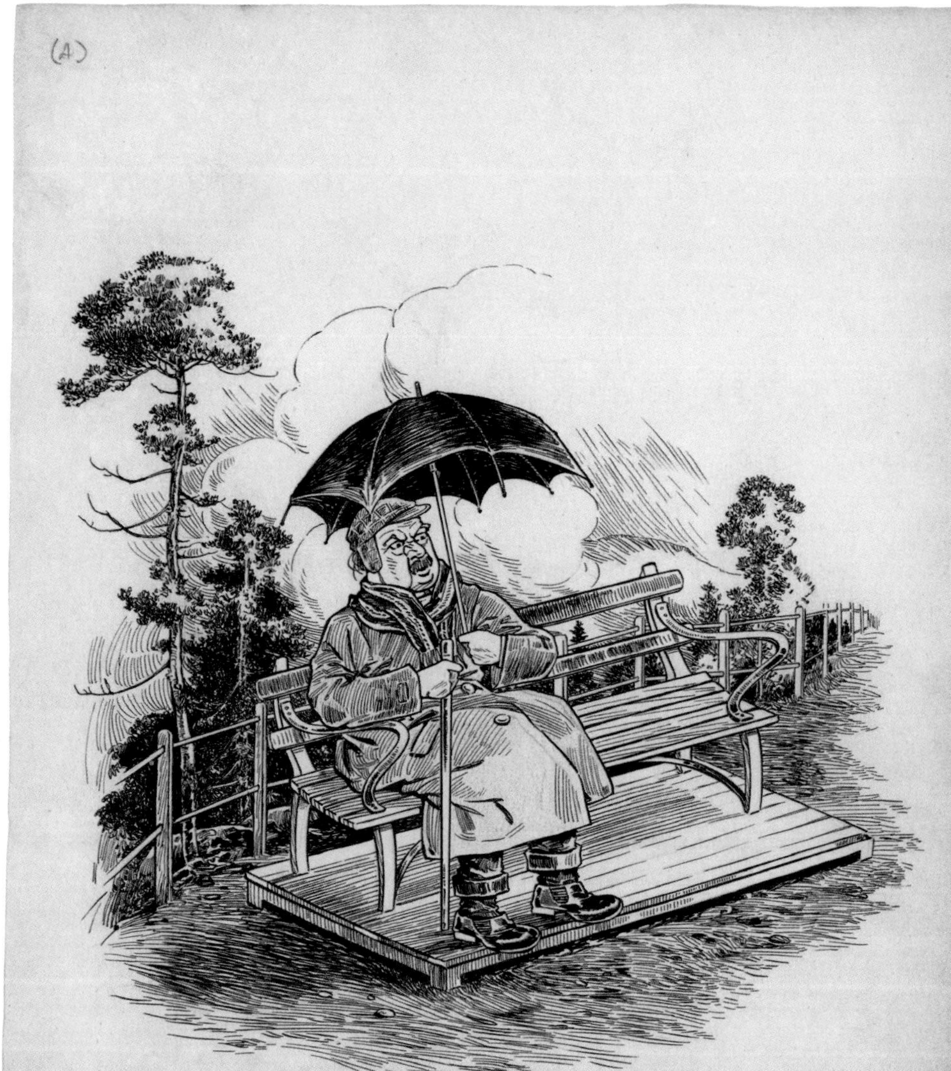

Illustration for *Kochi-Sansad* (*Kajjali*, 1928)

Bangla text: “Nakur-mama”.
Character: Nakur-mama (Uncle Nakur – Nakur Choudhury).

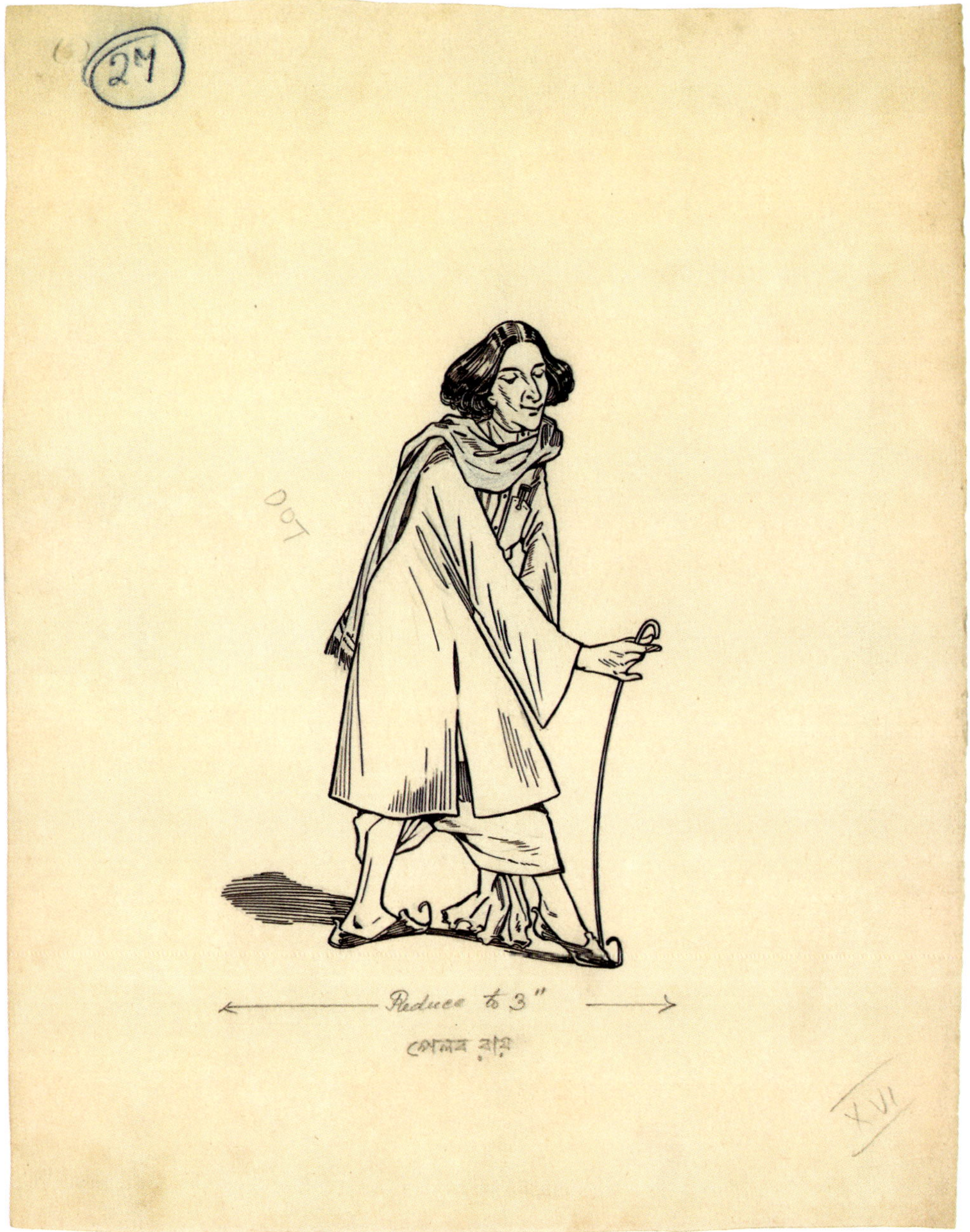

Illustration for *Kochi-Sansad* (*Kajjali*, 1928)

Bangla text: “Pelab Ray”.
Character: Pelab Ray.

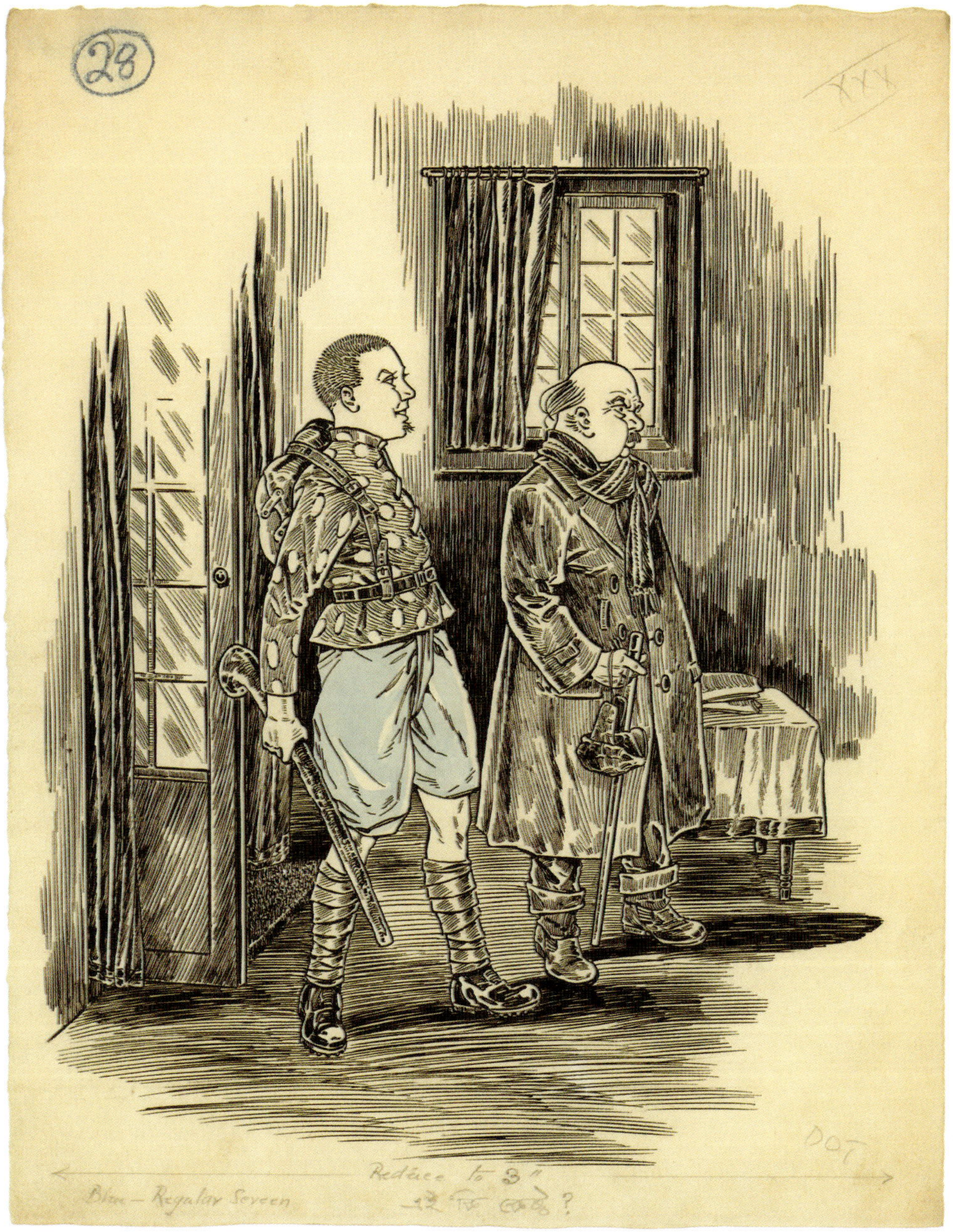

Illustration for *Kochi-Sansad* (*Kajjali*, 1928)

Bangla text: "Could it be Keshto?"
Characters: Nakur mama and Keshto.

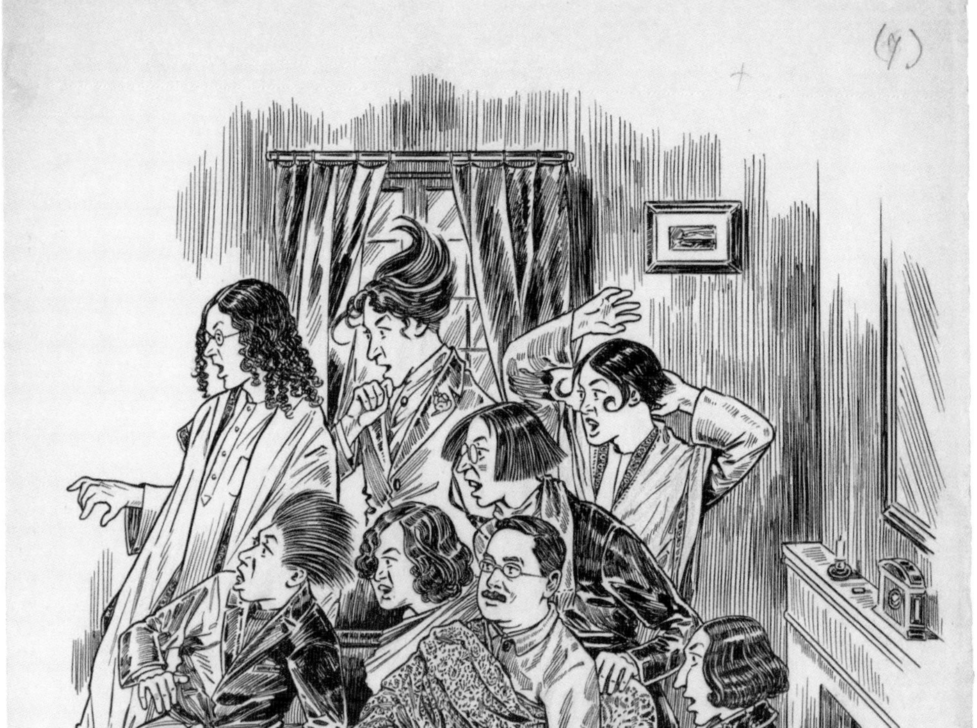

Illustration for *Kochi-Sansad* (*Kajjali*, 1928)

Bangla text: "All members of the Kochi Sansad gazed at him in wonder".

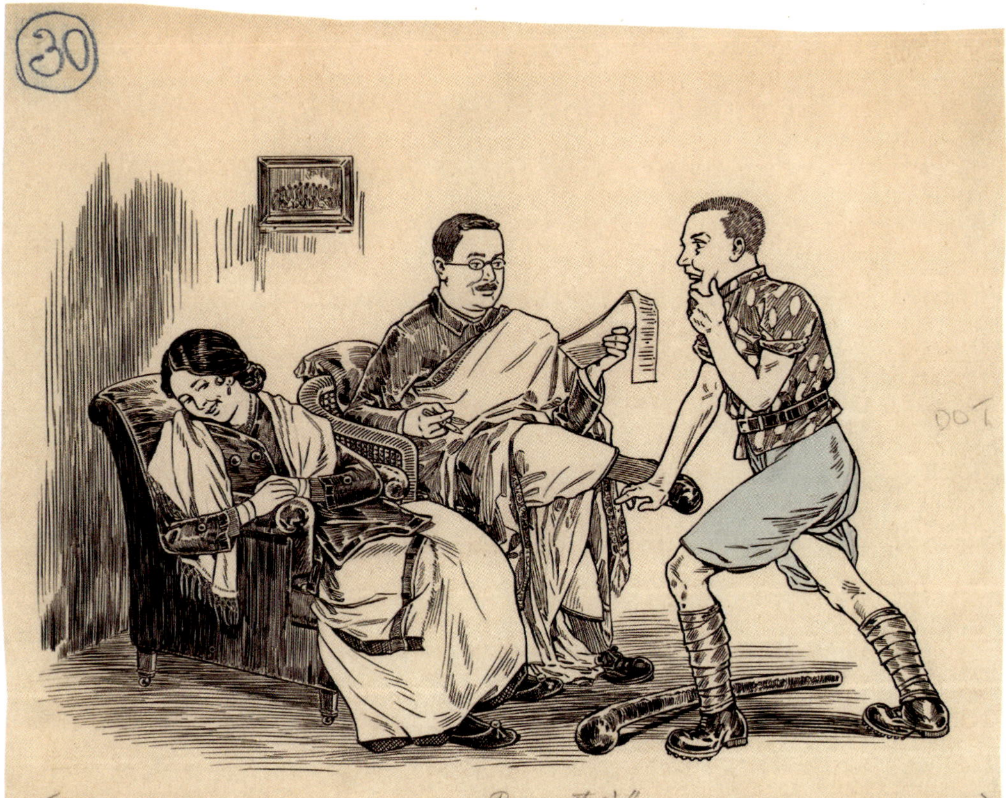

Illustration for *Kochi-Sansad* (*Kajjali*, 1928)

Bangla text: "Just take another look".
Characters: (From left) Padma, Brajen and Keshto.

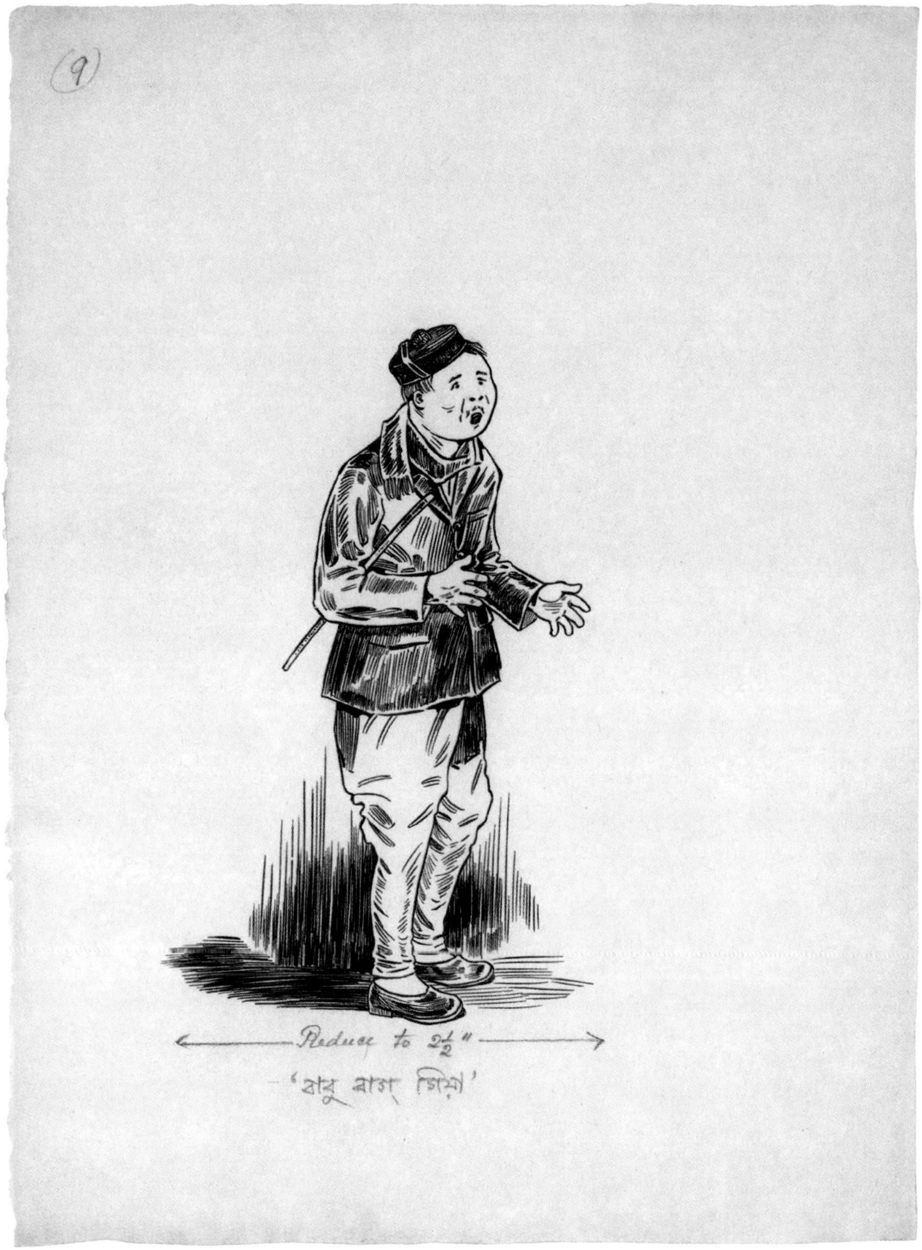

Illustration for *Kochi-Sansad* (*Kajjali*, 1928)

Bangla text: "The babu has run away".
Character: Boda.

(10)

Tail-piece

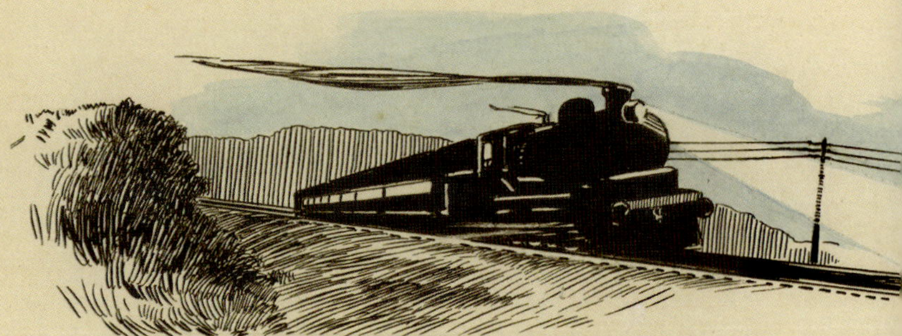

← Reduce to 3 " —

Blue (in paint) indicates—Regular Screen with o

Closing illustration of a train for *Kochi-Sansad*.

ULAT PURAAN

Ulat Puraan, or The Scripture Read Backwards, imagines an alternative history in which Britain and Europe falls under Indian colonial rule. In this fantasy, the British now go through the kind of cultural and political domination that Indians had been actually made to go through. Names like Mediterranean and Switzerland are rendered easy for the Indian tongue and become Metipukur and Chhachhurabad. An Indian governess teaches English children the proper Bengali accents and makes the family sit in the bathtub to practice the civilised way of eating mangoes. And when British women go on a militant protest march against male oppression, Oriya sergeants cheer them on since the Indian authorities want to prove that the colonized British are not fit for self-governance!

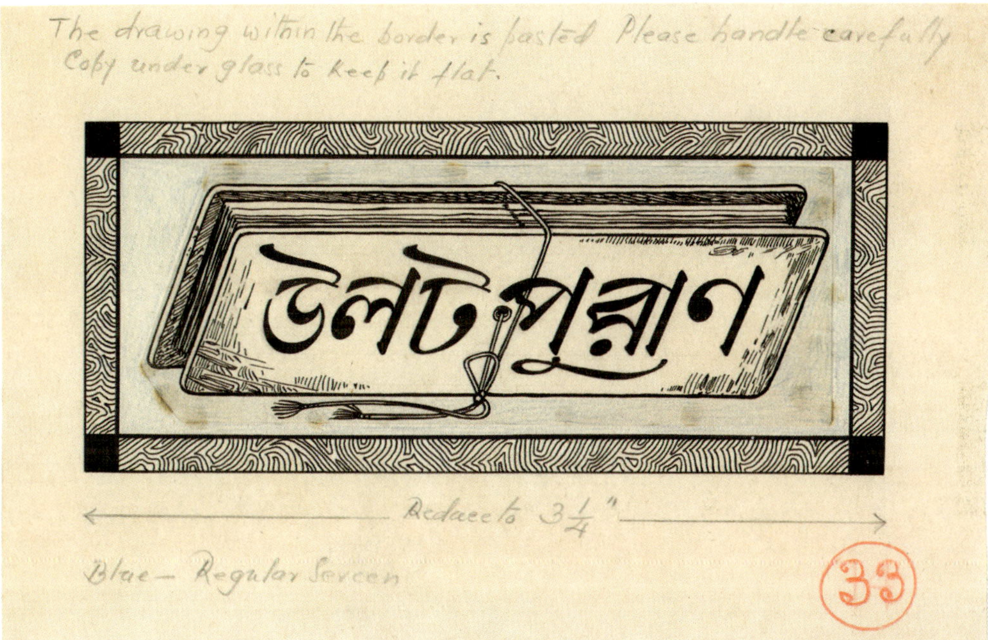

Illustration and title design for *Ulat Puraan* (published in the collection *Kajjali*, 1928).

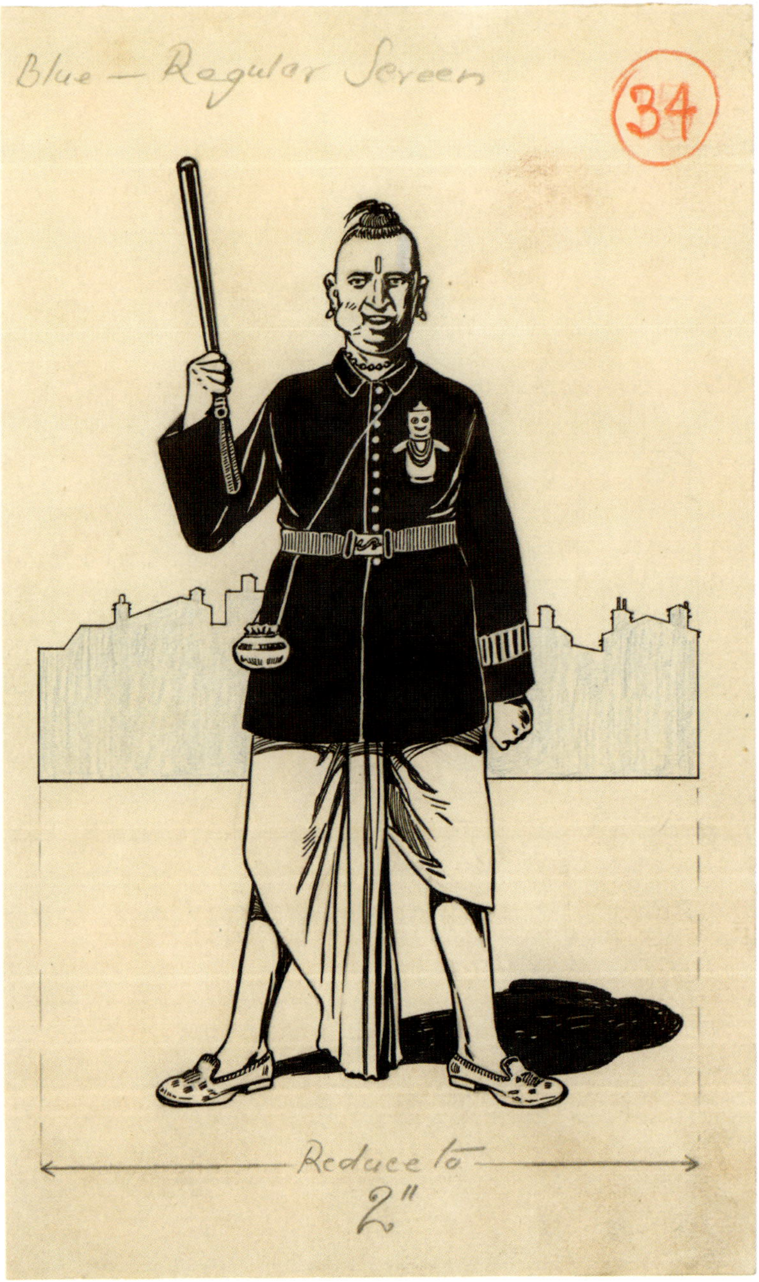

Illustration at the end of *Ulat Puraan* (*Kajjali*, 1928)

Character: Oriya sergeant.

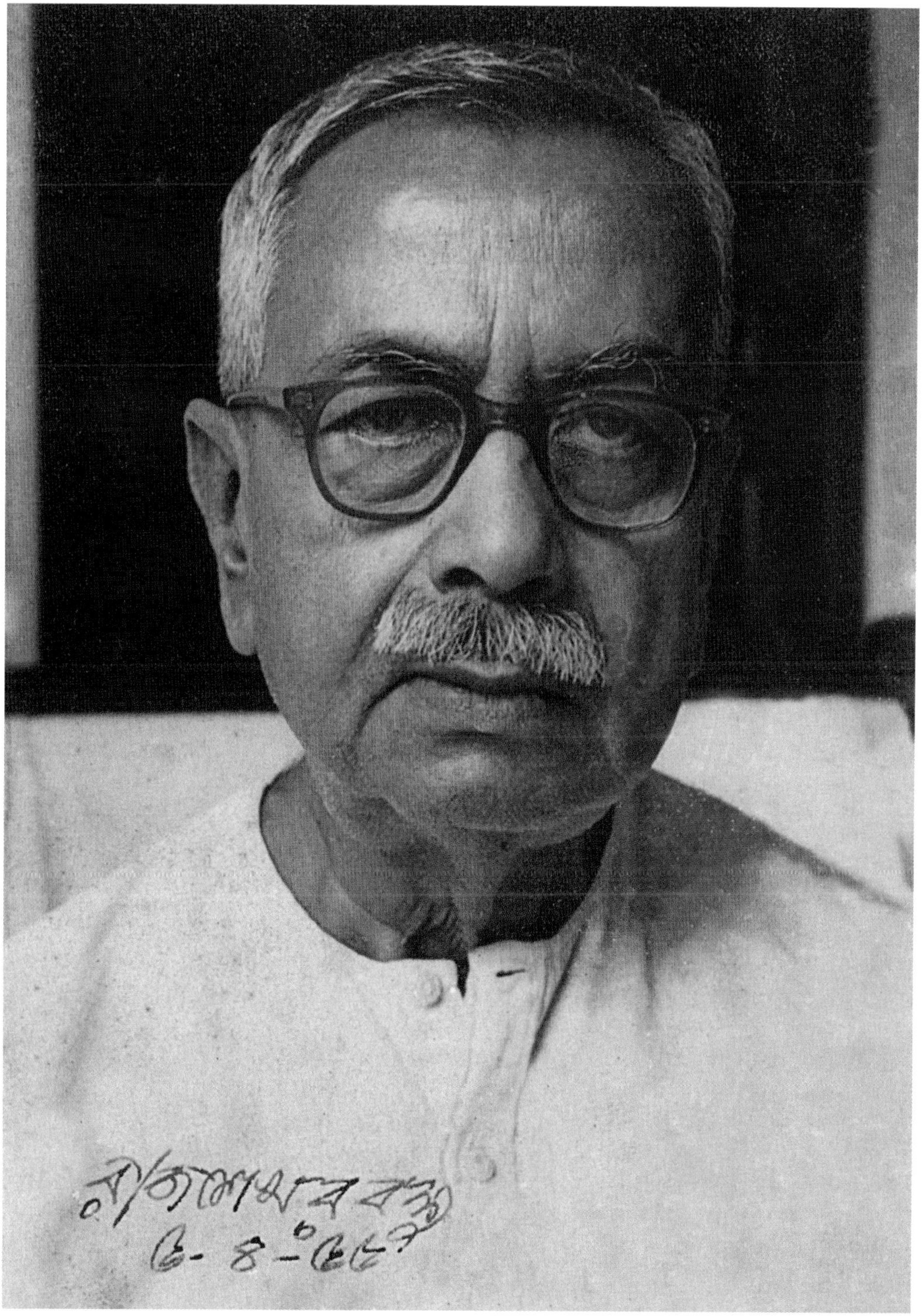

Rajshekhar Basu

STORIES FROM
HANUMANER SWAPNO ITYADI GALPO

COVER ILLUSTRATION FOR
HANUMANER SWAPNO ITYADI GALPO
(HANUMAN'S DREAM AND OTHER STORIES), 1937

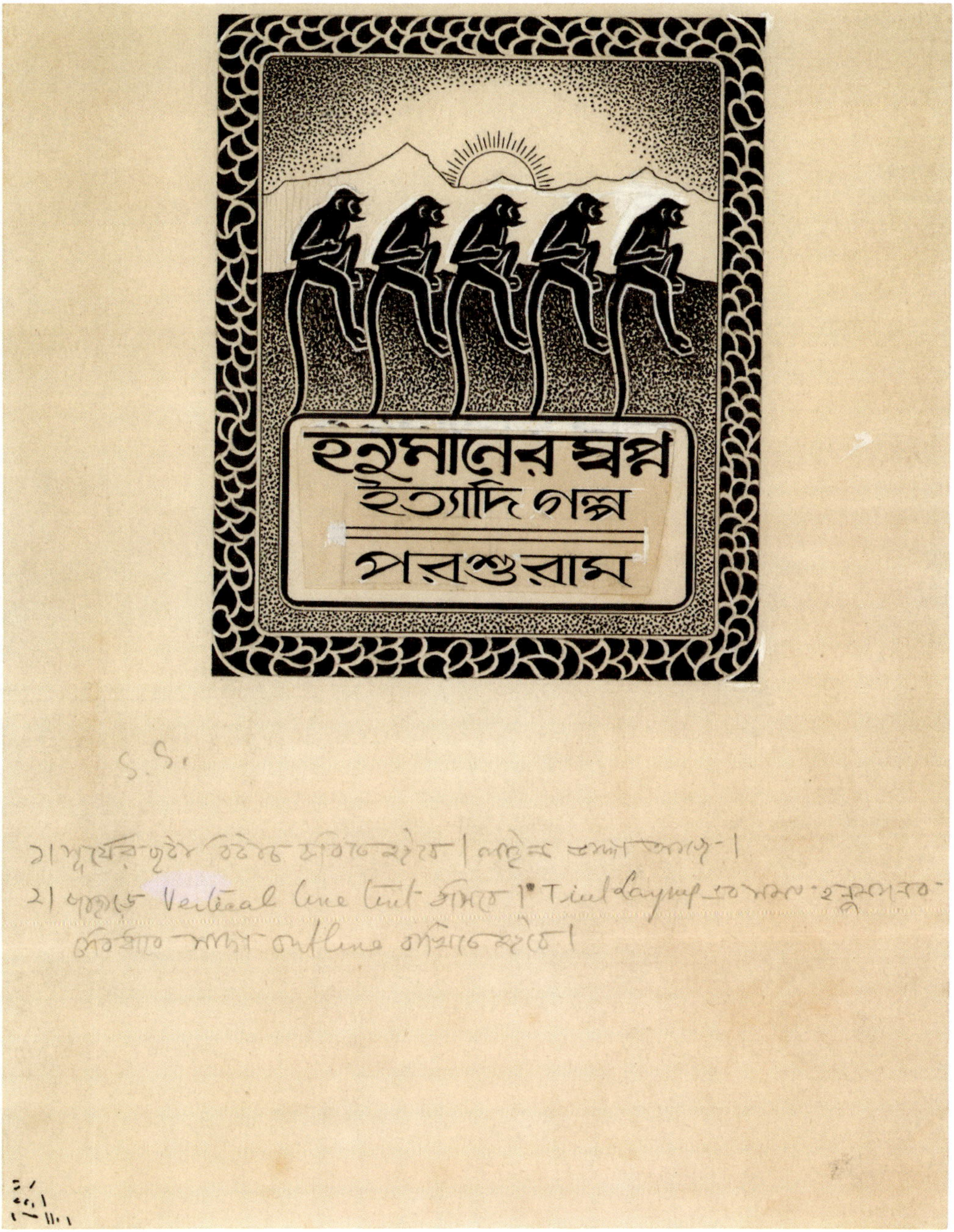

Bangla text: Parashuram's instructions to "detach" the sun rays, give vertical lines on the hills, and keep a white line around the Hanuman figures.

HANUMANER SWAPNO

When Lord Ram returns to rule Ayodhya, he gets a beautiful banana garden and a wooden home made for Hanuman. But Hanuman seems morose. Eventually, he confides in Sita that he dreamt of his ancestors sitting with sad faces, moving their hands over their bellies. He feels that his ancestors are hungry and worried about who will offer them *pinda* (the ritual offerings to a departed soul by their descendants) after Hanuman's death, since he has no children. Following Sita's advice, he goes to Kishkindha looking for his bride. After an eventful journey, he meets the simian princess Chilimpa and wishes to marry her. But he realises his mistake. His heart is occupied by Sita and Ram and there is no place for a wife and children. Hanuman returns to Ayodhya and asks Sita for a boon of immortality, so that he can offer *pinda* to his ancestors forever.

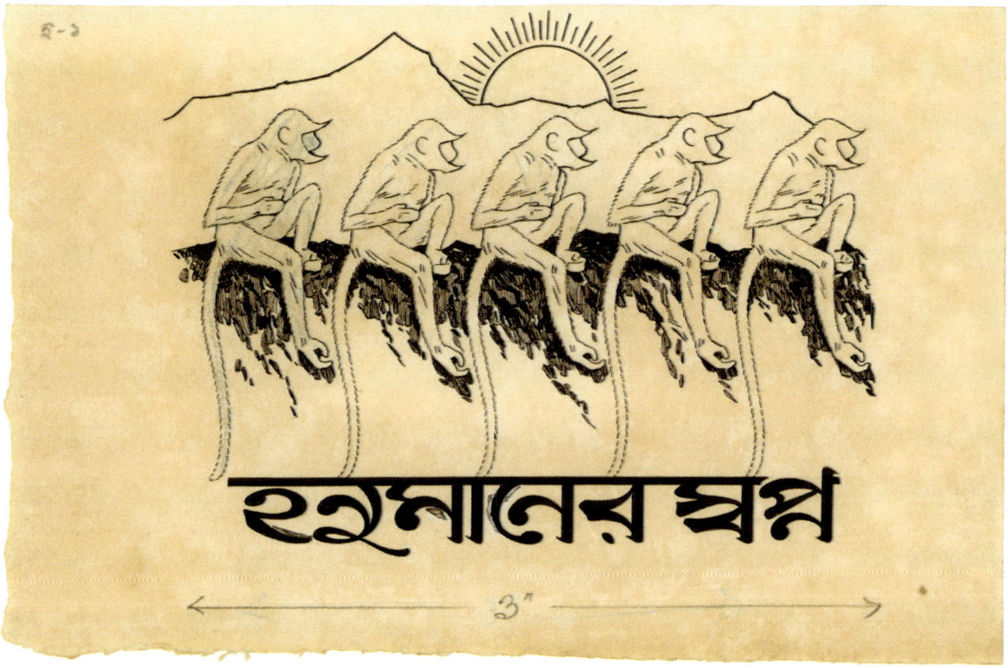

Illustration and title design for *Hanumaner Swapno* (published in the collection *Hanumaner Swapno Ityadi Galpo*, 1937)

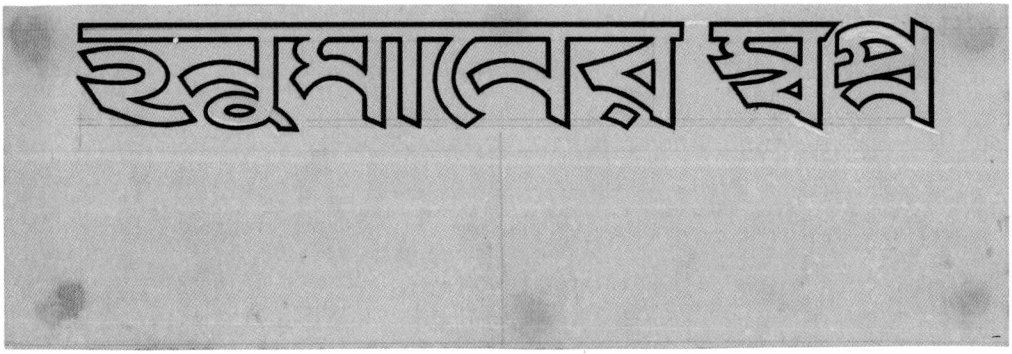

Draft sketches for the title of *Hanumaner Swapno* (*Hanumaner Swapno Ityadi Galpo*, 1937)

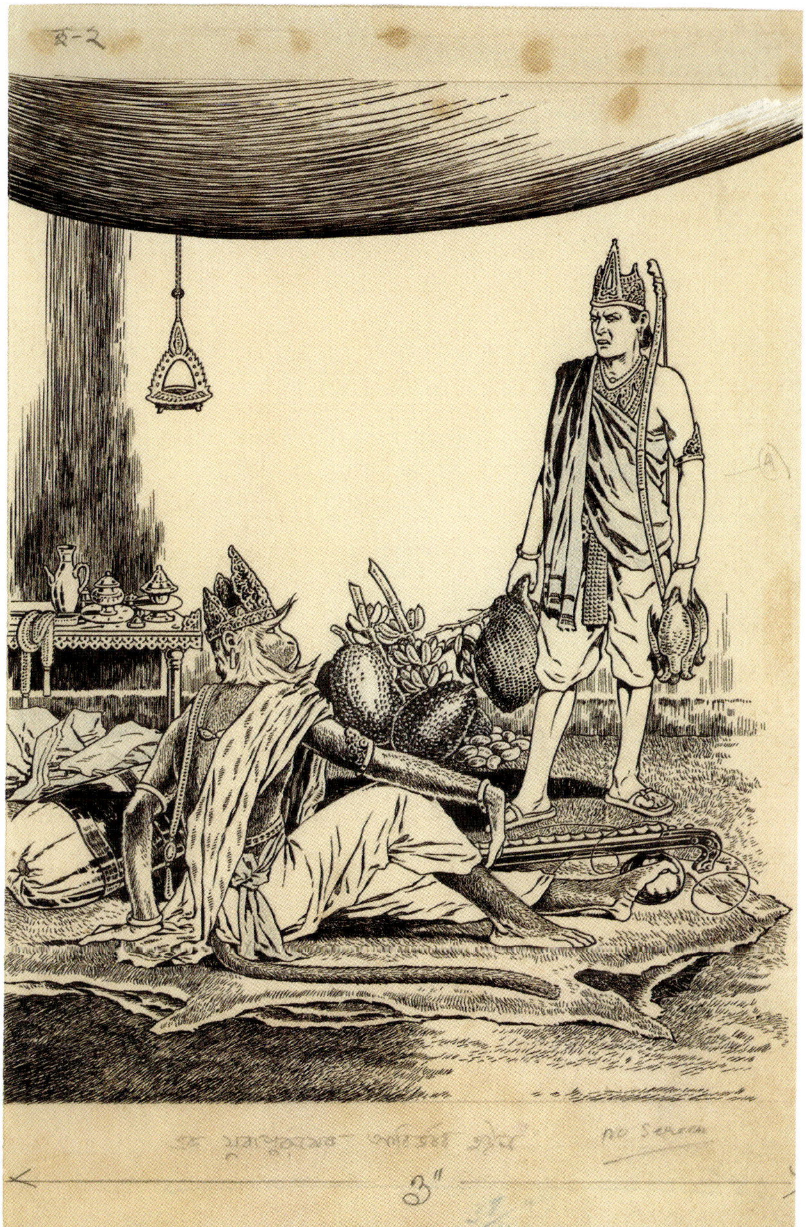

Illustration for *Hanumaner Swapno* (*Hanumaner Swapno Ityadi Galpo*, 1937)

Bangla text: "A young man appeared".
Characters: Hanuman and King Chancharik.

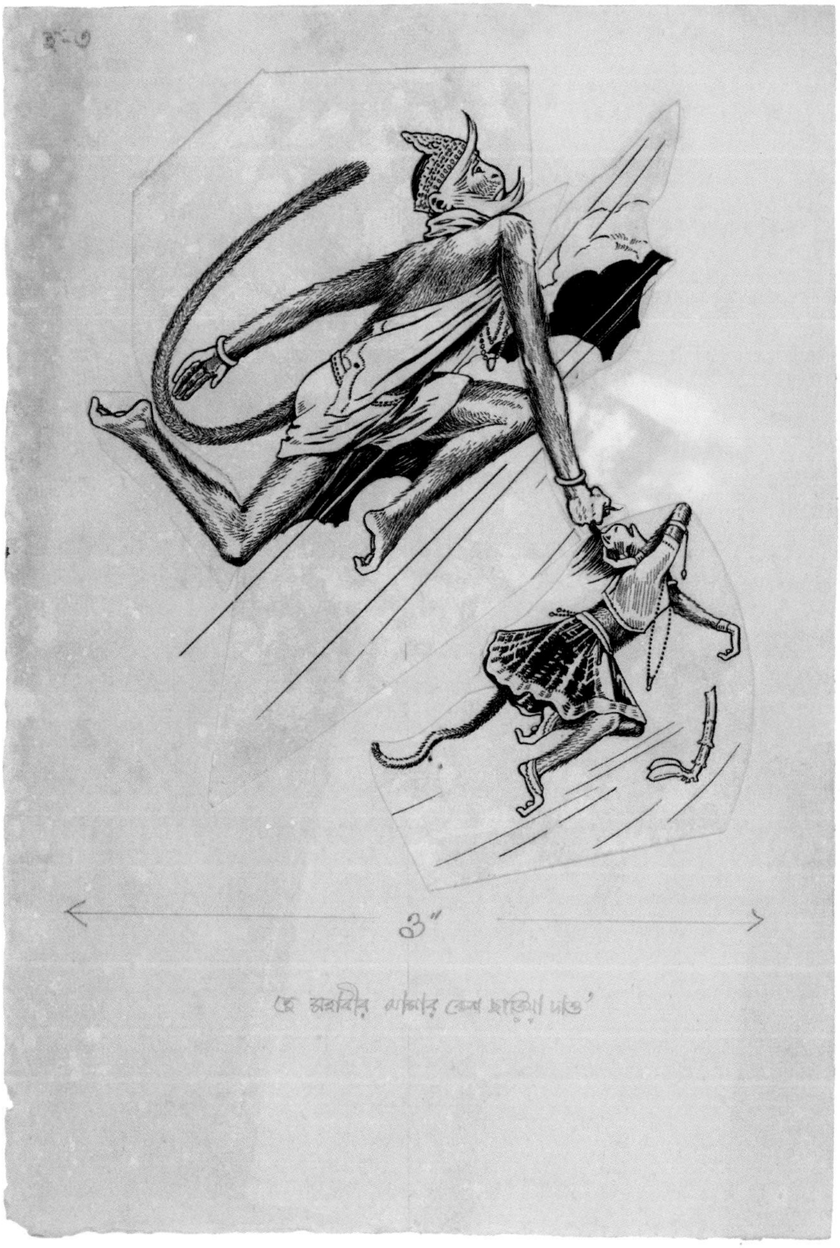

Illustration for *Hanumaner Swapno* (*Hanumaner Swapno Ityadi Galpo*, 1937)

Bangla text: “O Mahavir, let go of my hair”.
Characters: Hanuman and Chilimpa.

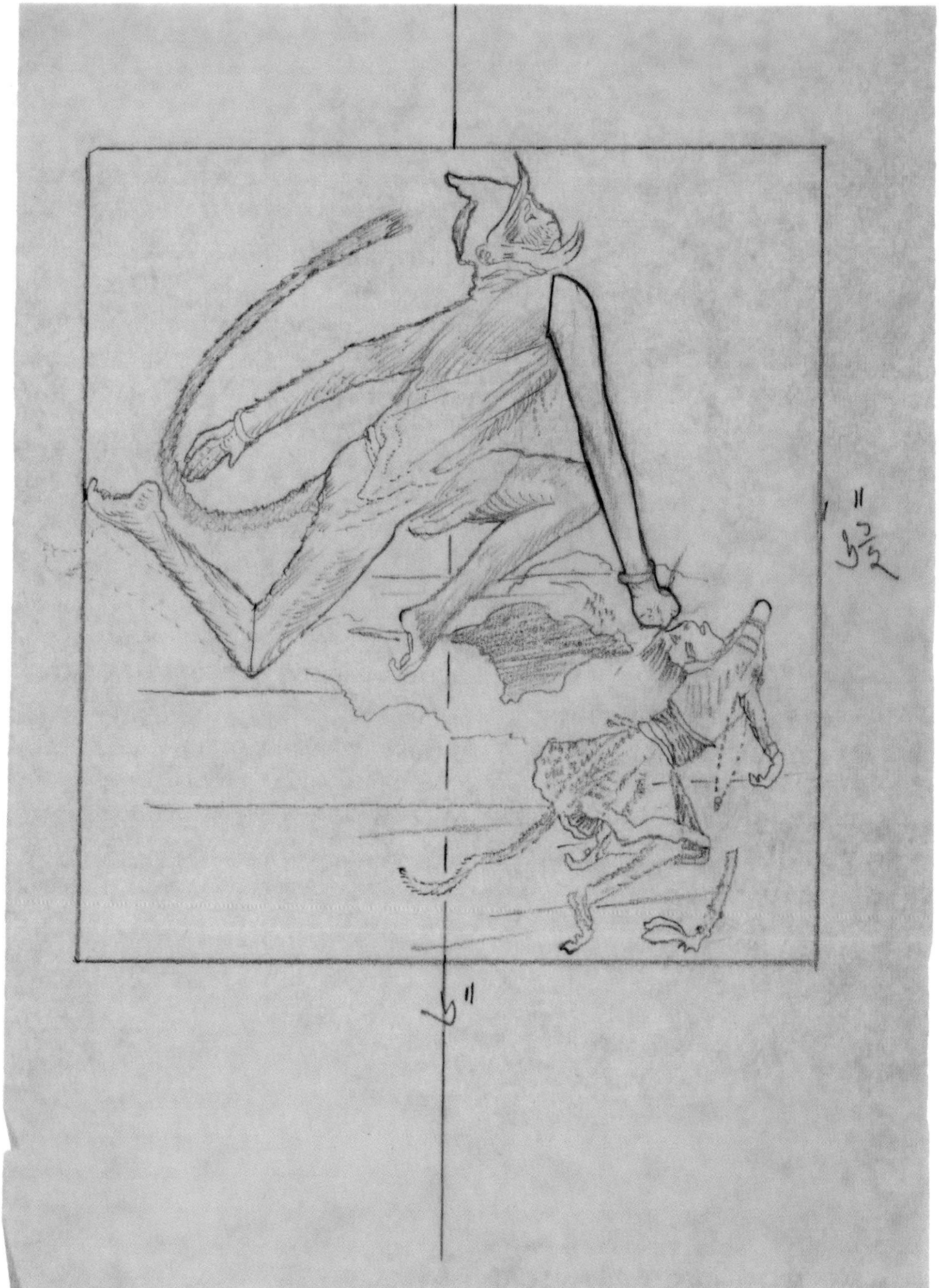

Trial sketch for *Hanumaner Swapno* (*Hanumaner Swapno Ityadi Galpo*, 1937)

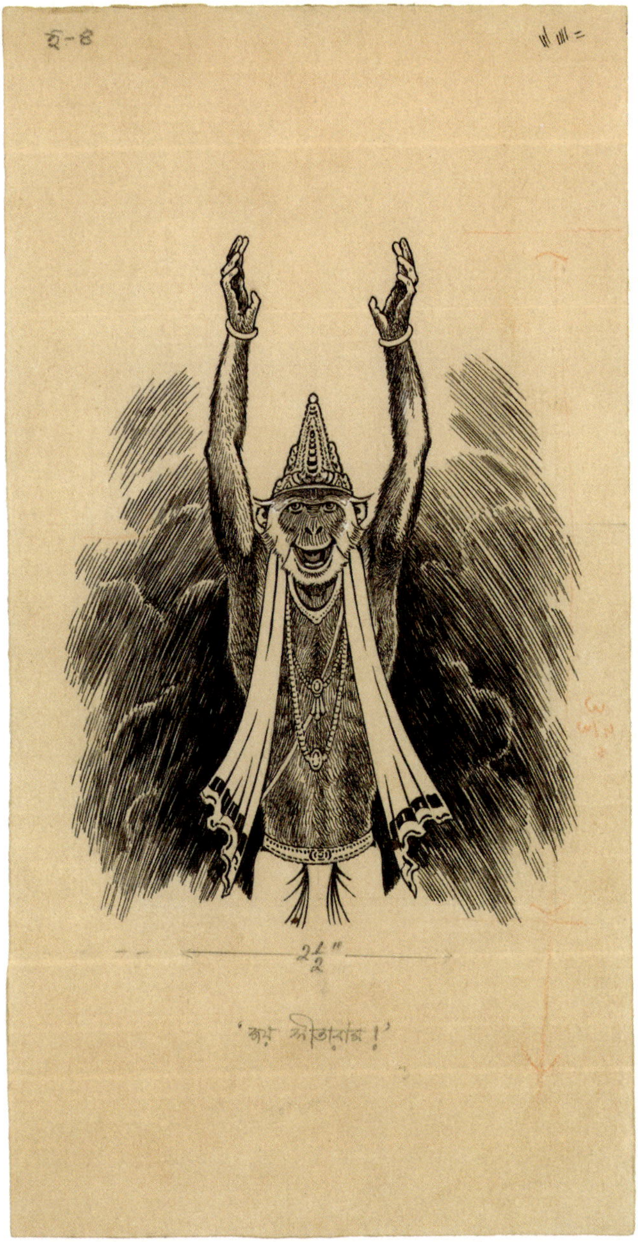

Illustration for *Hanumaner Swapno* (*Hanumaner Swapno Ityadi Galpo*, 1937)

Bangla text: "Jai Seeta-Ram".
Character: Hanuman.

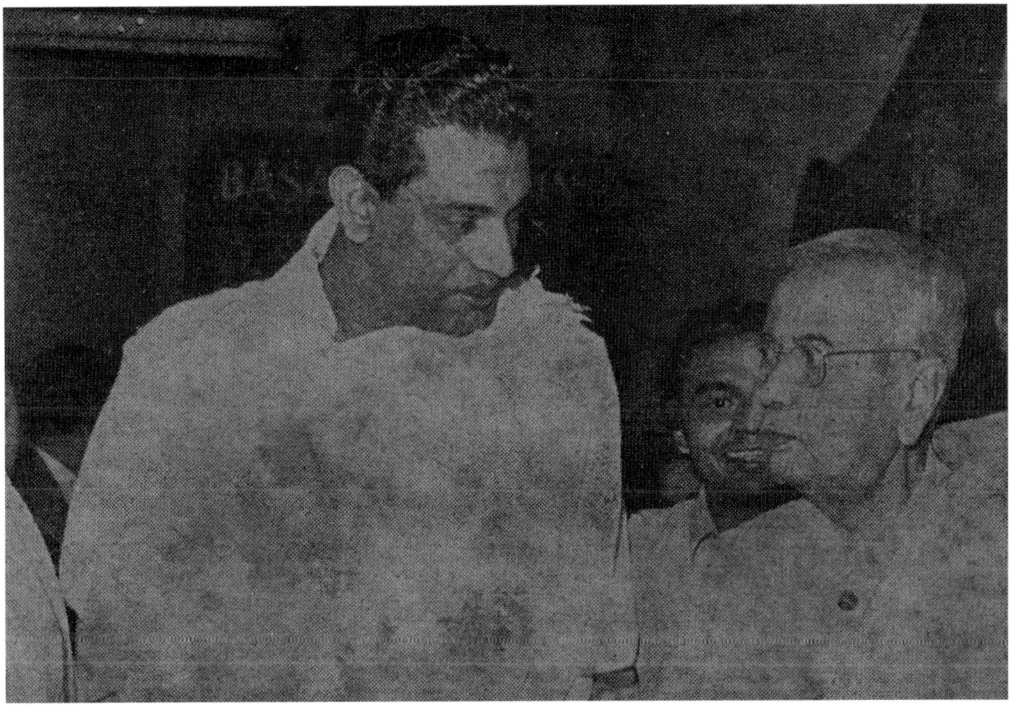

Rajshekhar Basu with Satyajit Ray

PUNARMILON

Inspired by the play *Madhyam* written by Bhasa, Parashuram tells us the story of the reunion of the Pandava Bheem and his demon wife Hidimba. Exiled in the forest with his family, Bheem loses his way while hunting and encounters a young *rakshasa*. The *rakshasa* challenges him to fight but perceiving that he is a mere boy, Bheem says he will only fight with the boy's father. The young *rakshasa* insists that Bheem should admit defeat and become food for his hungry mother. A curious Bheem goes with him and comes face-to-face with his wife. The *rakshasa* is his son Ghatotkach and the mother is his wife Hidimba.

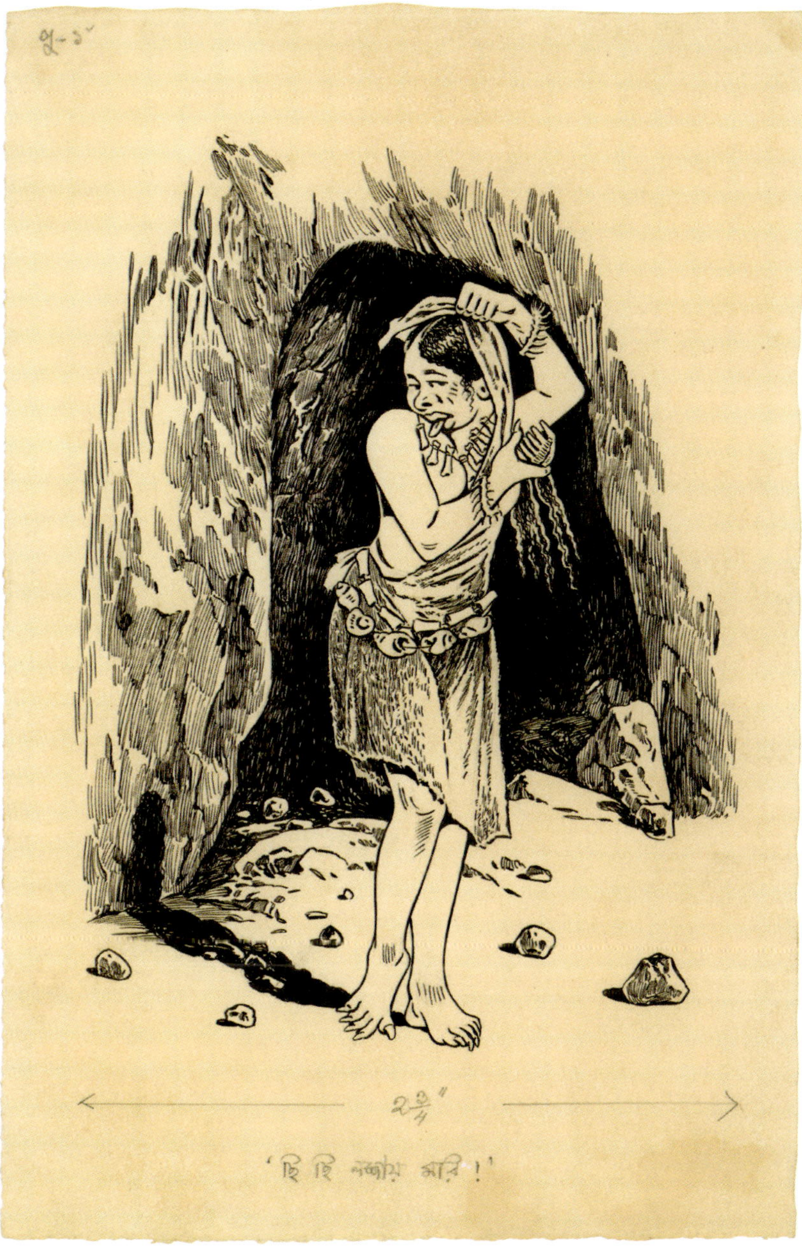

Illustration for *Punarmilon* (published in *Hanumaner Swapno Ityadi Galpo*, 1937)

Bangla text: "Chhi, chhi, I am dying of shame".
Character: Hidimba (Bheem's wife).

UPEKKHITO

Commander Kofta Khan impudently asks Shehzadi Jabarunnisa if she would marry him. The princess reminds him that he is a mere commander and she is the princess. Scorned, he takes out his sword to kill her. The sword flashes in the hand of Kofta Khan. A little shout, a little convulsion, and it's all over. After some time, the darkness of the evening thickens. Jabarunnisa is singing and her pet tiger is licking his lips with great satisfaction. To the tiger's left lies Kofta Khan's turban, to his right the tattered cloak, and in front of him lie some bones...

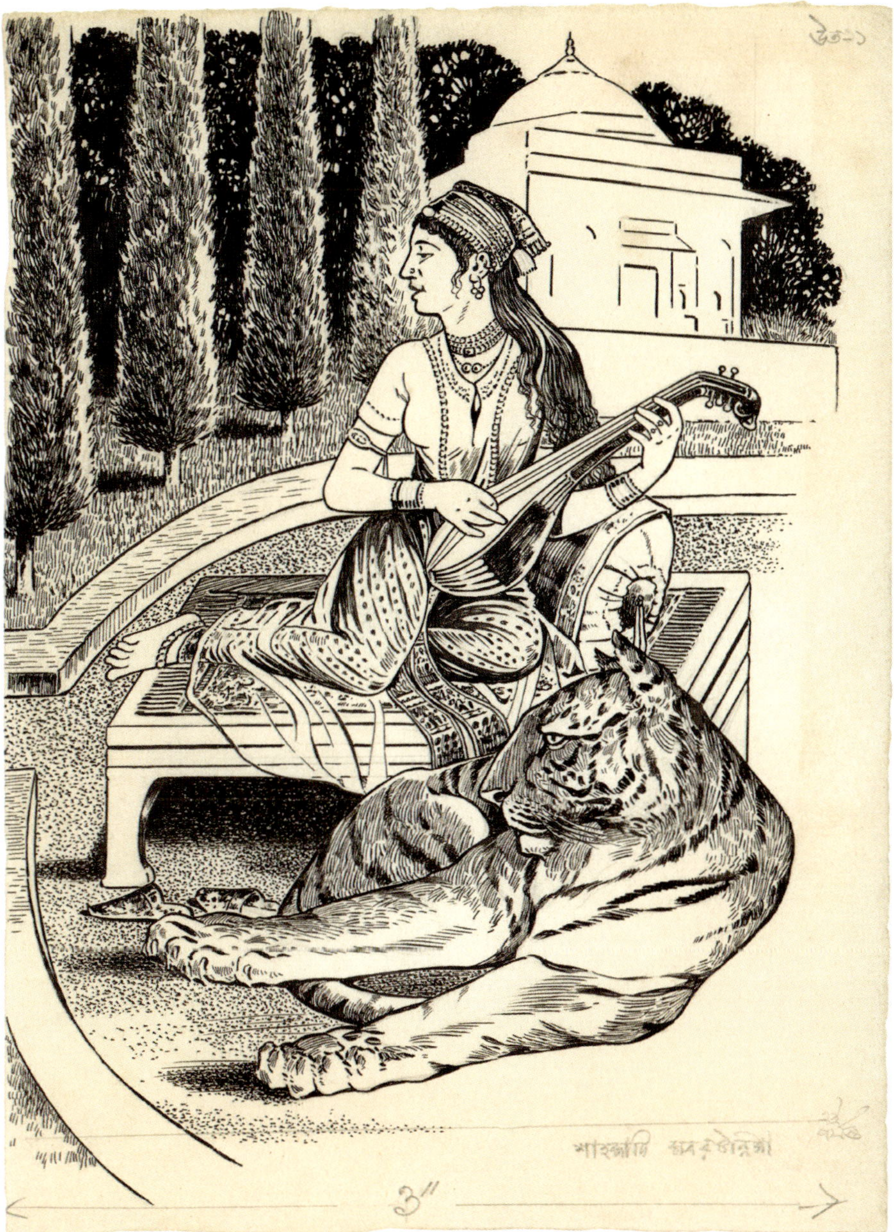

Illustration for *Upekkhito* (published in *Hanumaner Swapno Ityadi Galpo*, 1937)

Bangla text: Shehzadi Jabarunnisa.
Character: Shehzadi Jabarunnisa.

UPEKKHITA

The heroine Garima Ganguly and the hero Chatak Roy are sitting side by side on a rainy evening. Garima's parents want their daughter to marry Chatak and she is keen to win his heart. Trying to please him, she sings one song after another. But Chatak is clearly impatient to get up and go. The more she tries, the more his restlessness increases. Soon, he leaves as if unable to bear it any longer. Disconsolate, the heroine throws herself on the chair where Chatak had been sitting. The truth is revealed. "Poor Chatak! Countless bedbugs on that chair."

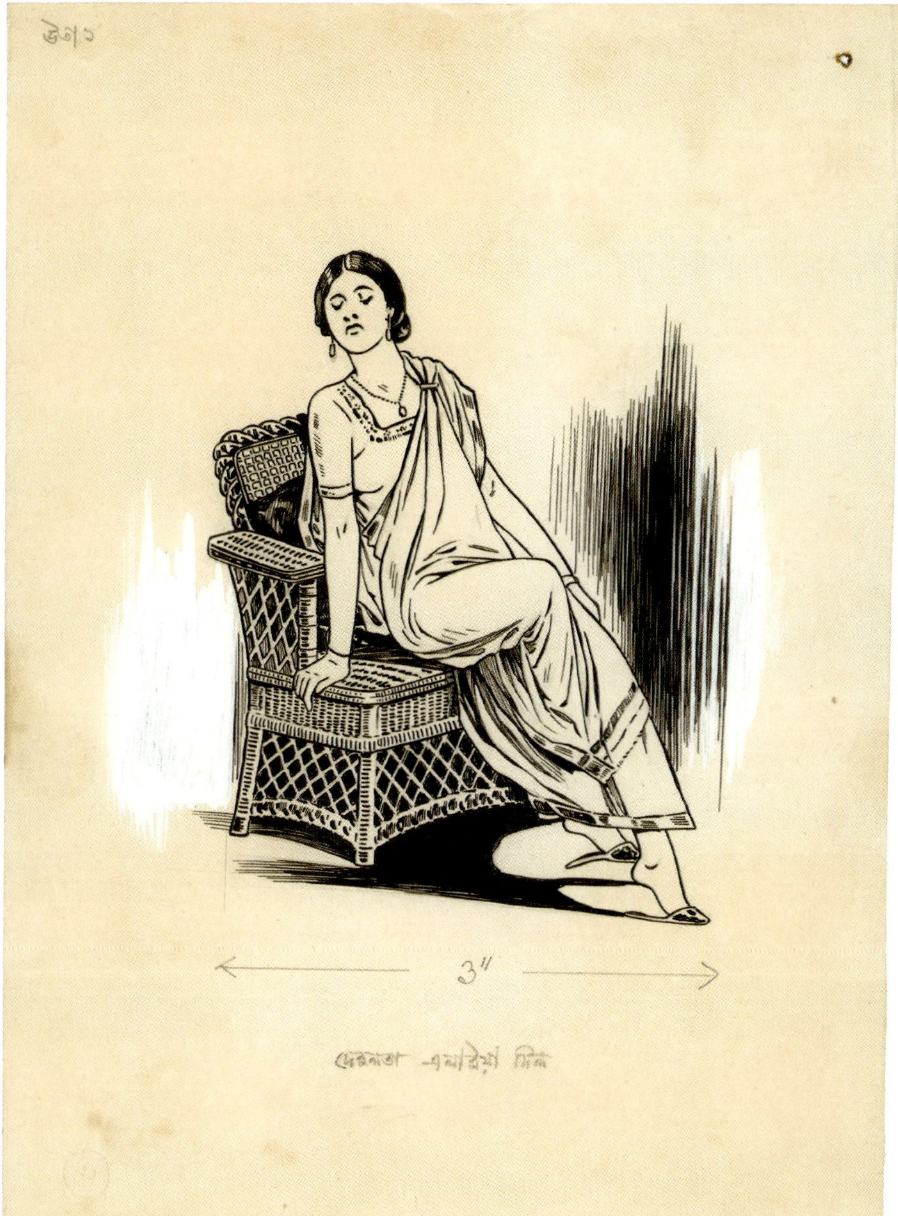

Illustration for *Upekkhita* (published in *Hanumaner Swapno Ityadi Galpo*, 1937)

Bangla text: "Her body leaned backwards".
Character: Garima.

GURUBIDAAY

Parashuram delighted in exposing the hypocrisies in society and frequently targetted religious frauds. Here, Banshalochan babu's spiritually minded wife Manini Debi wants to take a mantra initiation from a Guru. Along comes Khalwidong Swami from Ballygunge. Swamiji talks incessantly about love and mercy but when the family's pet goat Lambakarna pushes him over, he becomes vindictive. His insistence that Lambakarna be thrown out of the house makes Manini see the light. And it is the Swami who has to leave the house.

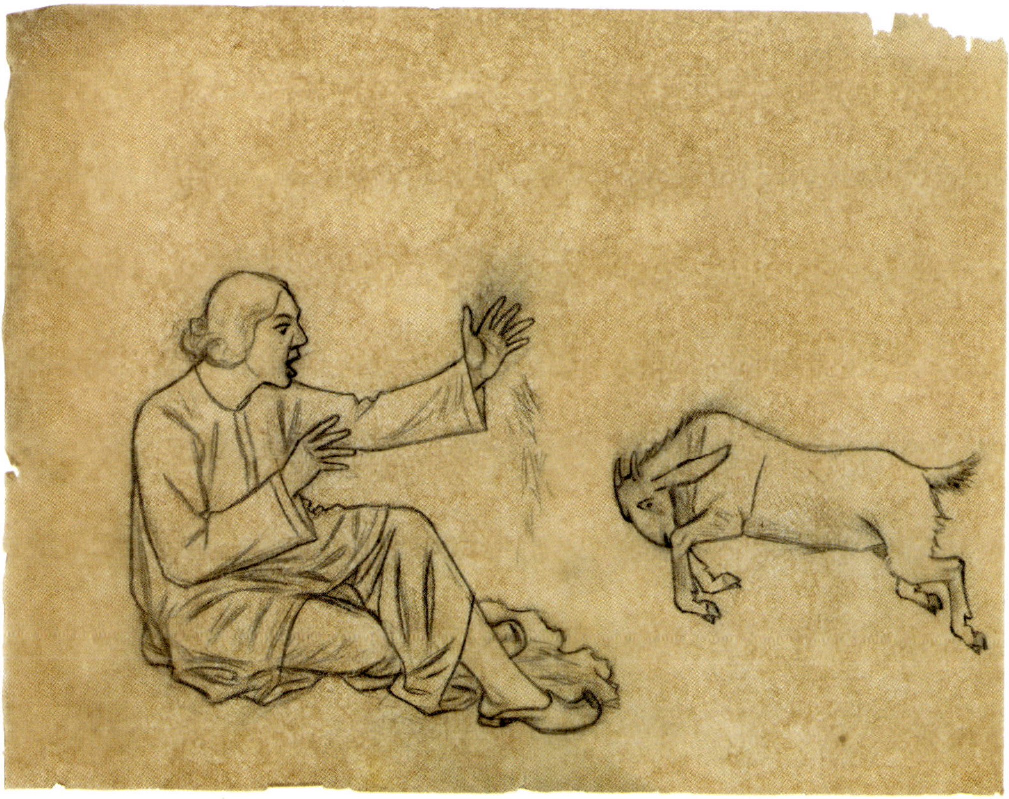

Draft sketch for *Gurubidaay* (*Hanumaner Swapno Ityadi Galpo*, 1937)

Characters: Khalwidong Swami and the goat Lambakarna.

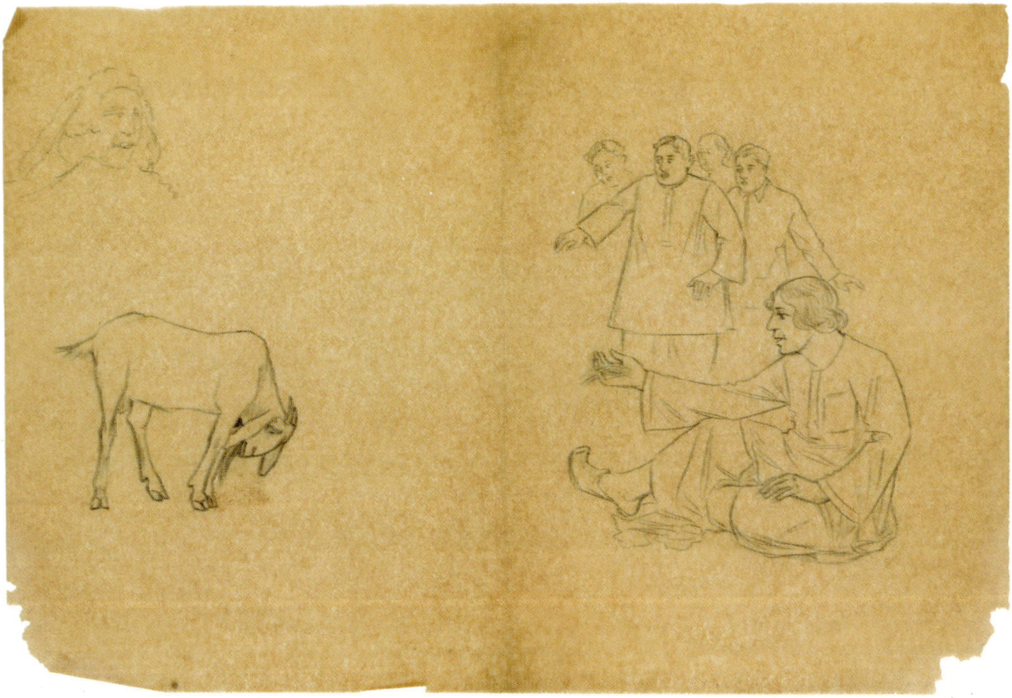

Draft sketch for *Gurubidaay* (*Hanumaner Swapno Ityadi Galpo*, 1937)

Characters: Swami Khalwidong and the goat Lambakarna with Raibahadur Banshalochan Bannerjee and others.

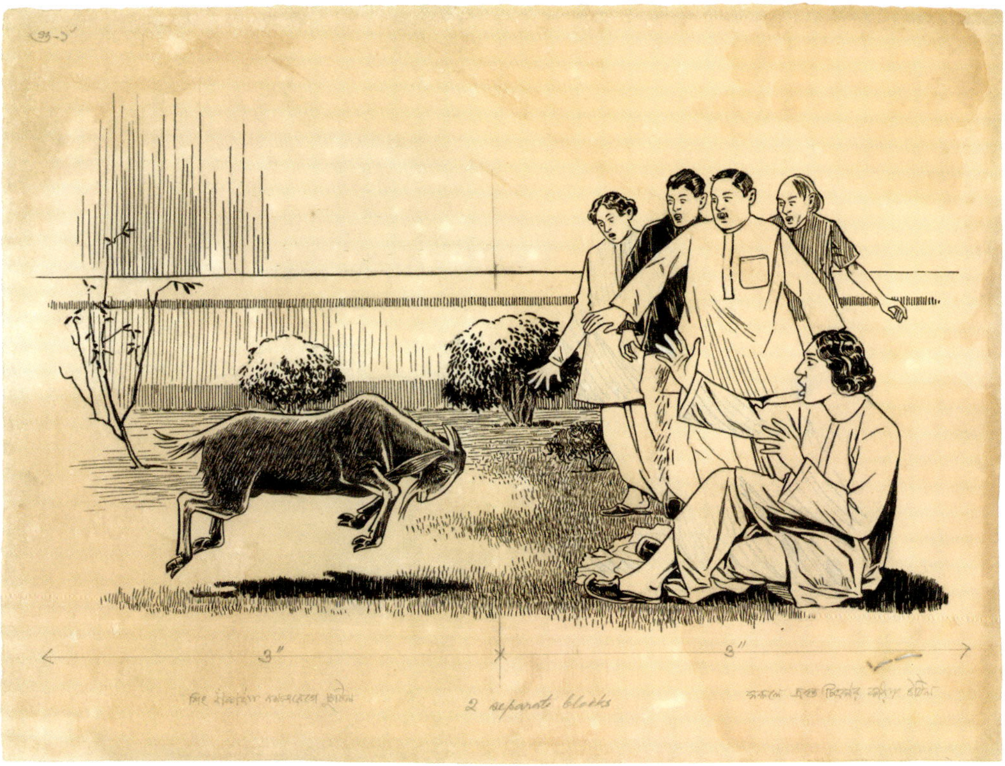

Final illustration for *Gurubidaay* (*Hanumaner Swapno Ityadi Galpo*, 1937)

Bangla text: "Horns bent forward, it ran at the speed of stars" and "All of them screamed in terror".
Characters: Swami Khalwidong and the goat Lambakarna with Raibahadur Banshalochan Bannerjee and others.

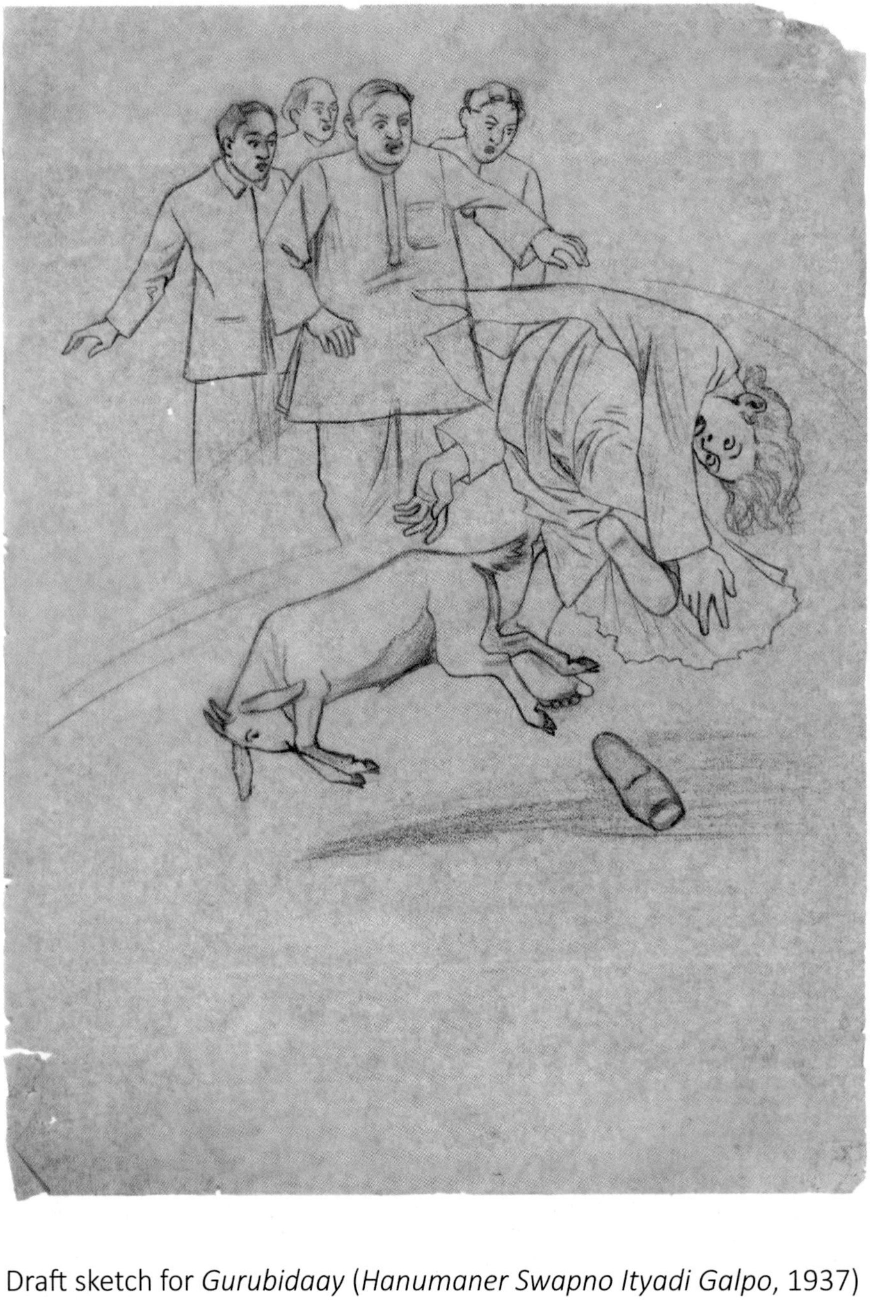

Draft sketch for *Gurubidaay* (*Hanumaner Swapno Ityadi Galpo*, 1937) [*The sketch was not used in the book*].

Characters: Swami Khalwidong and the goat Lambakarna with Raibahadur Banshalochan Bannerjee and others.

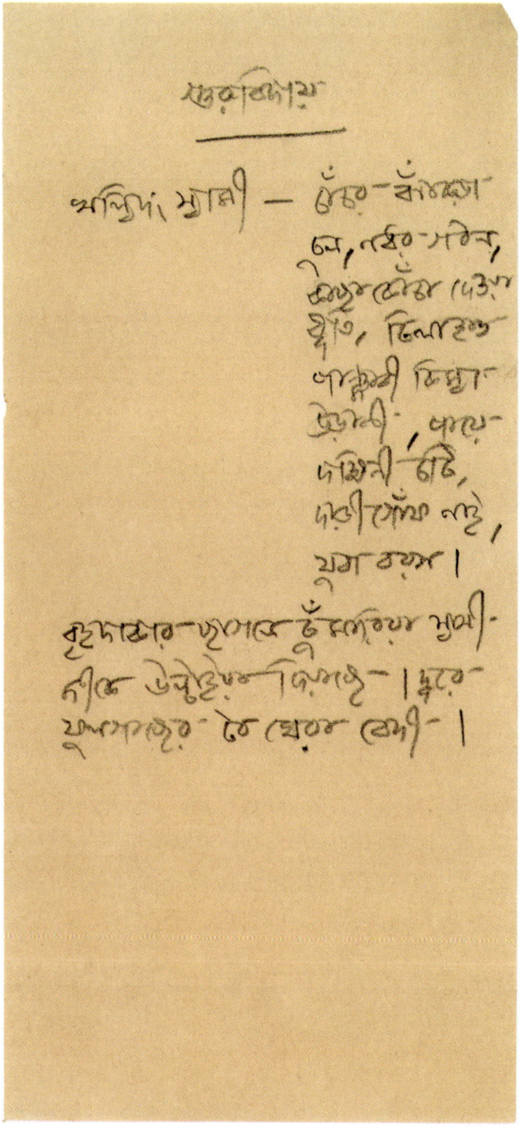
গুরুবিদায়

খল্বিদং স্বামী — কোঁকড়া-ঝাঁকড়া চুল, নধর-গড়ন, ফিটফাট ধুতি, ঢিলাহাত পাঞ্জাবী কিন্তু উড়ানী, পায়ে দক্ষিণী চটি, দাড়ী গোঁফ নাই, যুবা বয়স।

বৃহদাকার ছাগলে ঢুঁ মারিয়া স্বামী-জীকে উল্টাইয়া দিয়াছে। দূরে ফুলগাছের টব ঘেরা বেদী।

Parashuram's instructions for the appearance of Khalwidong Swami (*Gurubidaay*)

Khalwidong Swami – Curly, long clusters of hair, plump and fleshy structure, neatly dressed in a dhoti, loose sleeved kurta but with a stole, 'southern' chappal in feet, without beard and moustache, young in age.
Pushing with its head, the big goat overturns the Swamiji. At a distance, there is an altar surrounded by tubs of flowering plants.

MAHESHER MAHAJATRA

Another story narrated by Kedar Chatterji, *Mahesher Mahajatra* deals with the vexed subject of ghosts. Close friends Mahesh Mittir and Harinath Kundu are professors of mathematics and philosophy, respectively. They have almost a running feud about ghosts – Mahesh does not believe in ghosts (or gods or an afterlife) while Harinath wants to prove that ghosts exist. Mahesh gets addicted to reading books about ghosts and getting enraged. He starts losing his sleep and his health. Eventually he makes a will, instructs Harinath to not waste money on his funeral rituals, and soon dies. As his increasingly enigmatic funeral procession moves along, Mahesh appears to Harinath waving his hands. His voice reaches Harinath as if from a great distance. "Harinath", Mahesh calls out to him... "Everything is there, everything is true..."

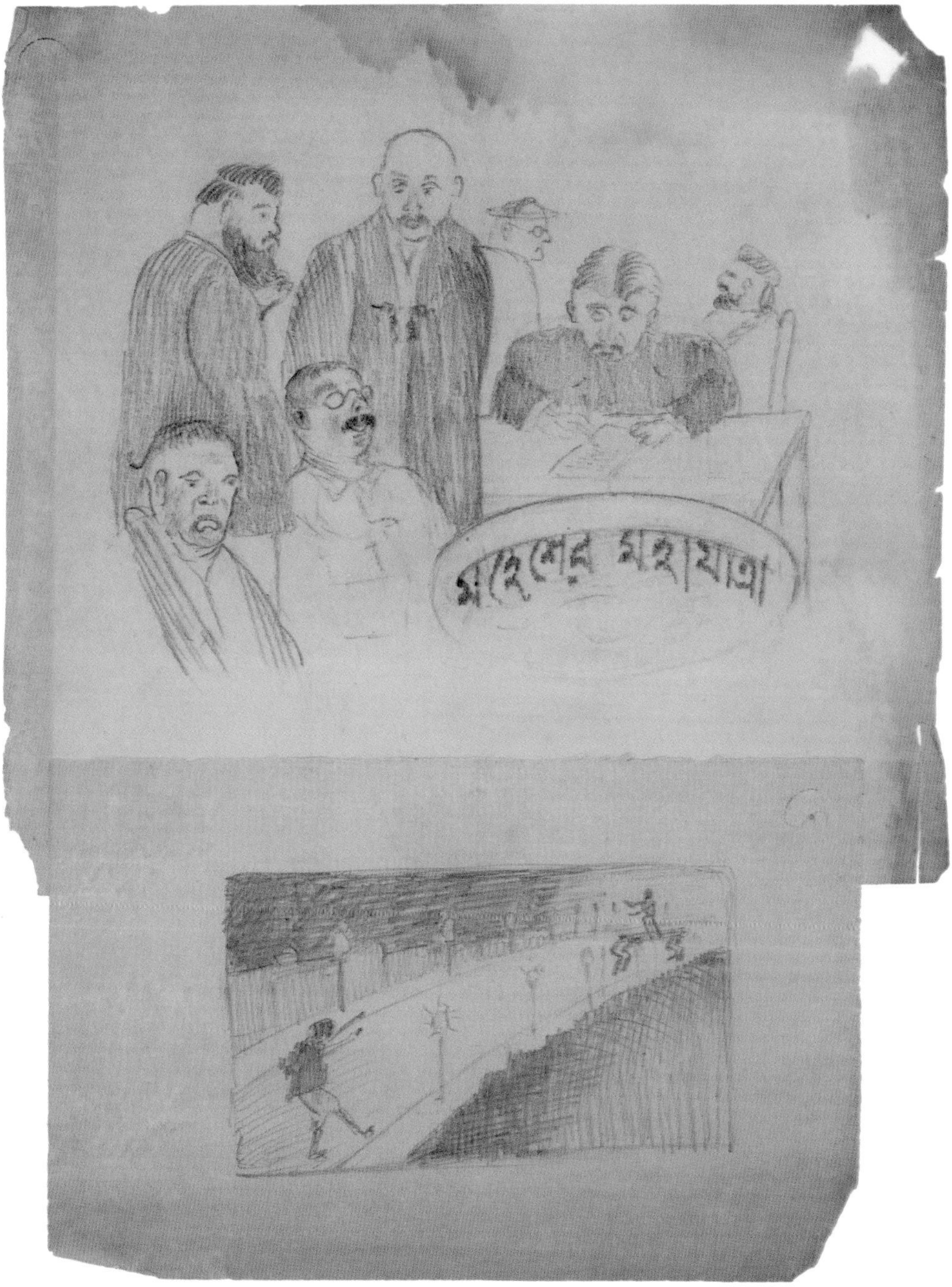

Parashuram's sketches for *Mahesher Mahajatra* (*Hanumaner Swapno Ityadi Galpo*, 1937)

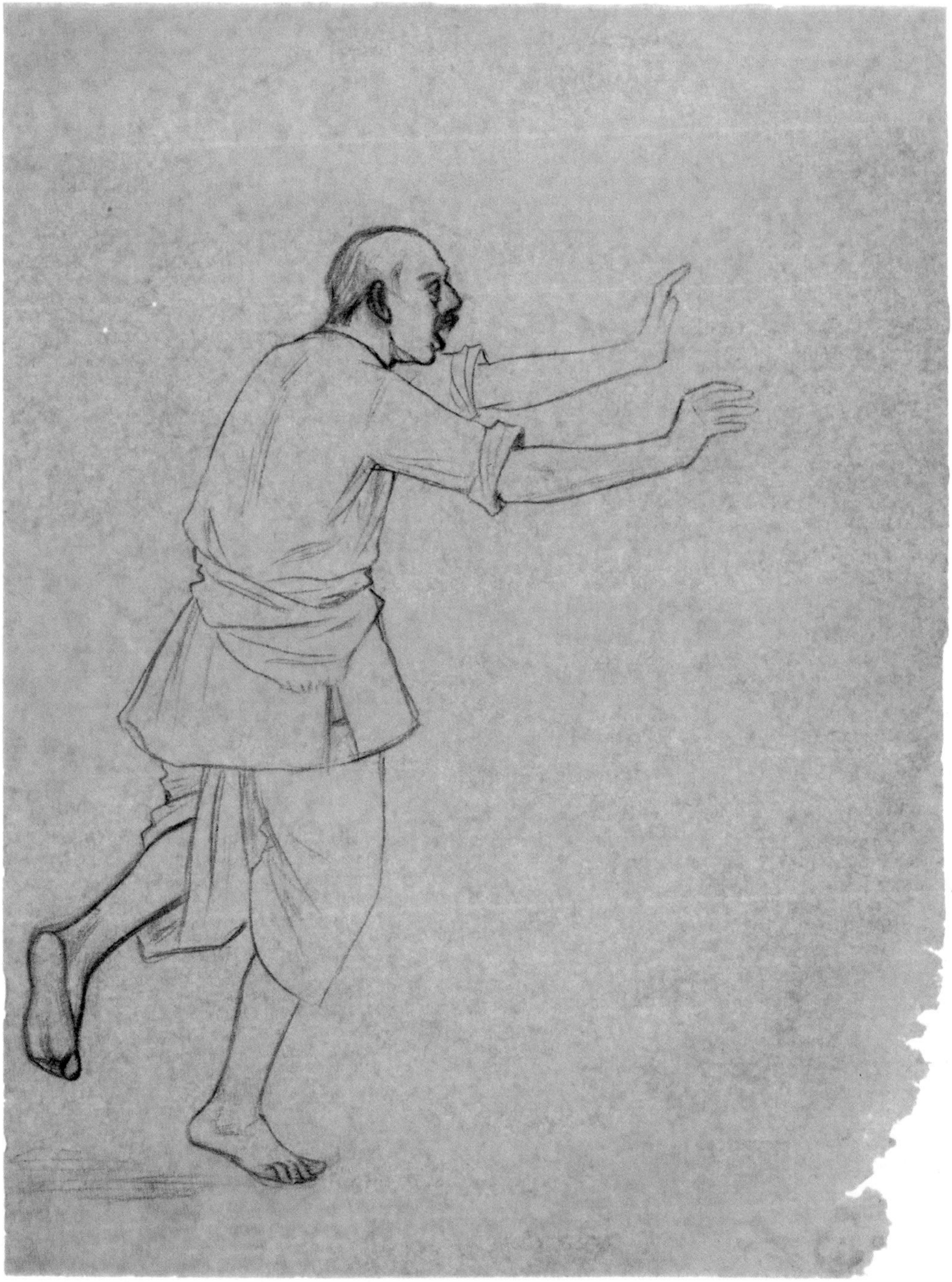

Draft sketch for *Mahesher Mahajatra* (*Hanumaner Swapno Ityadi Galpo*, 1937)

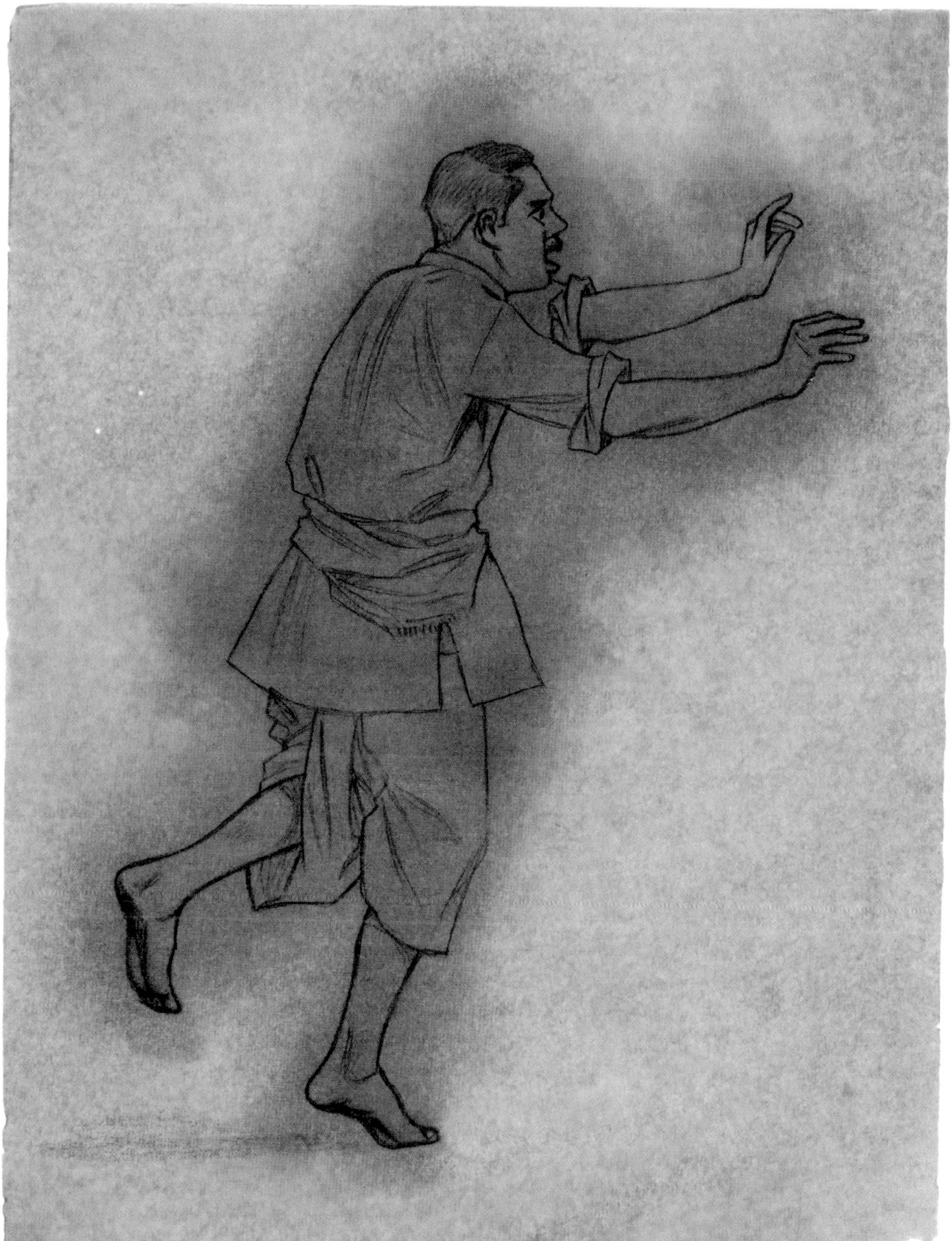

Draft sketch for *Mahesher Mahajatra* (*Hanumaner Swapno Ityadi Galpo*, 1937)

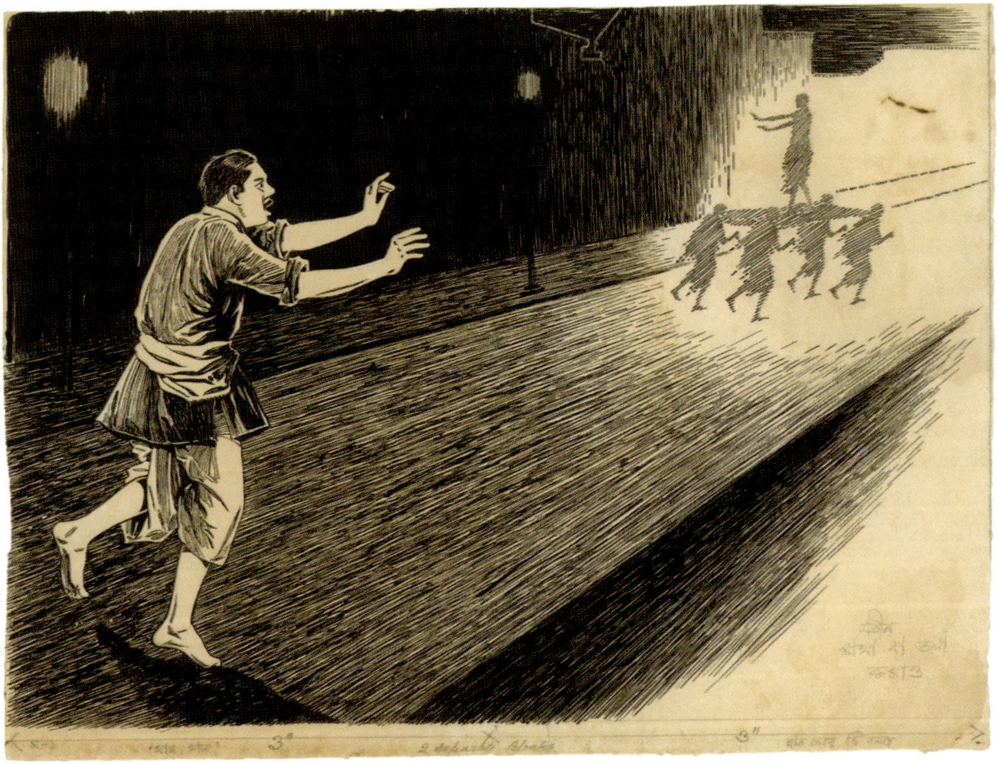

Final illustration for *Mahesher Mahajatra*, published in *Hanumaner Swapno Ityadi Galpo* (1937)

Characters: Harinath and Mahesh's ghost rising from his funeral procession.

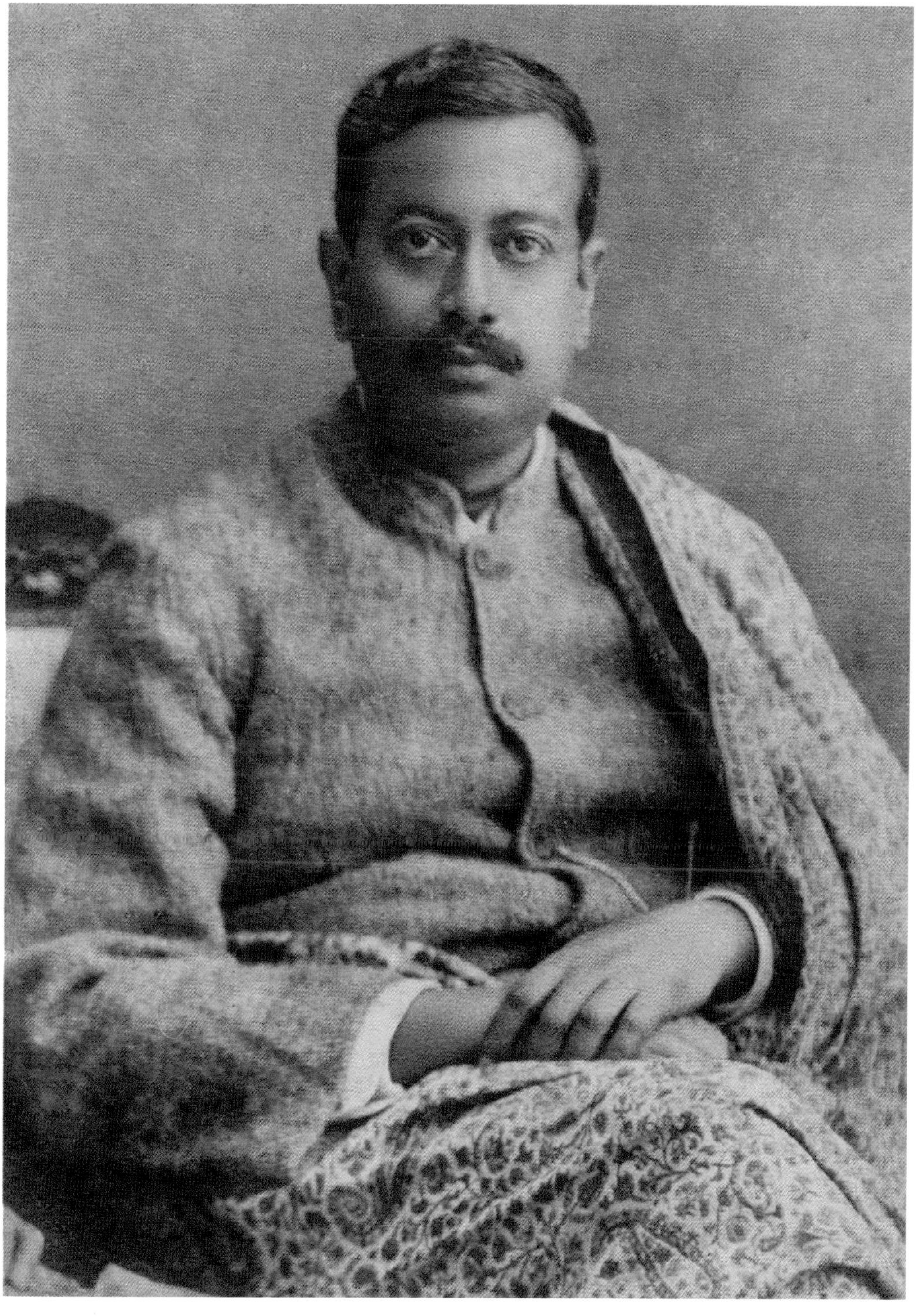

Rajshekhar Basu

RAATA-RAATI

Kartik dreams of a woman who is the epitome of beauty, courage and humour, apart from being exceptionally talented at singing, dancing and writing. He has specific examples of such paragons whom his prospective bride must measure up to. There is no doubt that he will *not* marry the girl who is his father's choice – Neri. How Neri becomes Kartik's dream girl is described comically in *Raata-raati* (overnight), helped along by the presence of Parashuram regular Kedar Chatterjee.

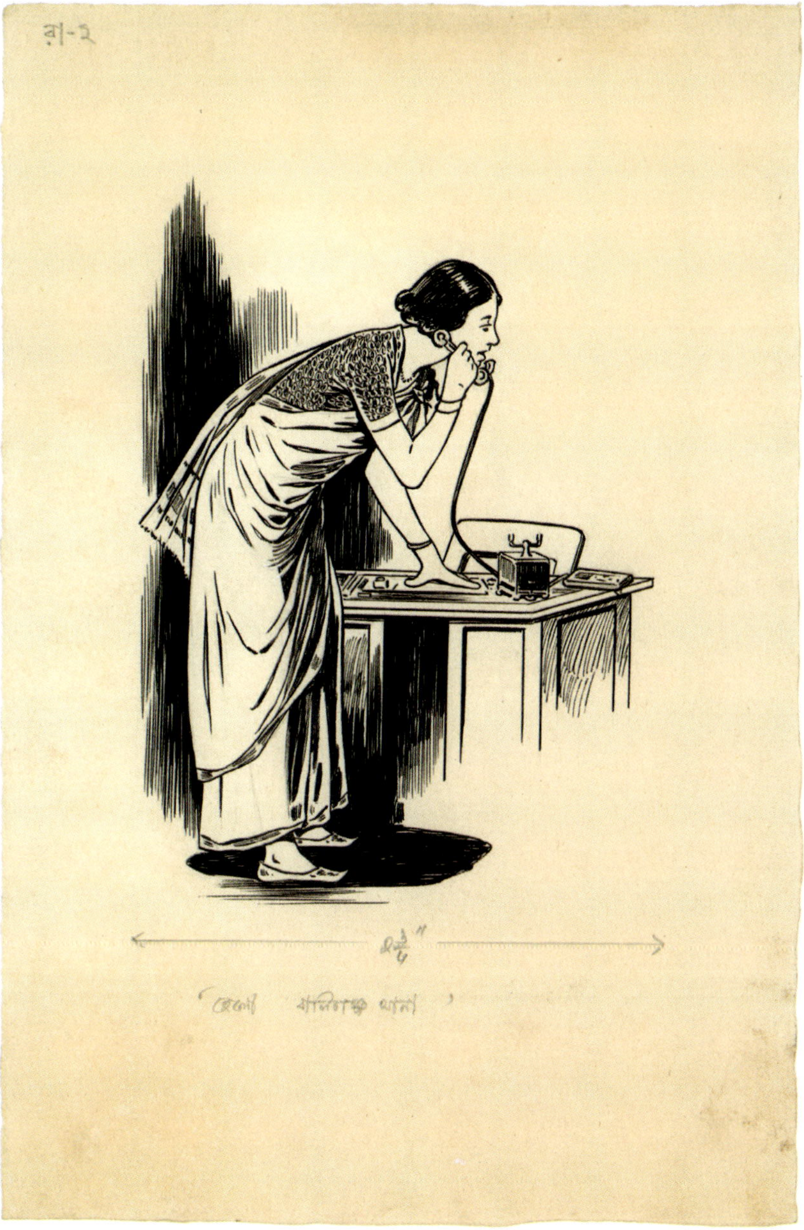

Illustration for *Raata-Raati* (*Hanumaner Swapno Ityadi Galpo*, 1937)

Bangla text: "Hello, Ballygunge Police Station".
Character: Neri.

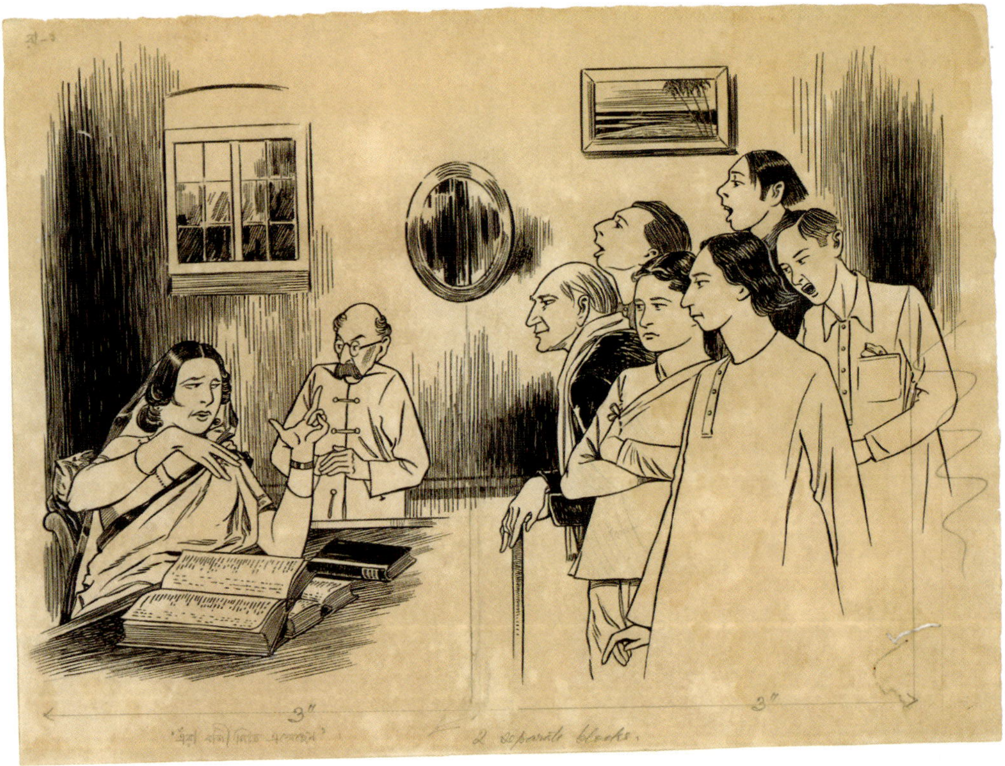

Illustration for *Raata-Raati* (*Hanumaner Swapno Ityadi Galpo*, 1937)

Bangla text: "They have come to receive your assurance".
Characters: Jigisha Debi and her husband Sushen babu, facing Kedar Chatterjee, Kartik, and Kartik's friends.

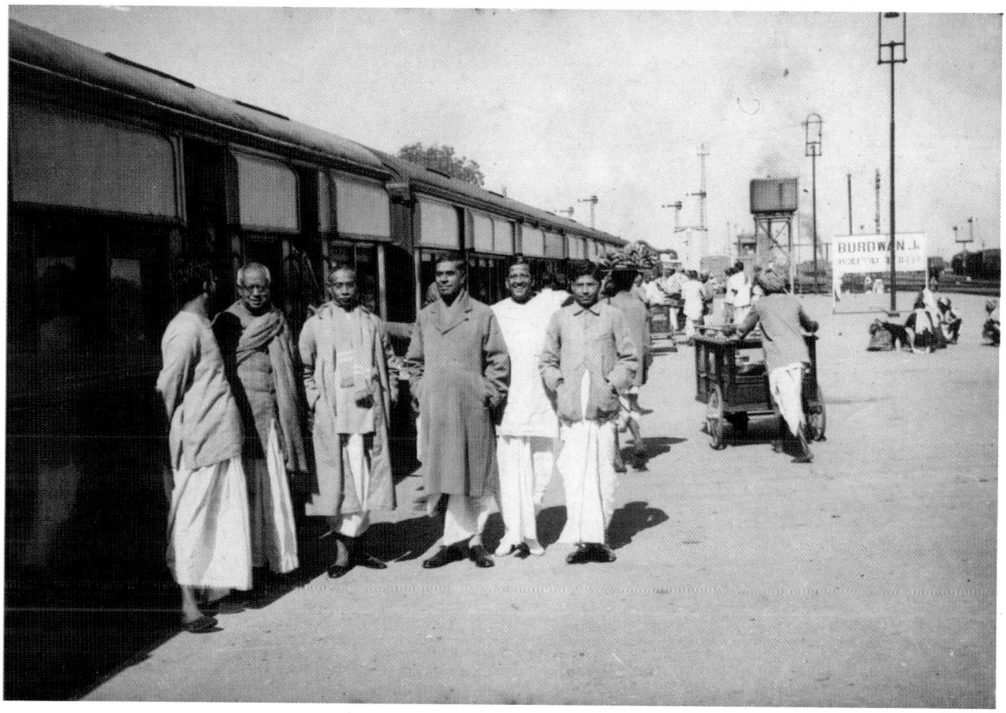

Charuchandra Bhattacharya, Jatindrakumar Sen, Krishnashekhar Bose and Satya Prasanna Sen

PREMCHAKRA

In Premchakra, there is such a complex situation around three pairs of lovers that Parashuram calls it a "hopeless hexagon". Harit, Jarit and Larit are in love with Samita, Jamita, and Tamita. Harit loves Samita, who wants Jarit... who wants Jamita, but she is attracted to Larit... who loves Tamita but she prefers Harit!

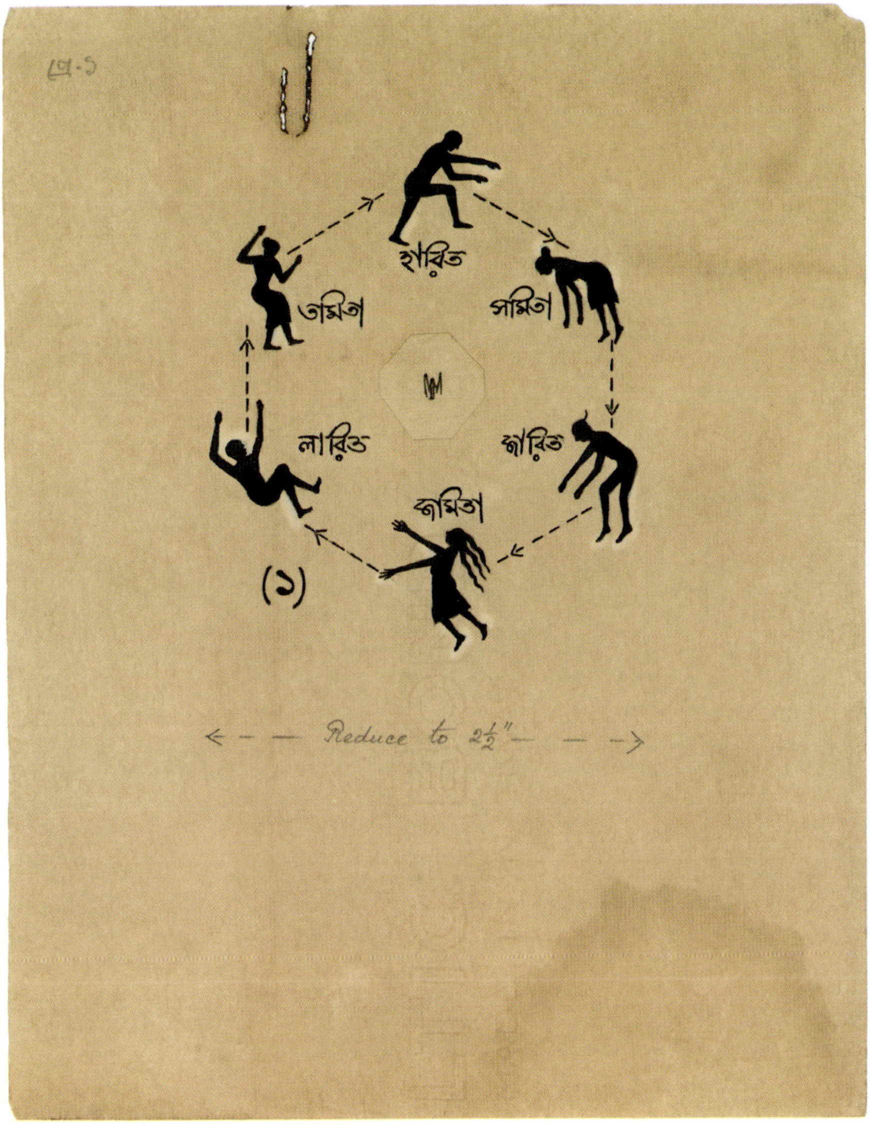

Parashuram's illustration for *Premchakra* (*Hanumaner Swapno Ityadi Galpo*, 1937)

Bangla text (clockwise from top): "Harit, Samita, Jarit, Jamita, Larit, Tamita". Bangla number at bottom left: "1".
Characters: Harit, Samita, Jarit, Jamita, Larit, Tamita. (*In the story, Parashuram calls this the "hopeless hexagon" since each is in love with the next!*)

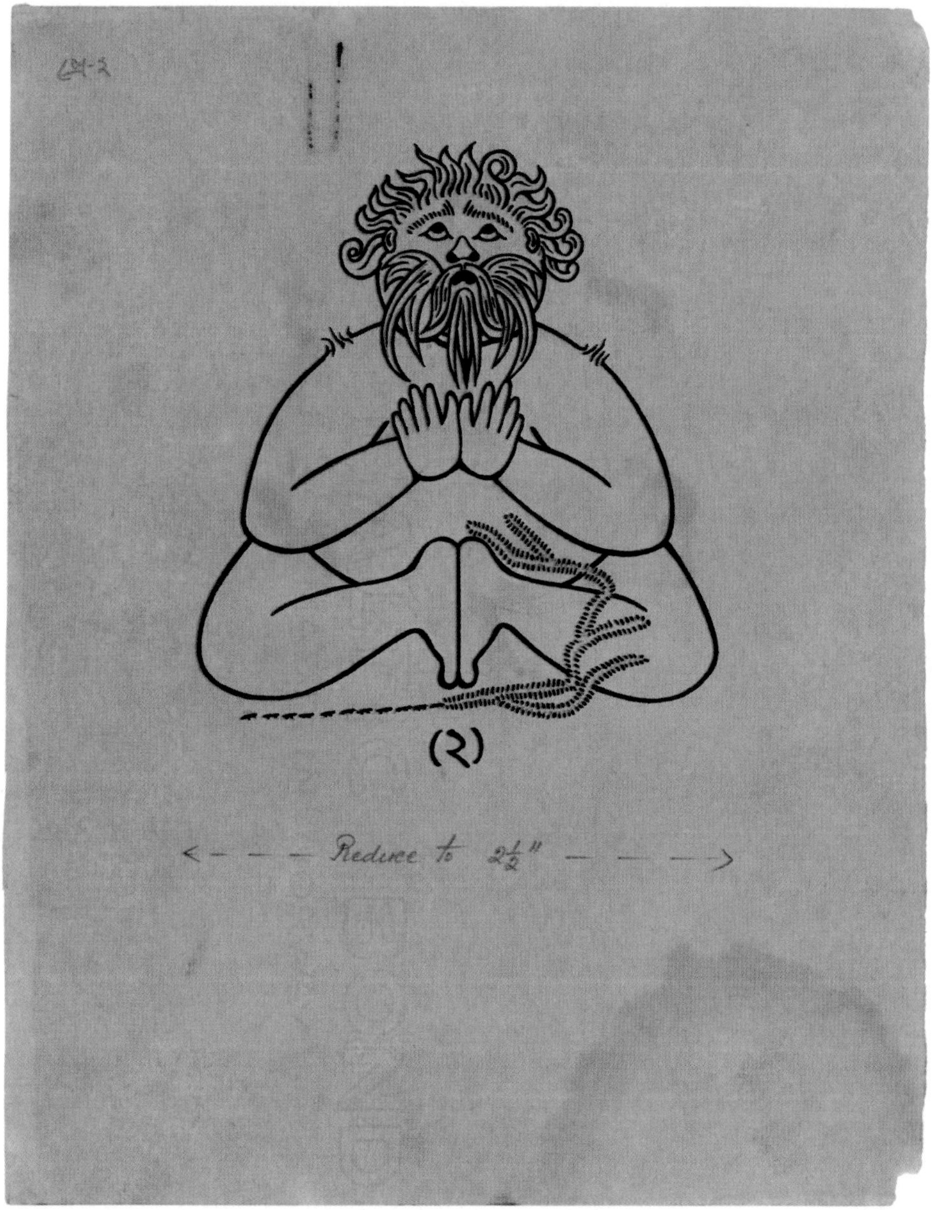

Parashuram's illustration for *Premchakra* (*Hanumaner Swapno Ityadi Galpo*, 1937)

Bangla number at the bottom: "2".
Character: Bhundil Muni.

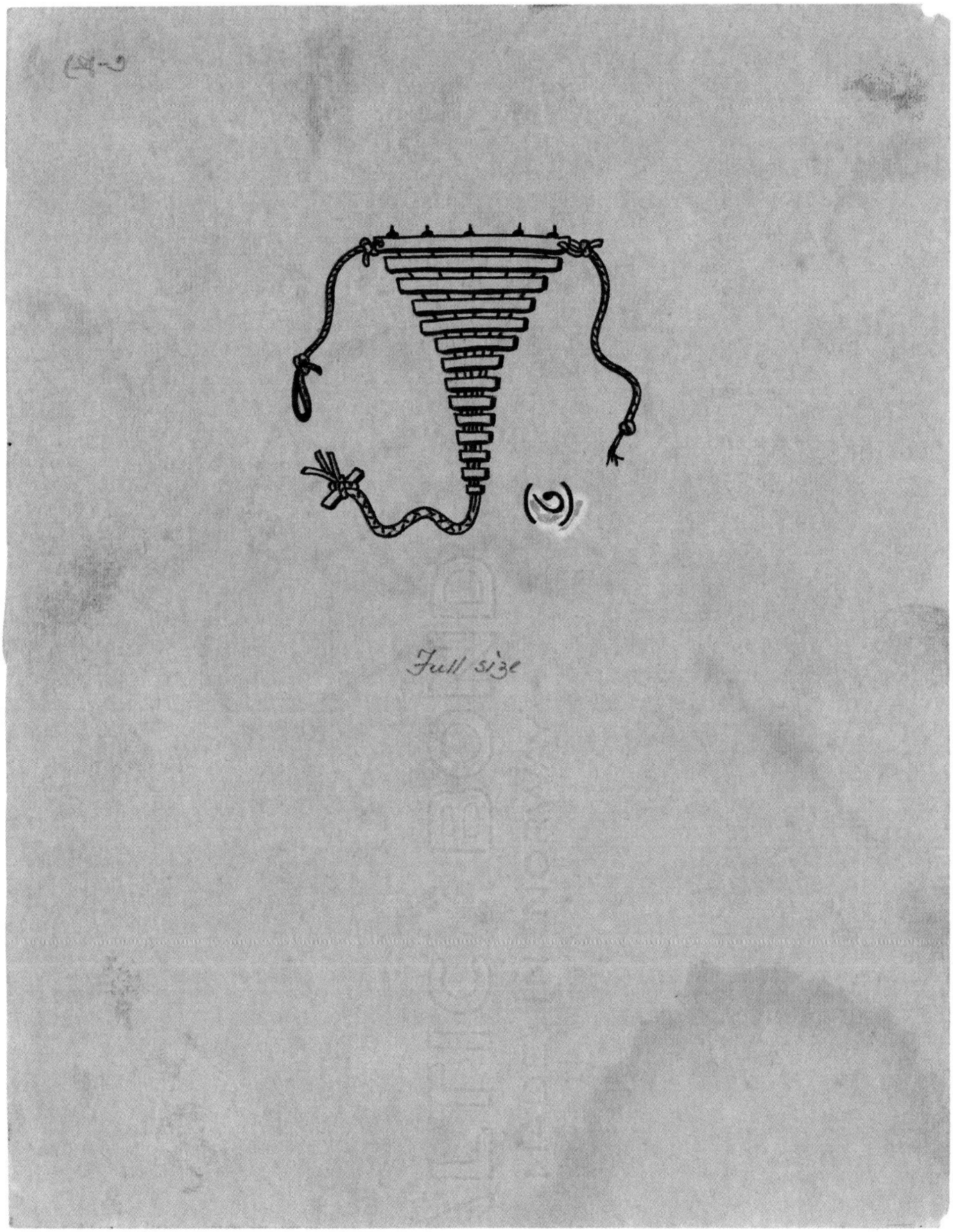

Parashuram's illustration of "loin cloth made of bael wood" for *Premchakra* (*Hanumaner Swapno Ityadi Galpo*, 1937)

Bangla number at bottom right: "3".

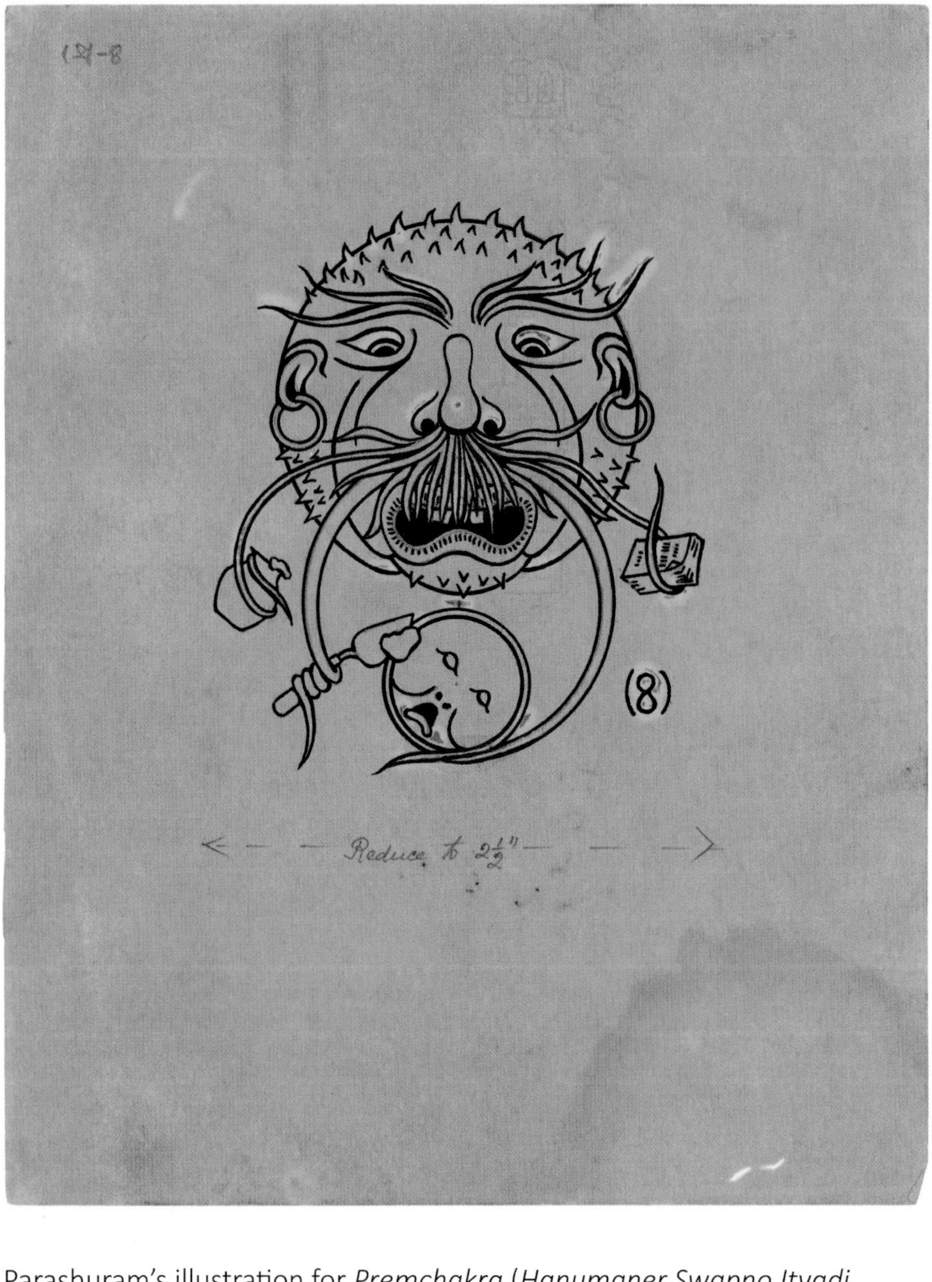

Parashuram's illustration for *Premchakra* (*Hanumaner Swapno Ityadi Galpo*, 1937)

Bangla number towards the right: "4".
Character: Rahu (celestial body in Hindu mythology; considered inauspicious).

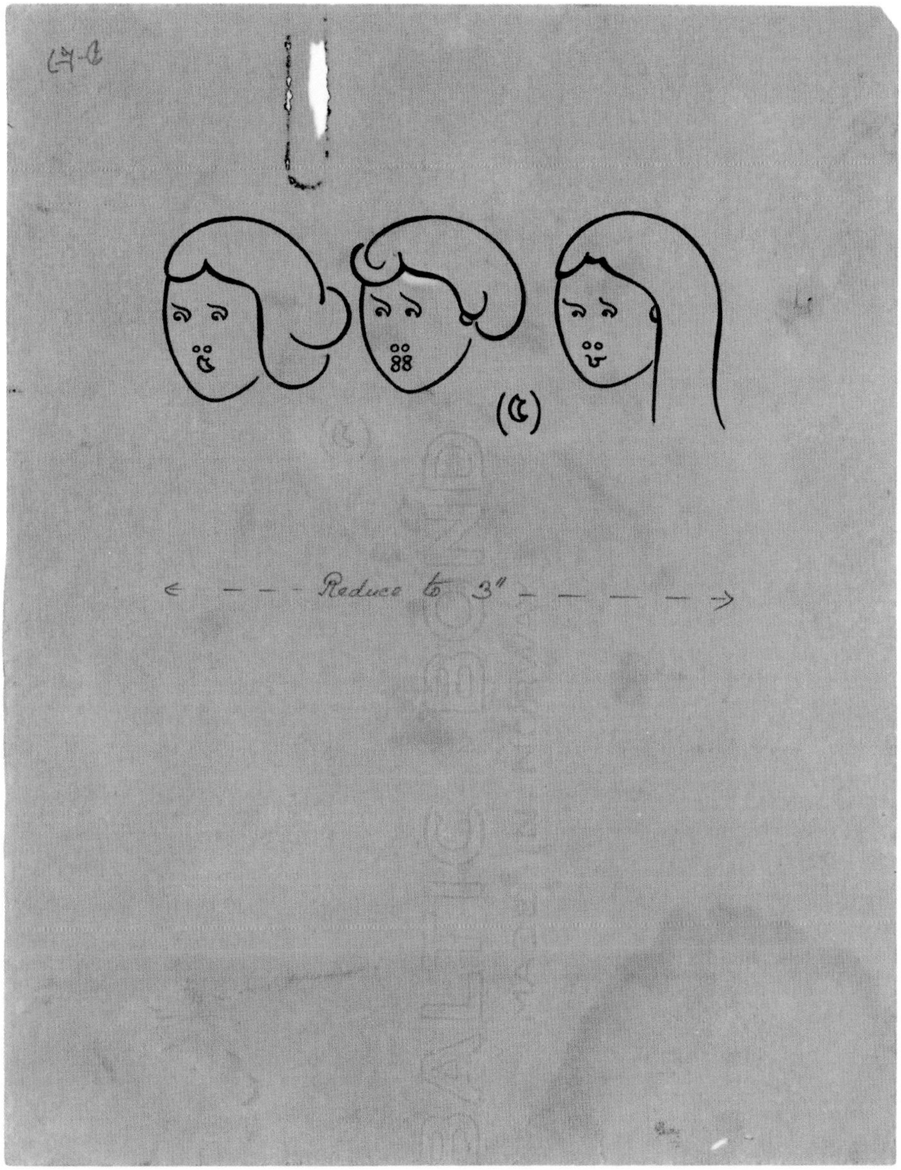

Parashuram's illustration for *Premchakra* (*Hanumaner Swapno Ityadi Galpo*, 1937)

Bangla number below the faces: "5".
Visual: The result of Chingdi teaching Mama how to draw someone looking askance using Bengali numbers and symbols.

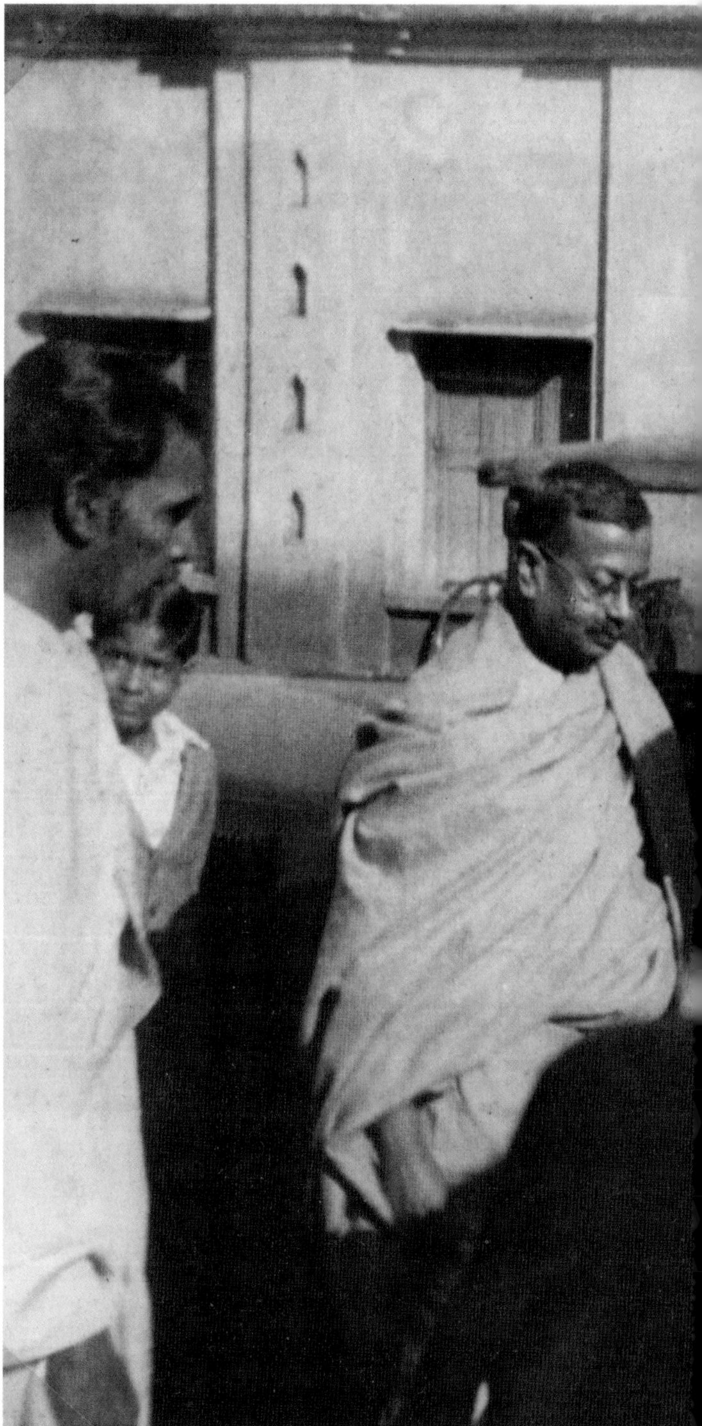

Rajshekhar Basu with
Rabindranath Tagore

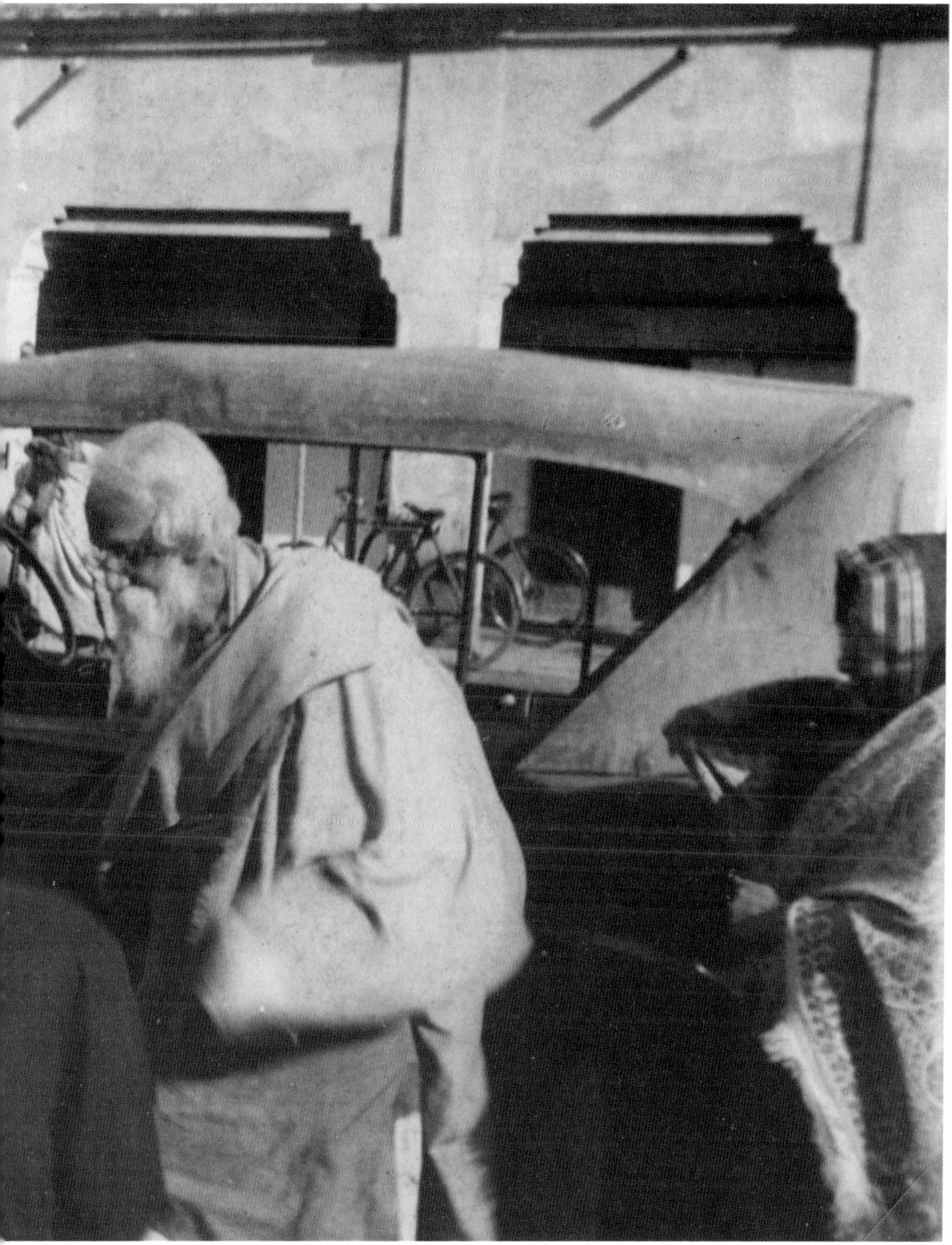

Parashuram's sketches for *Ramayana*, which was finally published without illustrations

বালকাণ্ড

১। নারদ-বাল্মীকি-সংবাদ

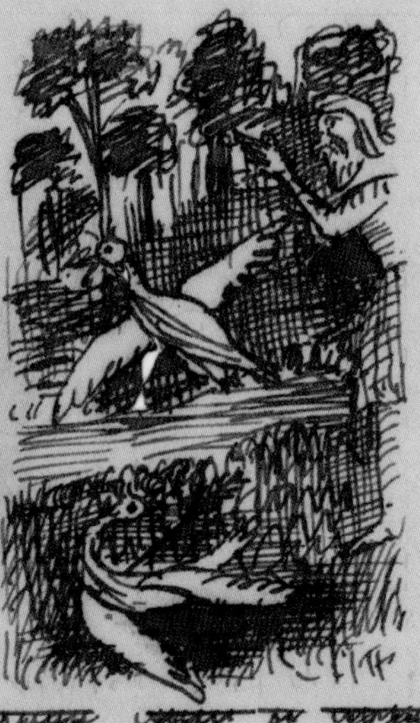

বেদজ্ঞ তপস্বী পণ্ডিতশ্রেষ্ঠ নারদকে মুনিবর বাল্মীকি জিজ্ঞাসা করলেন, সম্প্রতি পৃথিবীতে কে আছেন যিনি গুণবান্, বীর্যবান্, ধর্মজ্ঞ, কৃতজ্ঞ, সত্যবাদী ও দৃঢ়ব্রত; যিনি সচ্চরিত্র, সর্বভূতের হিতকারী, বিদ্বান্, কর্তব্যপালনে সমর্থ এবং অদ্বিতীয় প্রিয়দর্শন; যিনি আত্মসংযমী, কান্তিমান্, জিতক্রোধ ও অসূয়াশূন্য?

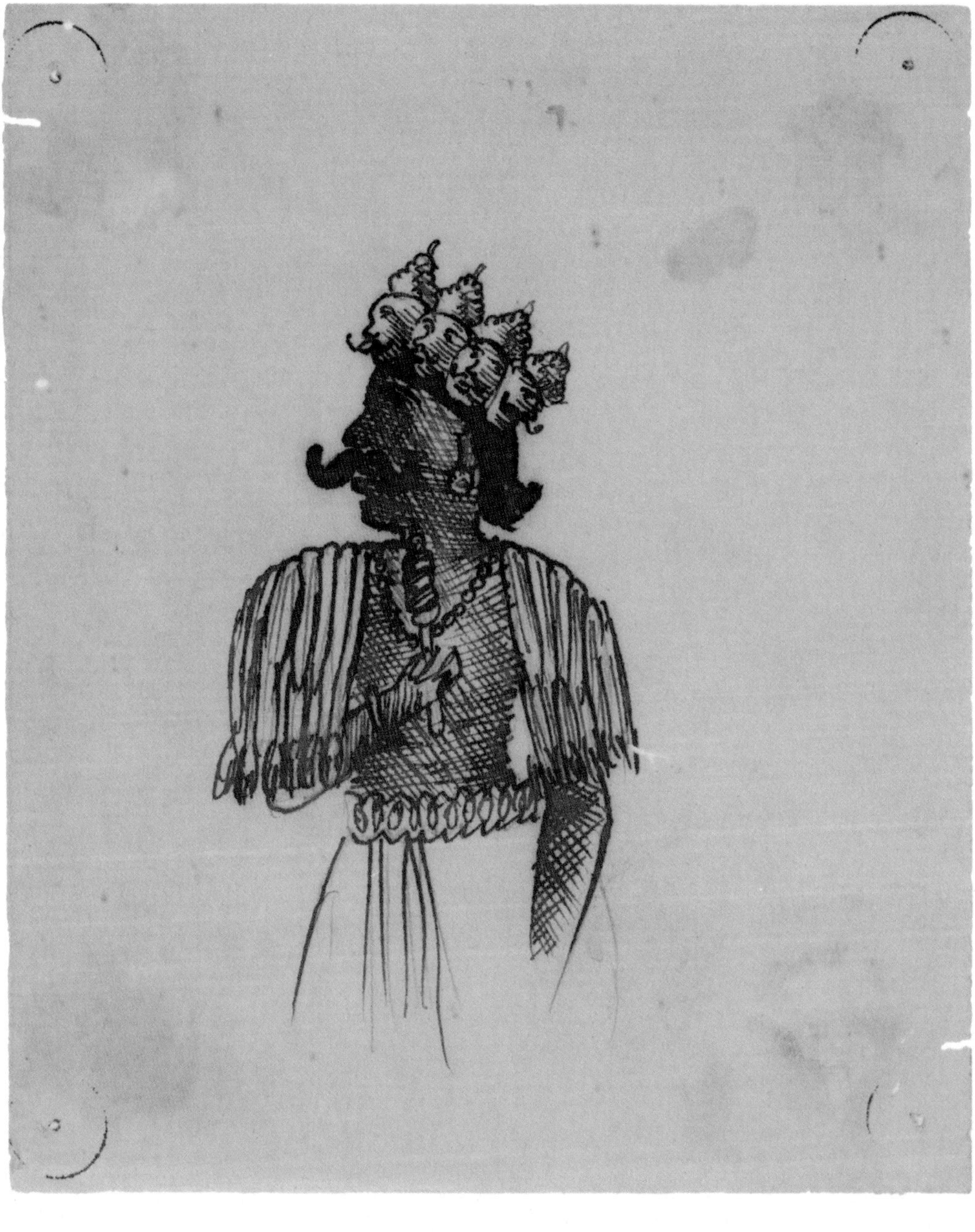

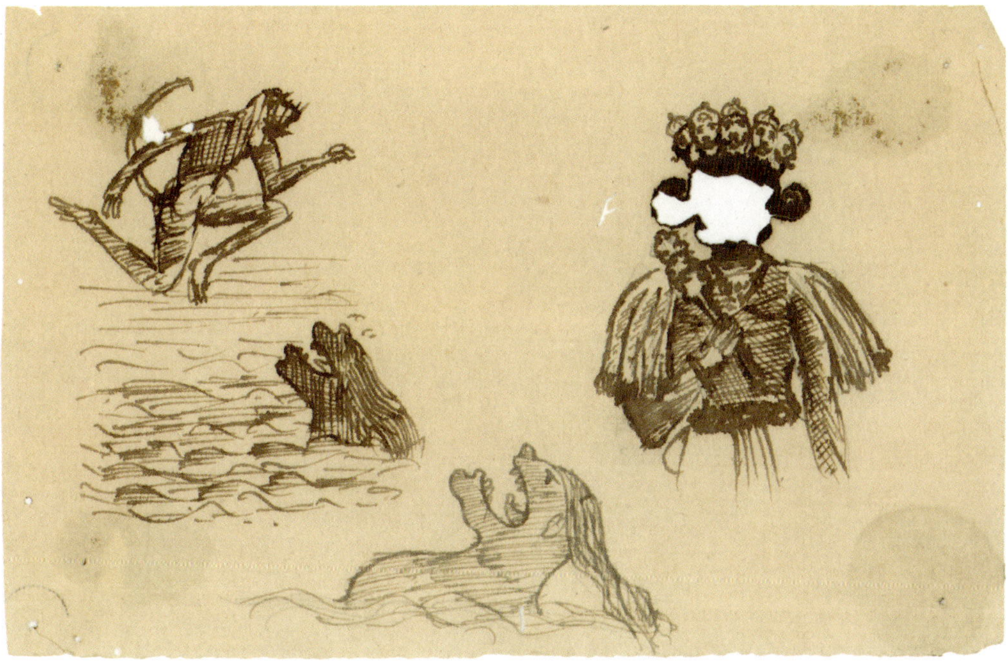

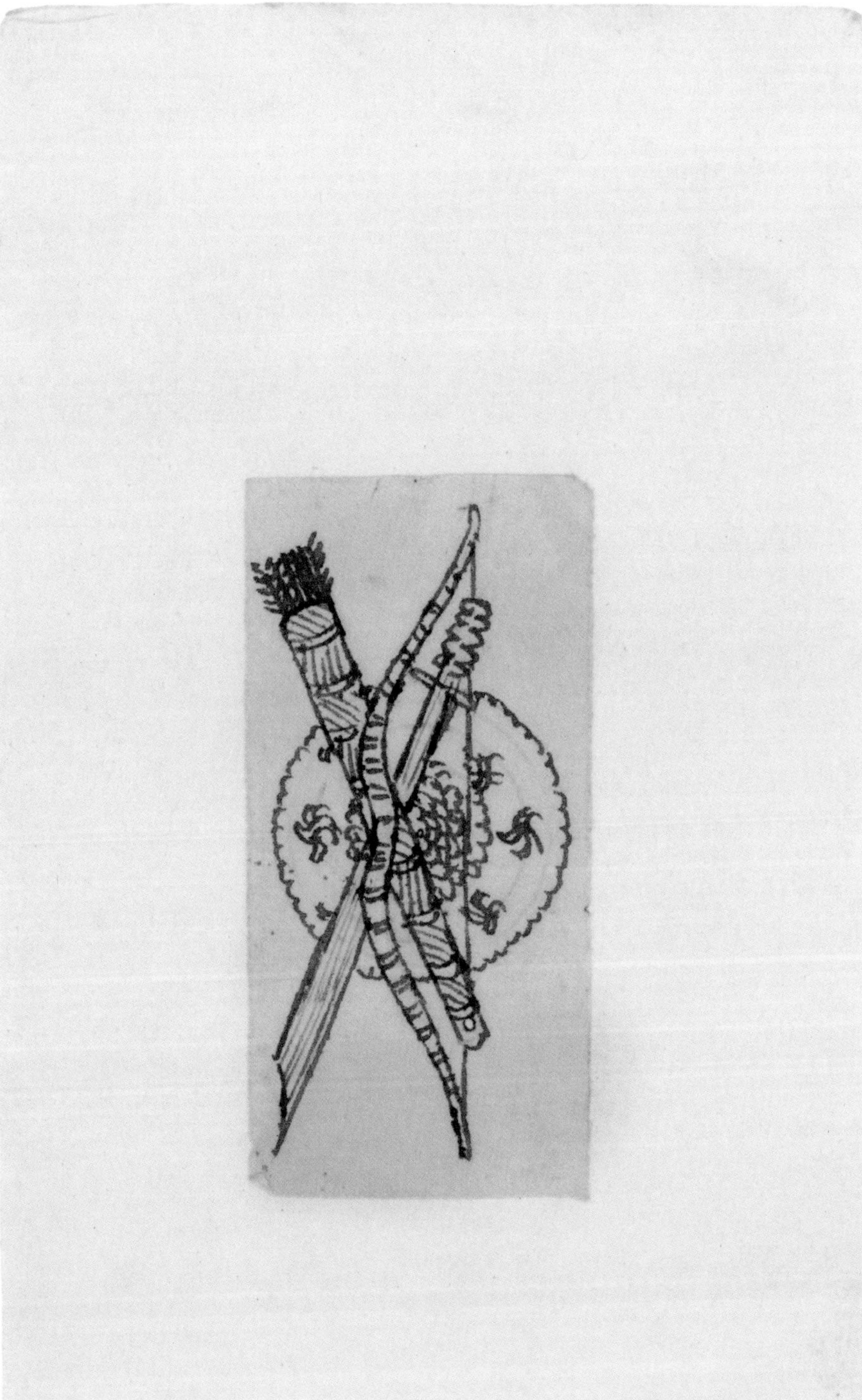

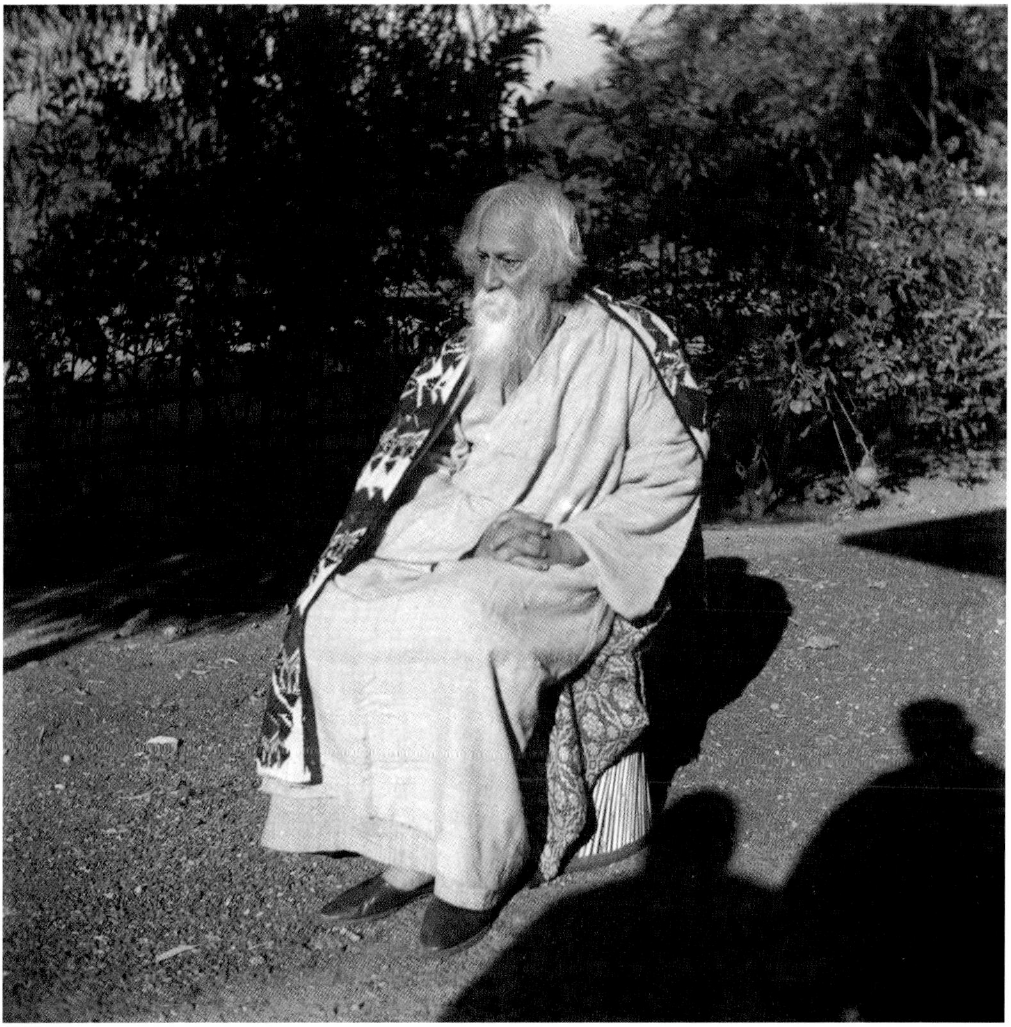

Rabindranath Tagore | Photograph by Jatindrakumar Sen

Jatindrakumar Sen's unused sketches

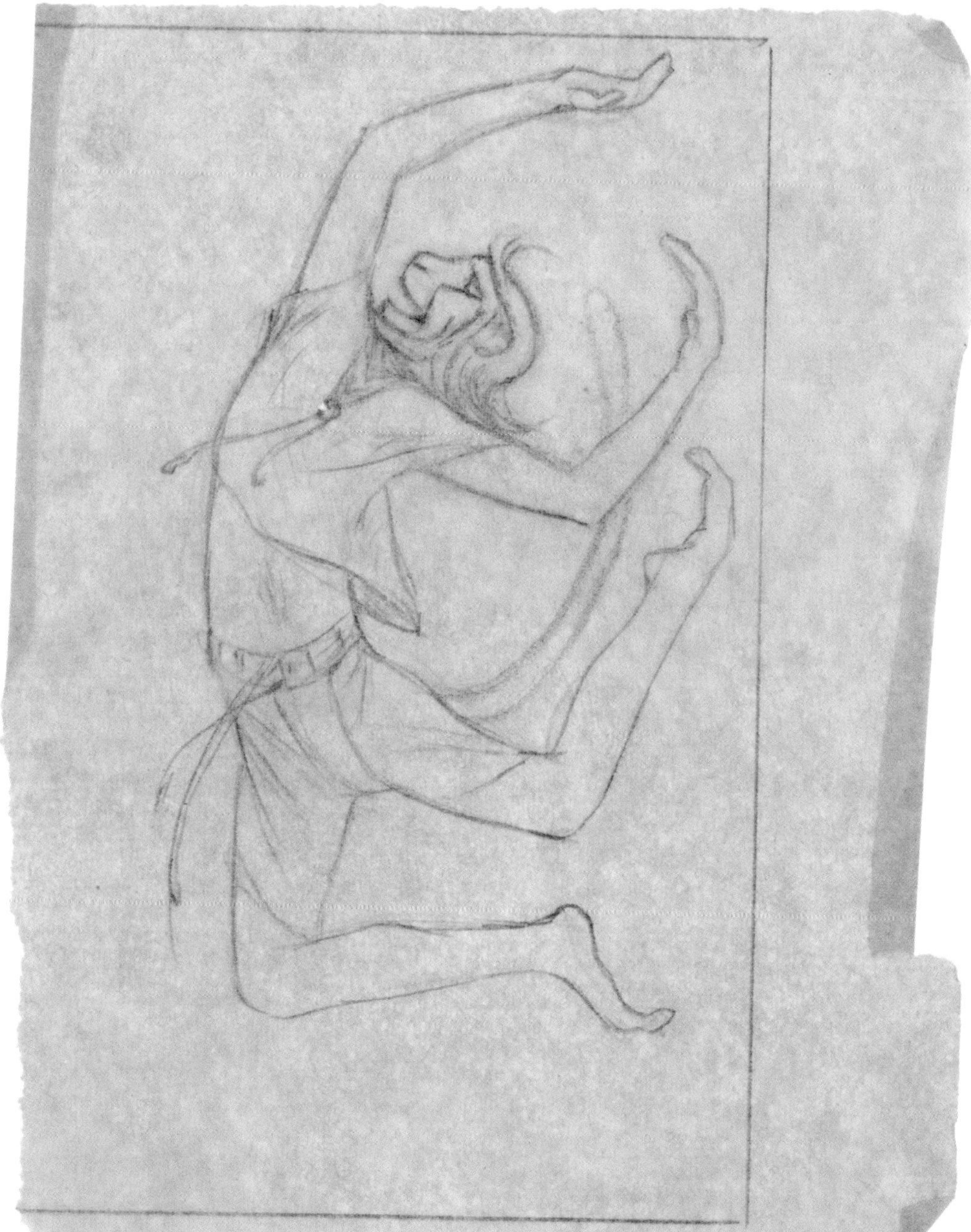

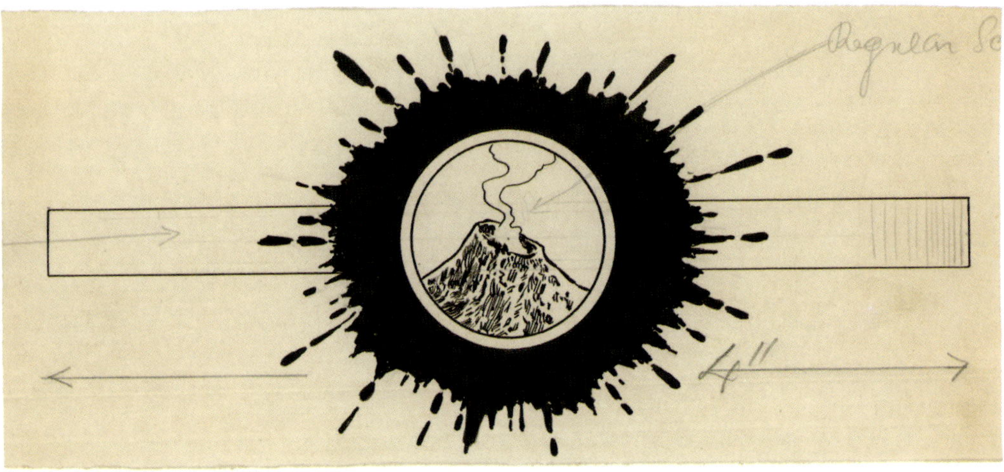

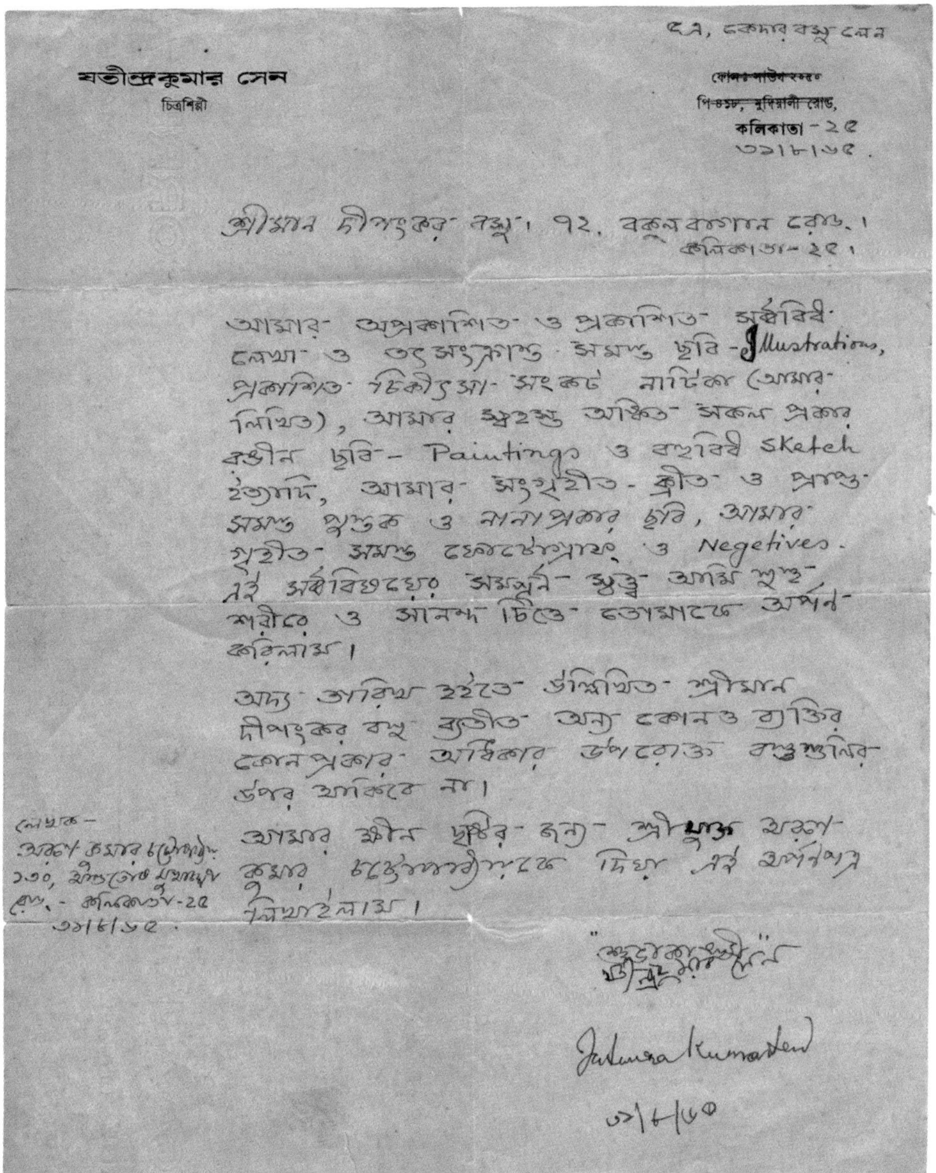

৫এ, কেদার বসু লেন

যতীন্দ্রকুমার সেন
চিত্রশিল্পী

~~ফোন: সাউথ [illegible]~~
~~পি-৪১চ, মুদিয়ালী রোড,~~
কলিকাতা - ২৫
৩১।৮।৬৫.

শ্রীমান দীপঙ্কর বসু। ৭২, বকুলবাগান রোড।
কলিকাতা-২৫।

আমার অপ্রকাশিত ও প্রকাশিত সর্ববিধ লেখা ও তৎসংক্রান্ত সমস্ত ছবি - Illustrations, প্রকাশিত চিকিৎসা সংকট নাটিকা (আমার লিখিত), আমার স্বহস্তে অঙ্কিত সকল প্রকার রঙীন ছবি - Paintings ও বহুবিধ Sketch ইত্যাদি, আমার সংগৃহীত - ক্রীত ও প্রাপ্ত সমস্ত পুস্তক ও নানাপ্রকার ছবি, আমার গৃহীত সমস্ত ফোটোগ্রাফ ও Negetives এই সর্ববিষয়ের সমস্ত স্বত্ব আমি সুস্থ শরীরে ও আনন্দ চিত্তে তোমাকে অর্পণ করিলাম।

অদ্য তারিখ হইতে উল্লিখিত শ্রীমান দীপঙ্কর বসু ব্যতীত অন্য কোনও ব্যক্তির কোনপ্রকার অধিকার উপরোক্ত বস্তুগুলির উপর থাকিবে না।

লেখক -
অরুণ কুমার চট্টোপাধ্যায়
১৩০, [illegible] মুখার্জী রোড, - কলিকাতা-২৫
৩১।৮।৬৫.

আমার ক্ষীণ দৃষ্টির জন্য শ্রীযুক্ত অরুণ কুমার চট্টোপাধ্যায়কে দিয়া এই অর্পণপত্র লিখাইলাম।

"শুভাকাঙ্ক্ষী"
যতীন্দ্রকুমার সেন

Jatindra Kumar Sen

৩১।৮।৬৫

Letter from Jatindrakumar Sen (written in the hand of Arun Chattopadhyay, due to Sen's poor eyesight), dated 31.08.1965. The letter is a transfer of copyright to Dipankar Basu (Parashuram's great grandson) over all Jatindra Sen's published or unpublished writings, illustrations and paintings as well as all photographs, negatives and collectibles owned by him.

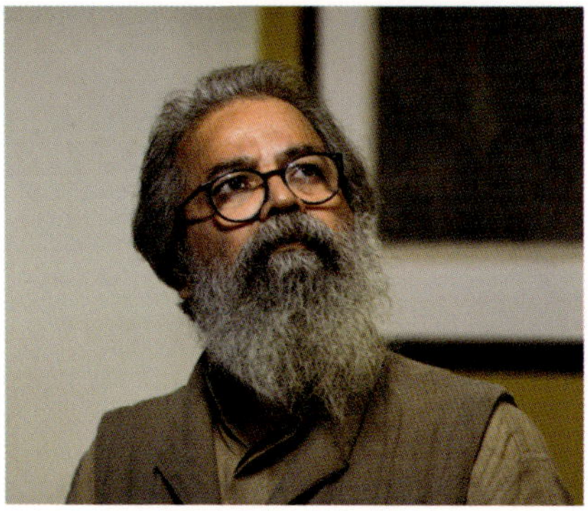

KS Radhakrishnan (born 1956) is a sculptor and is recognized as one of the most significant figures of contemporary Indian art. He studied art at Kala Bhavana, Viswa-Bharati University, Santiniketan, where he was mentored and trained by two important figures of Indian modernism – Ramkinkar Baij and Sarbari Roy Choudhury. Radhakrishnan has had numerous solo and group shows of his work in India as well as abroad. He curated the exhibition 'Ramkinkar Baij: A Retrospective' (2012) at National Gallery of Modern Art, New Delhi, Bangalore and Mumbai, and wrote the accompanying book *Ramkinkar's Yaksha Yakshi*. He curated 'Somnath Hore: A Centenary Exhibition' (2022) at Arthshila, Santiniketan and Emami Art Gallery, Kolkata, and produced the companion volume *Somnath Hore*. He also curated 'Iti, Satyajit Da' (2022) an exhibition in honour of Satyajit Ray's centenary at Emami Art Gallery, Kolkata and curated the book *Iti Satyajit Da, Letters to a Friend by Satyajit Ray*. A retrospective exhibition of his works is forthcoming at Bikaner House, Delhi (2023).

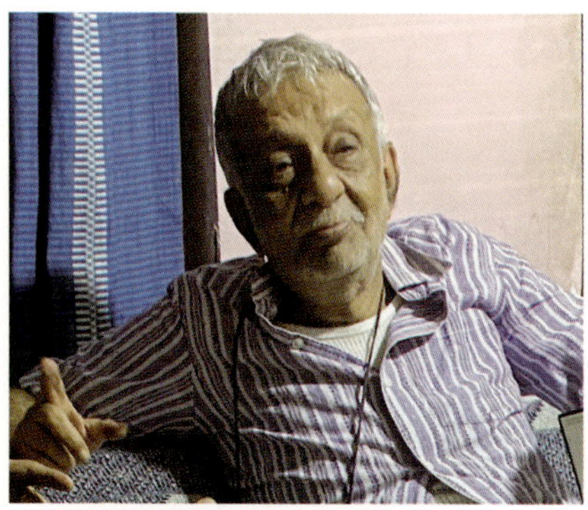

Gautam Bhadra is an eminent historian of South Asia. He taught for several years at the University of Calcutta and was a professor of history at the Centre for Studies in Social Sciences, Calcutta. He is now Honorary Professor at the Centre for Studies in Social Sciences (Jadunath Bhavan Museum and Resource Centre). He is also a recipient of the Bengali literary award Ananda Puraskar for his book *Nyara Bot-tolaye Jai Ko-bar* (2011).

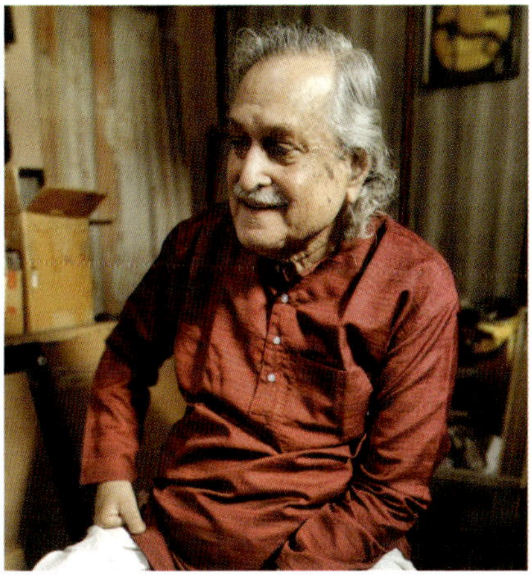

Parimal Ray is a senior and renowned Kolkata-based art collector and heritage enthusiast. Over the decades, he has researched, discovered, rescued and collected countless precious works in the fields of art, handicrafts, popular culture, photography, memorabilia, and much more. From books and magazines to letters and matchbox labels, from cinema posters and publicity materials to interesting street hoardings and signboards, he has preserved them all. He knew Satyajit Ray over a period of 30 years and often supplied the director with specific objet d'arts and authentic props required for his films such as *Ghare Baire*. Parimal Ray is now a living archive of memories of 20th century Calcutta, its cultural and literary figures and their legendary *addas*. He continues to energetically collect and promote artworks, handicrafts and needy artists.

Juhi Saklani is a writer, editor and photographer based in Delhi. Her articles have been published in magazines, newspapers and portals such The Hindu, Frontline, Outlook, Outlook Traveller, The Wire, Dark Mountain, Lonely Planet India, and Art & Deal. She won India Habitat Centre's Photosphere fellowship in 2019. She has edited the centenary volume *Somnath Hore* (2021) and *Iti Satyajit Da: Letters to a Friend from Satyajit Ray* (2022). Her essay on Somnath Hore, 'To My Eyes, They All Appeared To Be Wounds' will appear in *Aesthetics in the Fray: The Avant-Garde in India* (Routledge, forthcoming).

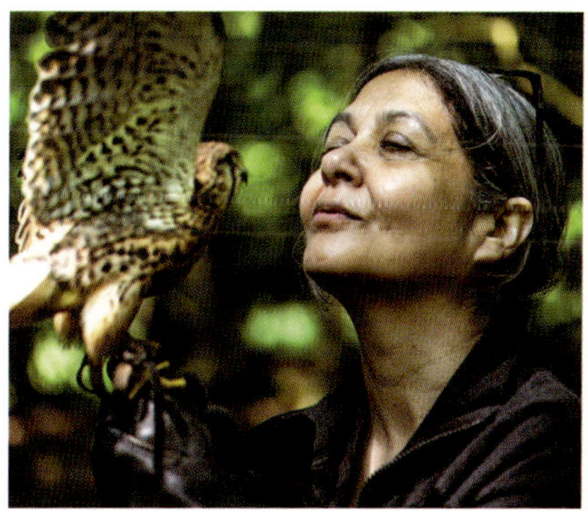

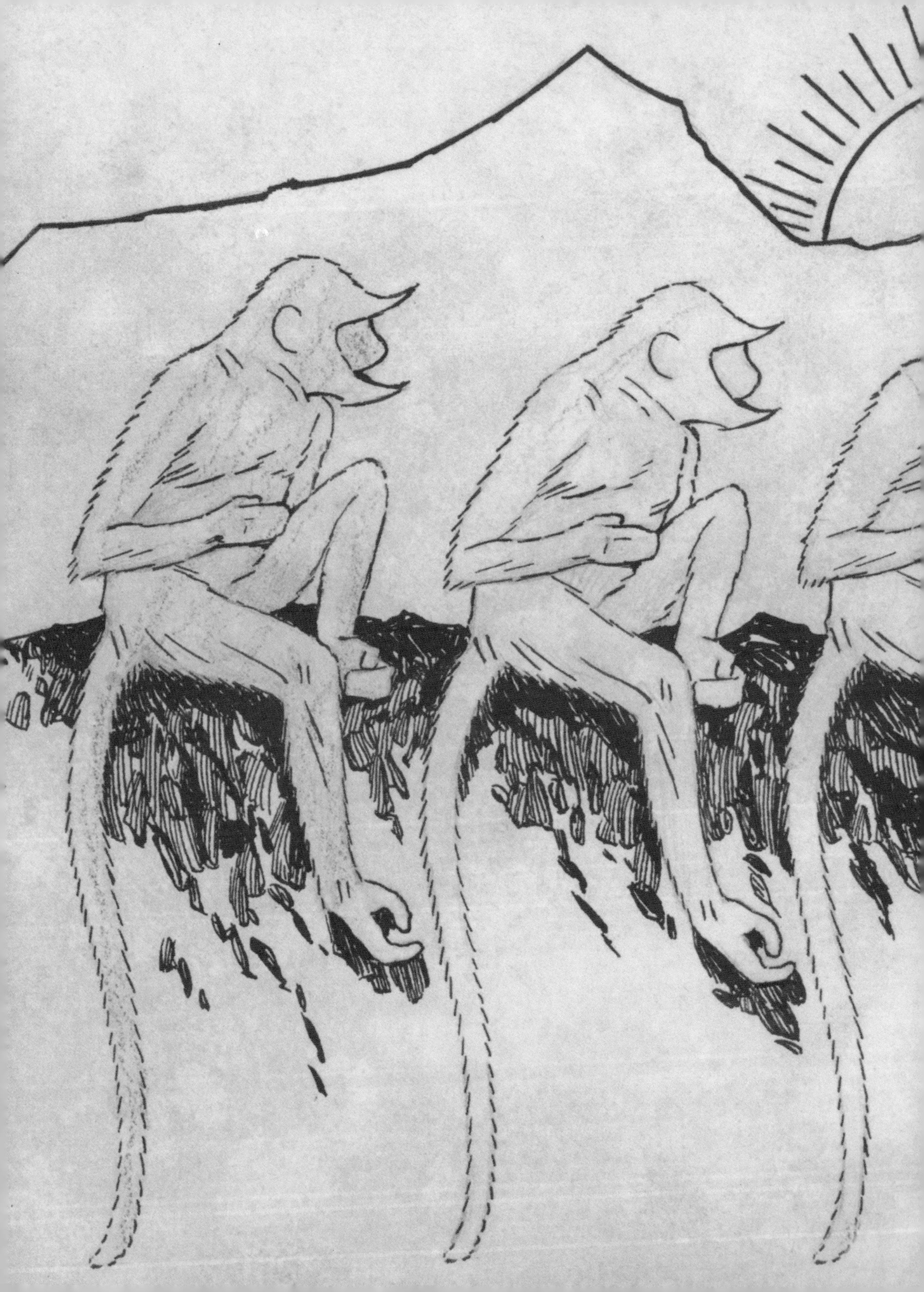